Maine

Unforgettable Vintage Images of the Pine Tree State

Note from the Publisher

Royalties from the sale of this book and the others in the Best of Series will be donated to the National Trust for Historic Preservation. These funds will be used to further their work and provide support to the preservation movement nationwide.

MAINE

Unforgettable Vintage Images of the Pine Tree State

ARCADIA
PUBLISHING

ISBN 978-0-7385-9714-0

Published by Arcadia Publishing
Charleston, South Carolina

Printed in the United States of America

Library of Congress Catalog Card Number: 00-105697

For all general information contact Arcadia Publishing at:
Telephone 843-853-2070
Fax 843-853-0044
E-mail sales@arcadiapublishing.com
For customer service and orders:
Toll-Free 1-888-313-2665

Visit us on the Internet at www.arcadiapublishing.com

Contents

ACKNOWLEDGMENTS

Arcadia would like to thank these generous authors for sharing their works with us.

John D. Bardwell

Ogunquit By-the-Sea

Old Kittery

Old York Beach

Old York

Diane & Jack Barnes

Lake Region

Maine Life at the Turn of the Century

The Sebago Lake Area

Dorothy A. Blanchard

Old Sebec Lake

Steven Burr

Kennebunk: Main Street

James Claflin

Light Houses and Life Saving Along the Maine and New Hampshire Coast

O.R. Cummings

York County Trolleys

Elin B. Dozois

Phippsburg

Rev. H. Kenneth Dutille

Lewiston & Auburn

Jim Harnedy

Around Wiscasset

Bonnie Pierpont

Auburn

Connie Porter Scott

Kennebunkport

Jeffrey A. Scully

INTRODUCTION

There is something in the Maine air that ignites the human spirit. Perhaps it is the spray of the Atlantic crashing against the coast. Maybe it is the sigh of pine trees covering some 17 million acres of forest. Whatever it may be, the state of Maine boasts an overwhelming pride in some of history's greatest Americans. Of course there is Henry Wadsworth Longfellow, whose poetry runs parallel with all that is the United States. There is Harriet Breecher Stowe, author of *Uncle Tom's Cabin*, a staple of America's constant struggle for liberty and freedom. There is Andrew Wyeth, whose art captured the simple beauty of New England amidst the violence of the twentieth century. There is Edwin Arlington Robinson and Edna St. Vincent Millary, two different sort of poets both sharing the Pulitzer Prize. However, the pages which follow are the images of men and women whom history may have forgotten but Mainers refuse to forget, proven in the over 75 Maine titles in the *Images of America* series.

In 1993, Arcadia began as a one woman office in Dover, New Hampshire. Seven years later, Arcadia has expanded to publish local histories nationwide, and in 2000 we are celebrating the publication of our 1000th title. Arcadia decided to celebrate this landmark by creating the "Best of" series in order to share the occasion with all of the authors, the historical societies, and all of the people who have made this achievement possible. Without readership, there would be no *Images of America* series. The publication of our 1000th book is a testament to the people of Maine and all over the United States who take pride in their town's history and love it enough to preserve it. We offer the *Best of Maine* for you, our reader, along with our thanks for making this landmark occasion possible.

Mike Spiegel
Editor, Arcadia Publishing

One

People

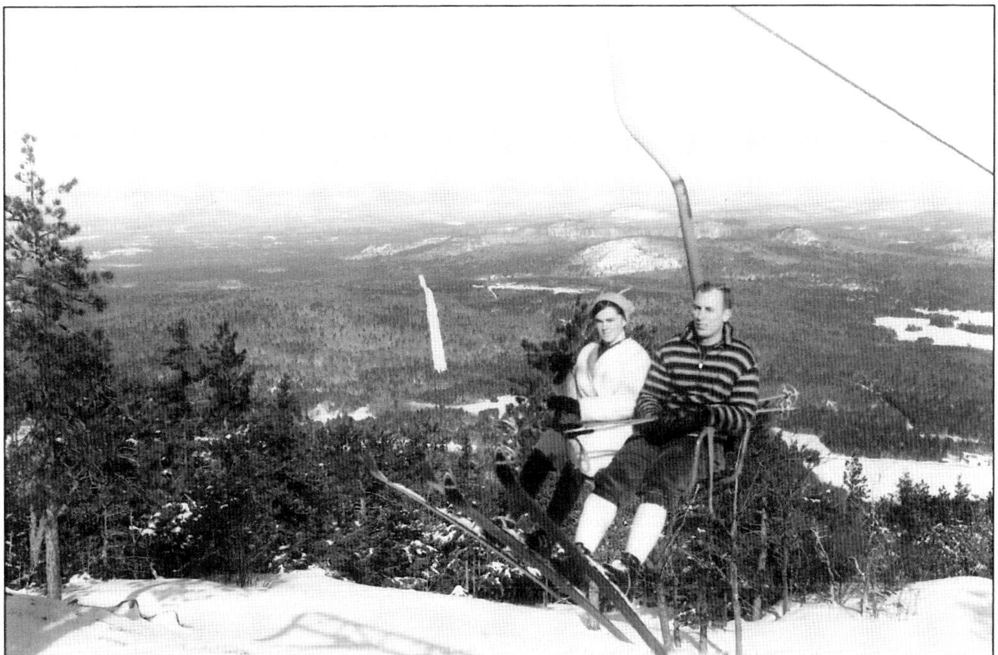

The second oldest ski area in Maine, Pleasant Mountain officially opened in January of 1938. Harry Sampson, headmaster of Bridgton Academy, along with his students and the help of the CCC and WPA, began clearing the forested slope in 1937. Russ Haggett and other civic leaders helped make Pleasant Mountain and Bridgton a popular ski resort. In 1988 the area was renamed Shawnee Peak at Pleasant Mt.

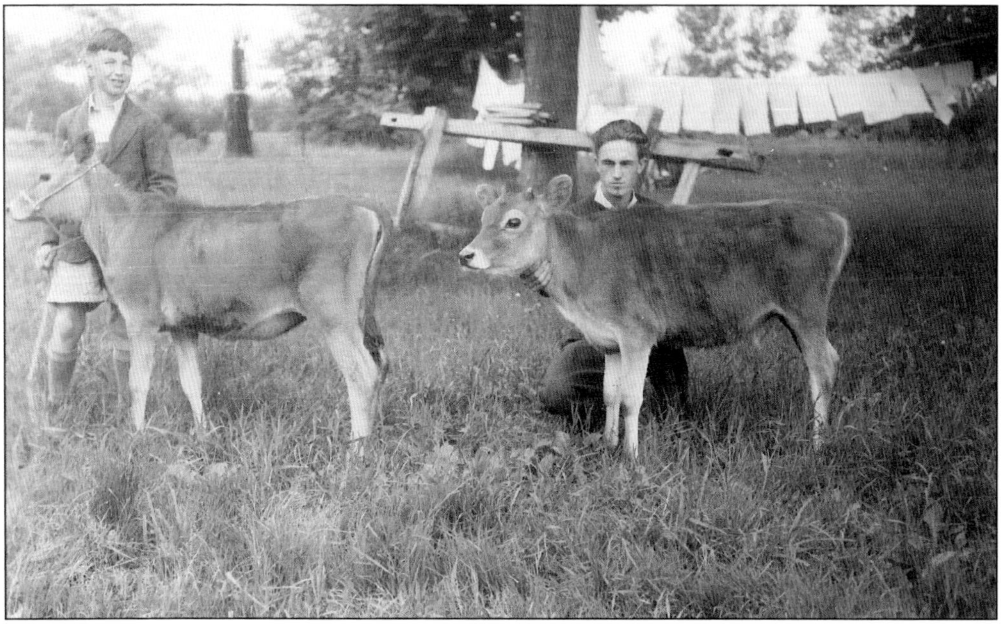

4-H clubs and related clubs in Harrison have played an important role over the years in building character and other noteworthy qualities that have enabled its young people to become successful in life. Here Dwight Sawin (left) and Wyman Dresser (right) are showing their Jersey heifers on the Dairy Club tour.

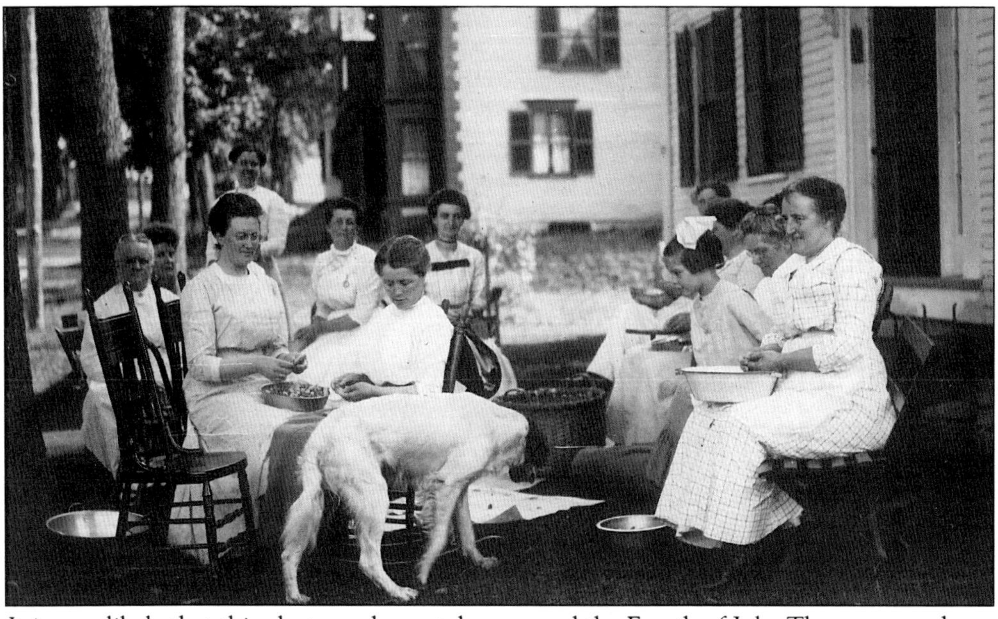

It is very likely that this photograph was taken around the Fourth of July. These women have gathered in front of the Wheeler House and are shelling peas for a family get-together or a community supper. Seated on the extreme left is Granny Greene; to the right near the door is Nell Davis.

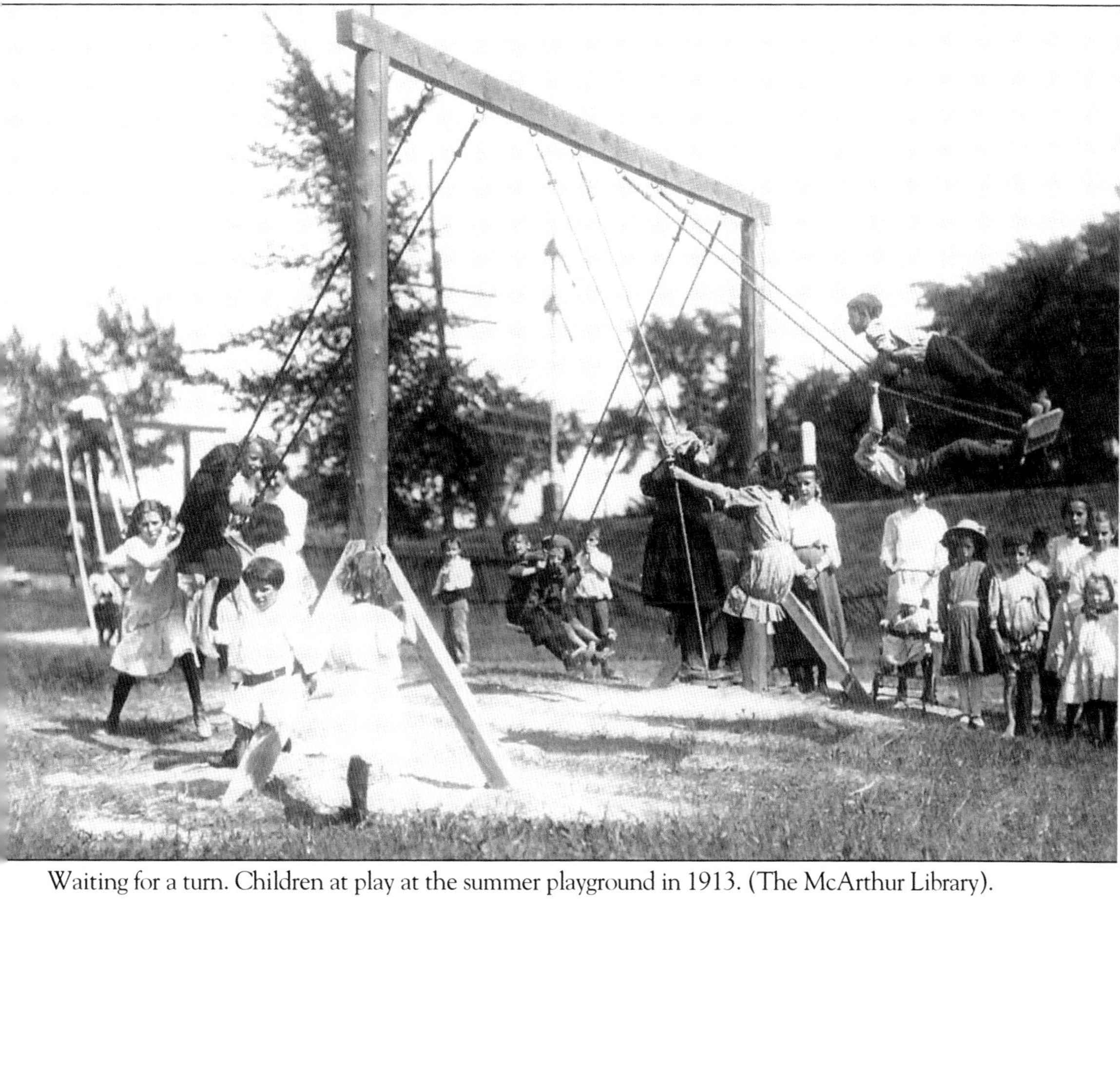

Waiting for a turn. Children at play at the summer playground in 1913. (The McArthur Library).

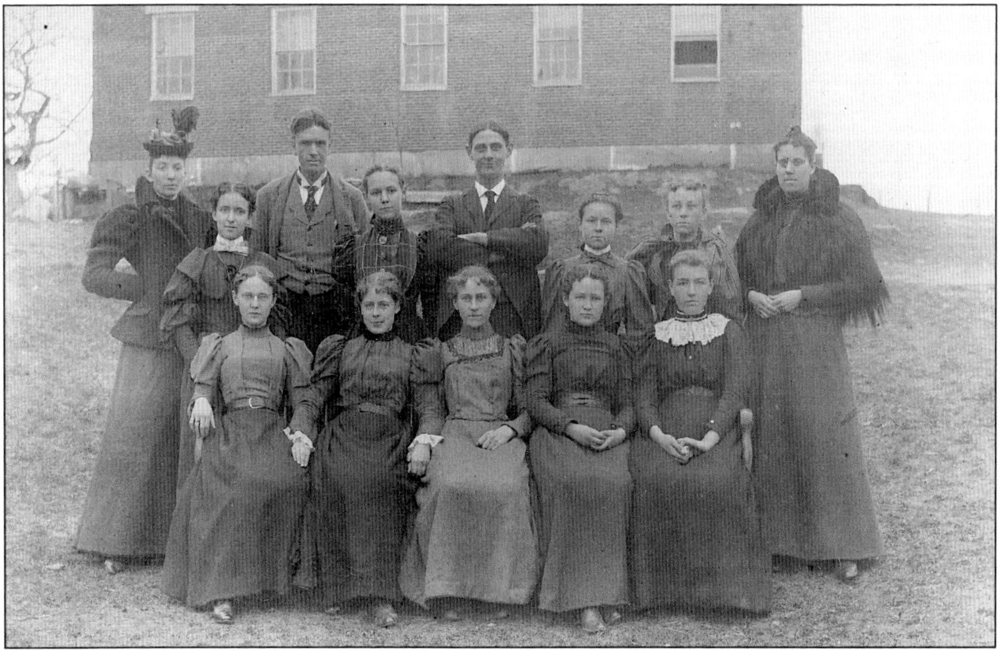

The class of 1899 poses in front of the Old Town House School, built in 1833 and later known as the Old Town Hall. It is now owned by the Windham Historical Society.

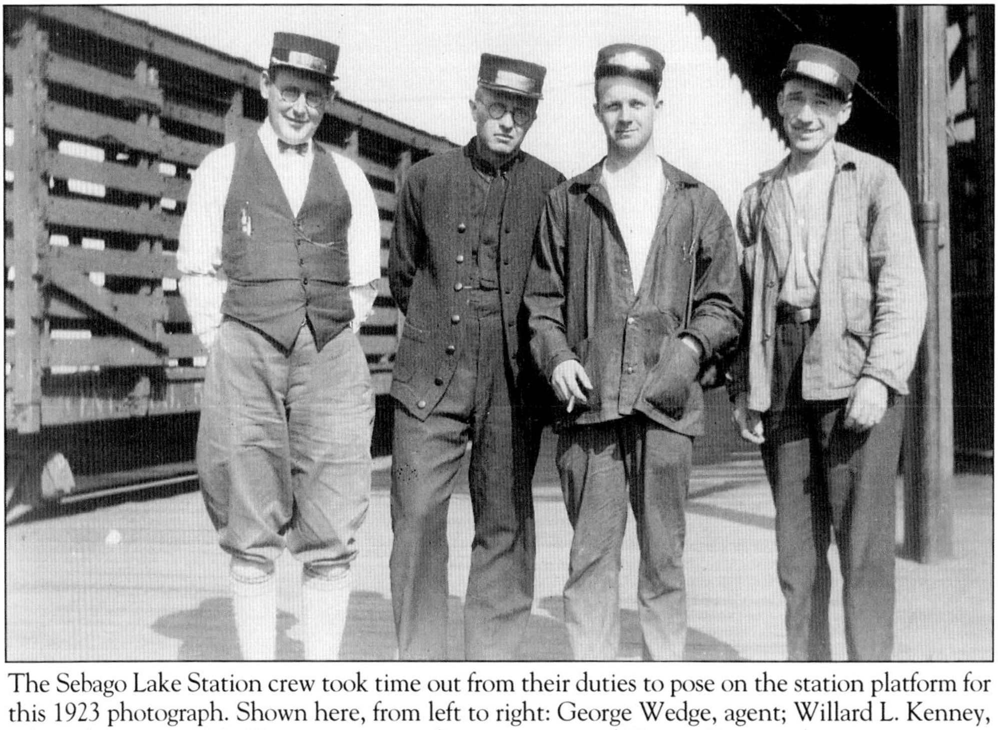

The Sebago Lake Station crew took time out from their duties to pose on the station platform for this 1923 photograph. Shown here, from left to right: George Wedge, agent; Willard L. Kenney, telegraph operator; Mr. Noonan, assistant baggage man; and Horace Ettinger, baggage man.

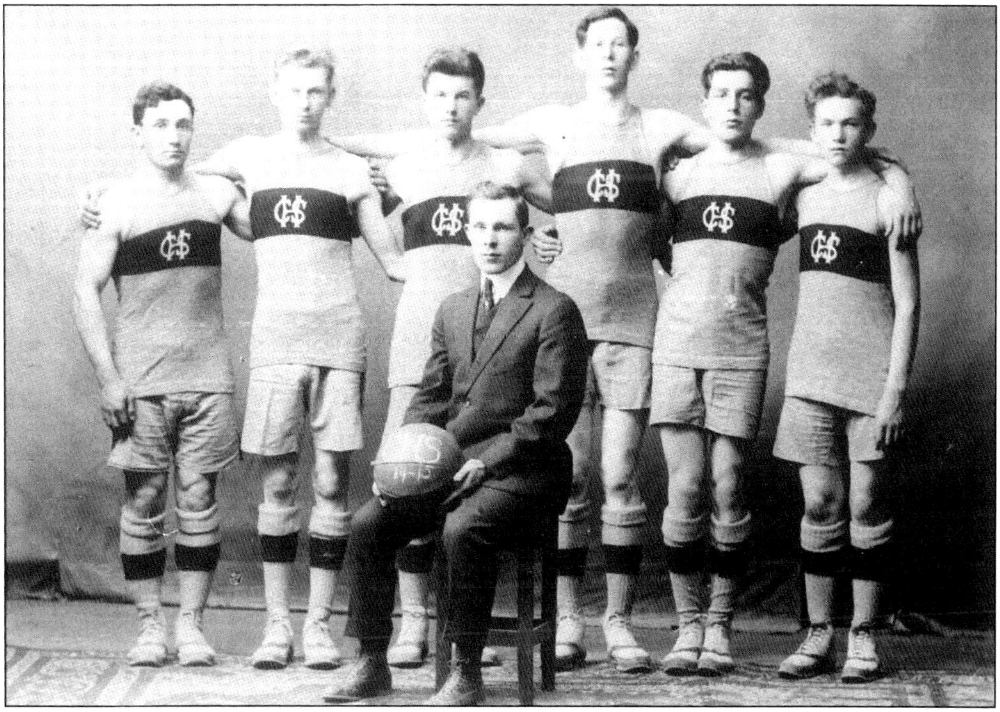

This 1914–15 squad was one of Casco High School's earliest basketball teams. At least two of these players, Melvin Shaw and George Burgess, were members of its first squad. The Casco HS boys won the coveted Class C State Championship under the tutelage of Conrad Hall in 1964. In 1966 they were the Western Maine Class C Champions.

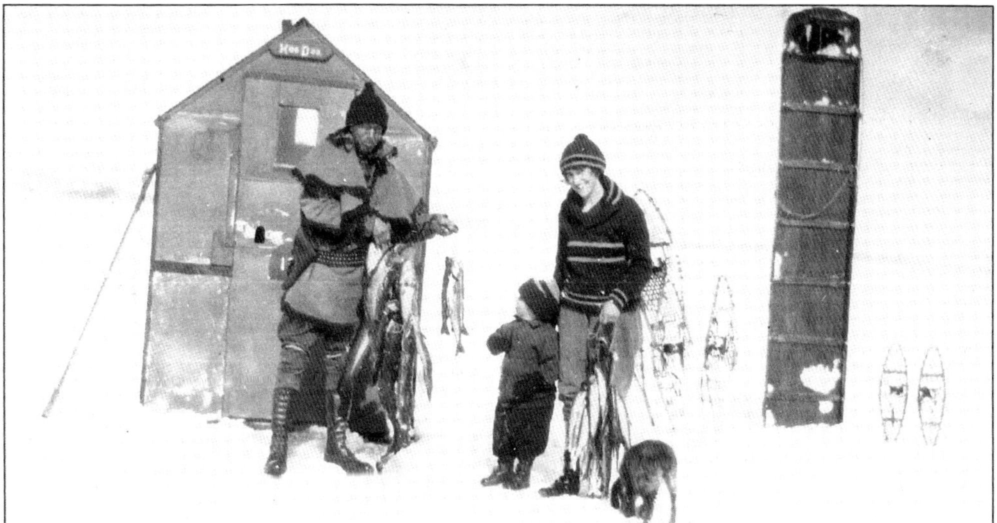

Cecil Lowell Barnes, his wife Rose (granddaughter of the famed Mellie Dunham), and their son Buddy (Dr. Lowell Barnes) certainly needed the toboggan (standing upright) to haul home this catch. Mellie Dunham made the snowshoes.

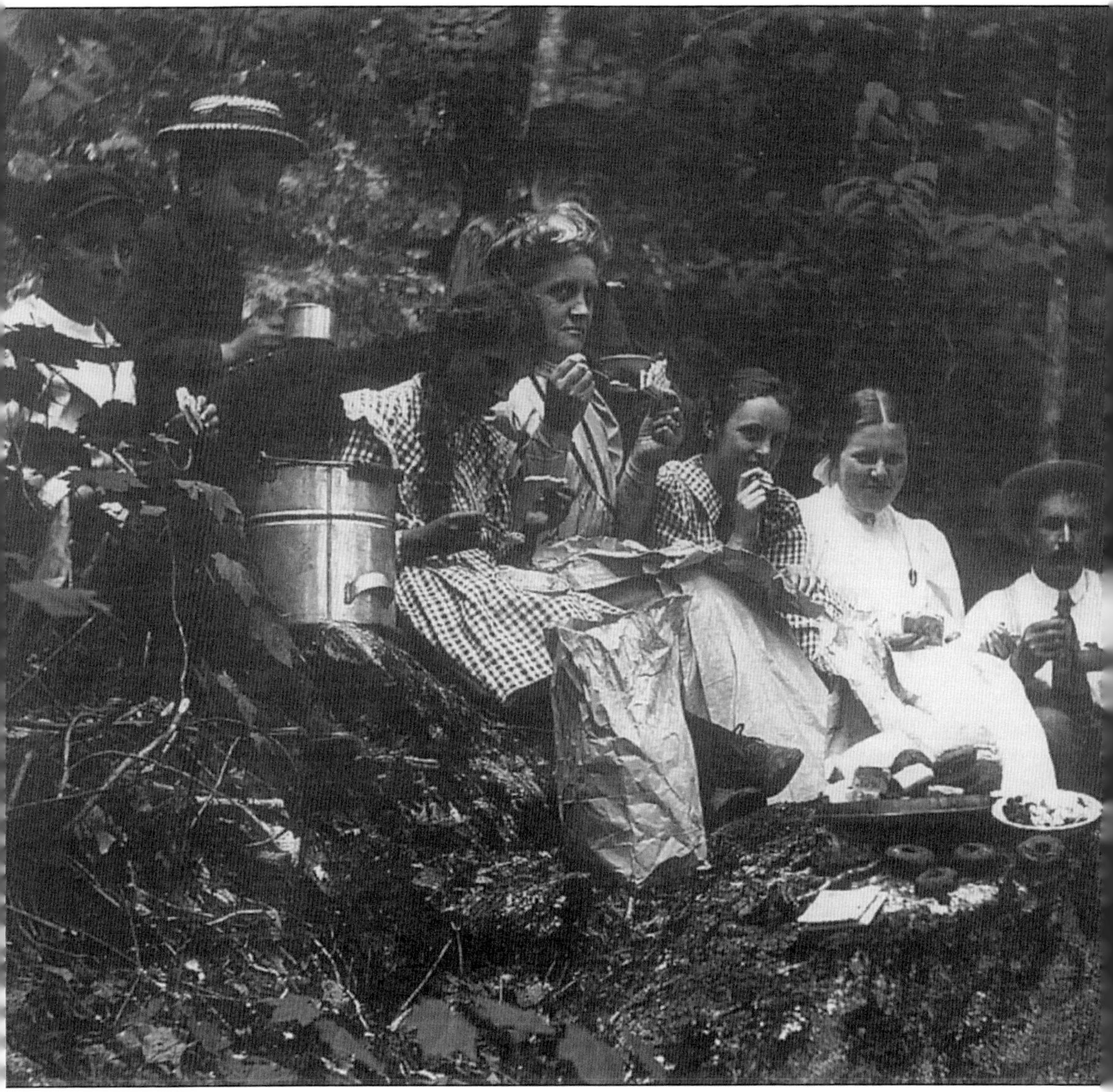

In this self-portrait, as in many of her portraits, Nettie Cummings Maxim used a painted scenic canvas backing which she attached to the side of the Maxim barn. She is either holding behind her back the leather bellows that controlled the shutter or had someone—very likely one of her three children—take this photograph. Interestingly she had only one tray containing flash powder for additional lighting. Therefore, the light all came from one side.

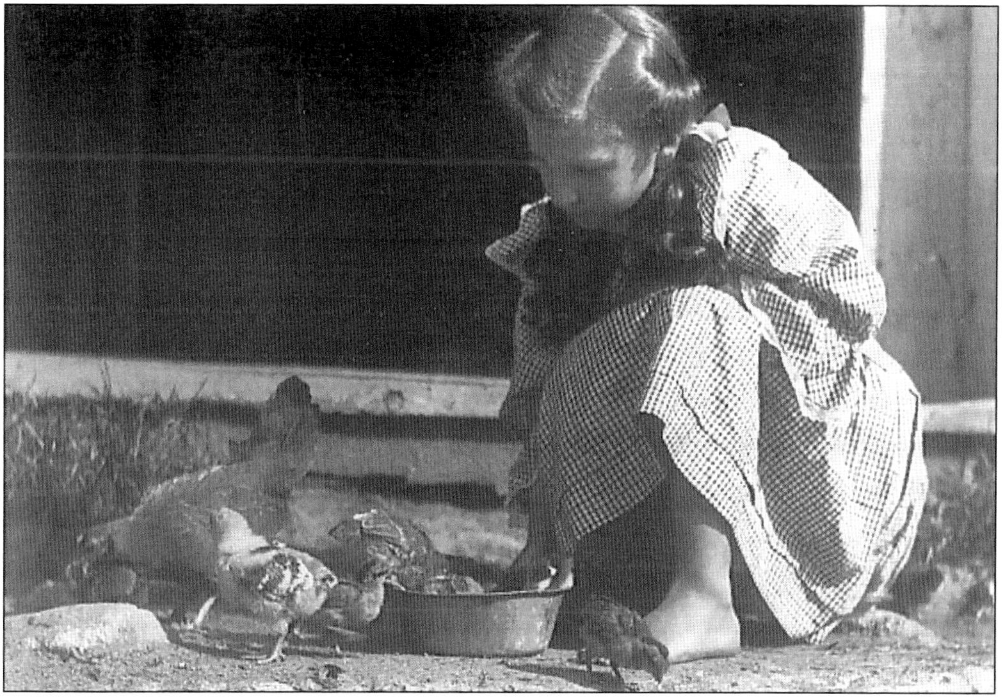

Bantams were popular pets for children living in rural areas. Nettie took this photograph of her daughter, Winnie, with a bantam hen and her little brood of month-old chicks sometime in late spring, 1904.

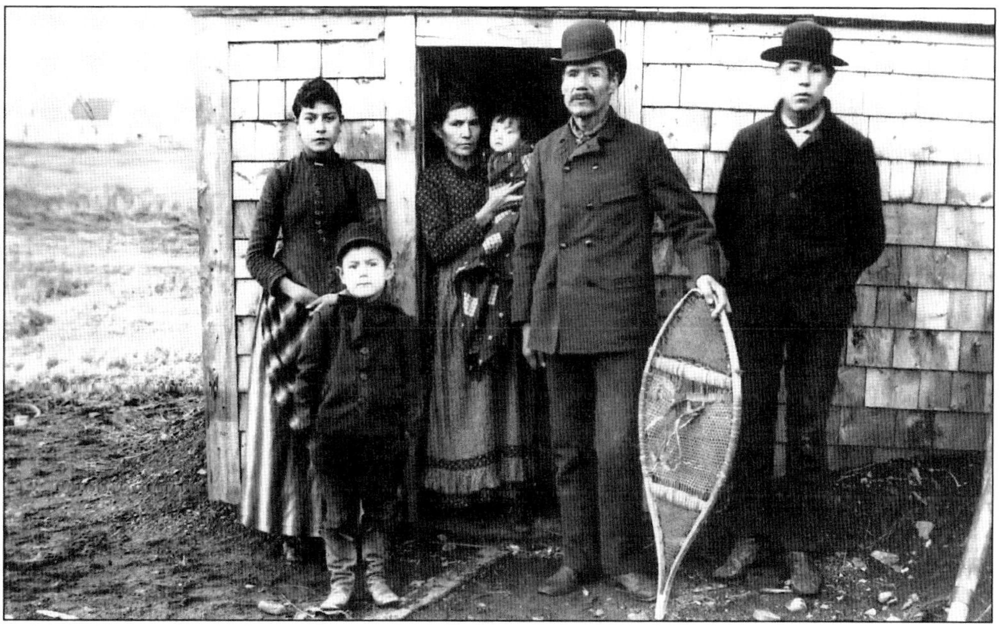

A Passamaquoddy family at Pleasant Point, *c.* 1885. The man is probably displaying his snowshoe-making craft. (Border Historic Society).

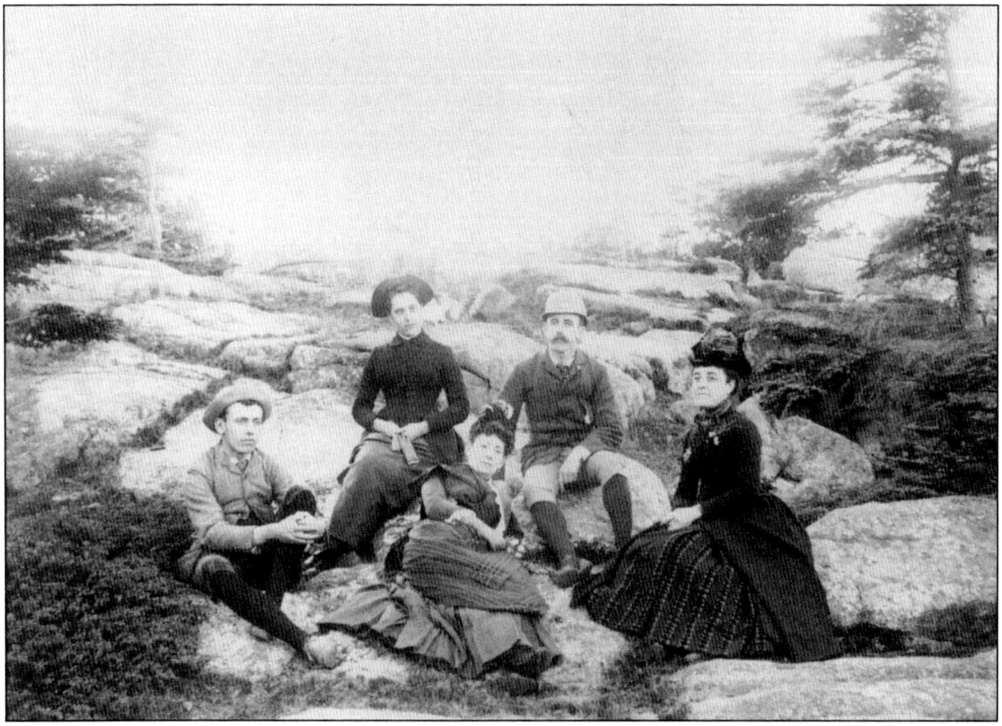

A photograph of Ms. Grace Kellog, "compliments of Wilfred A. French at Otter Cliffs—August 1883." (Raymond Strout).

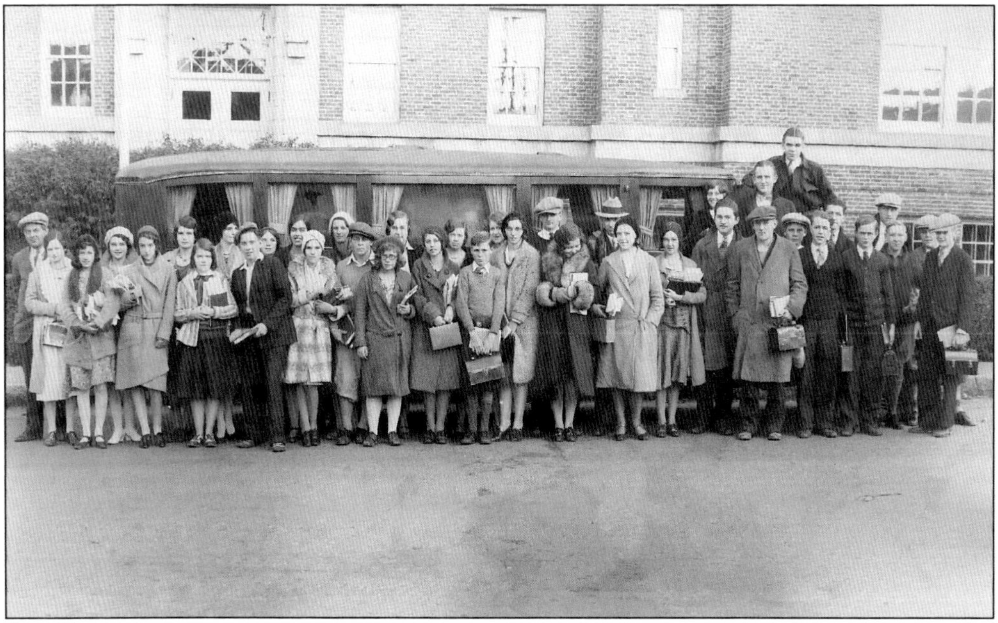

The school bus (curtains made by Mrs. Dolliver) and the fashionable students of the 1920s. Mr. Dolliver is the driver. (Robert Dolliver).

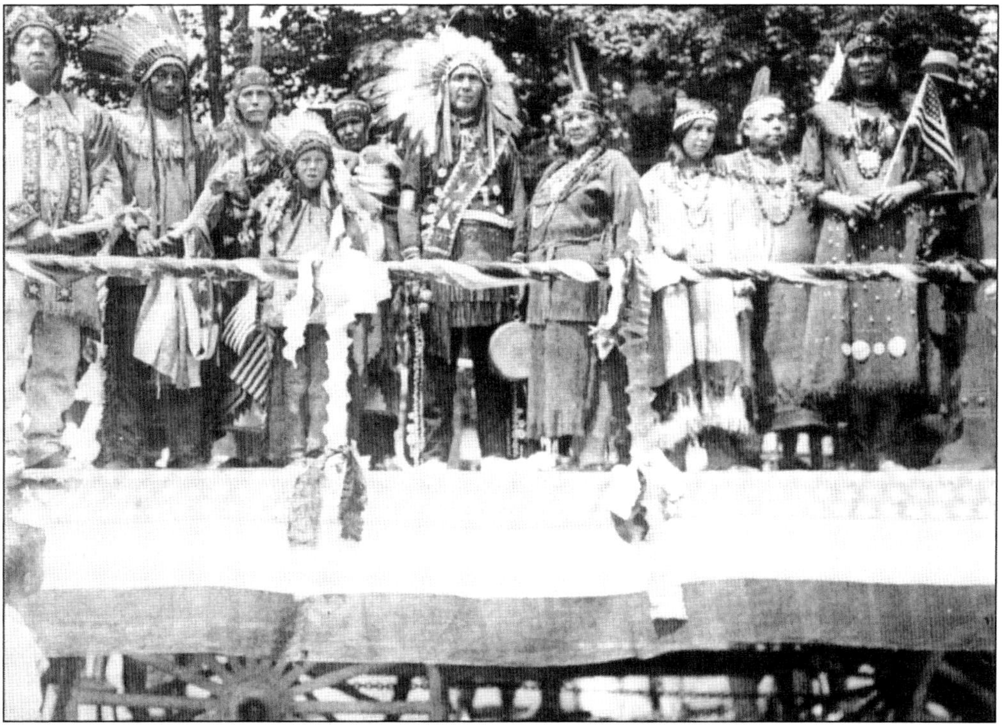

Passamaquoddy tribal members from Indian Township at the Princeton Centennial Celebration in 1932. By the 1930s their camps had disappeared from the Island where they had spent centuries of summers.

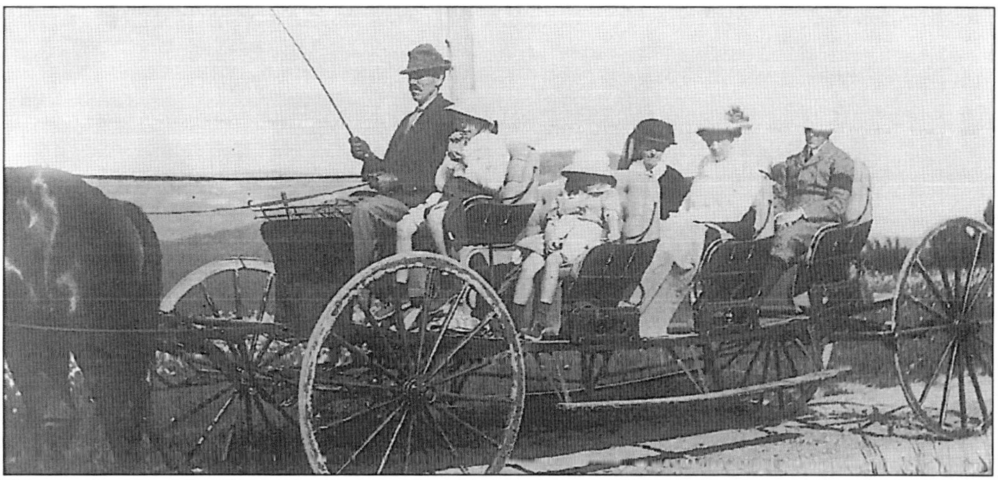

Carrying up to twelve passengers, the Bar Harbor buckboard remained the primary means of transportation on the island until a ban on automobiles was lifted in 1915. Whether meeting the steamer or providing the summer visitors with leisurely rides to the island's attractions, everyone depended on these locally made wagons. One visitor fondly recalled that she and her friends, clad in flowing dresses, took a half-day "drive up Beech Hill, saw the sunset, suppered at the Somes House, and returned by moonlight, all singing lustily." (Dunham Family Collection).

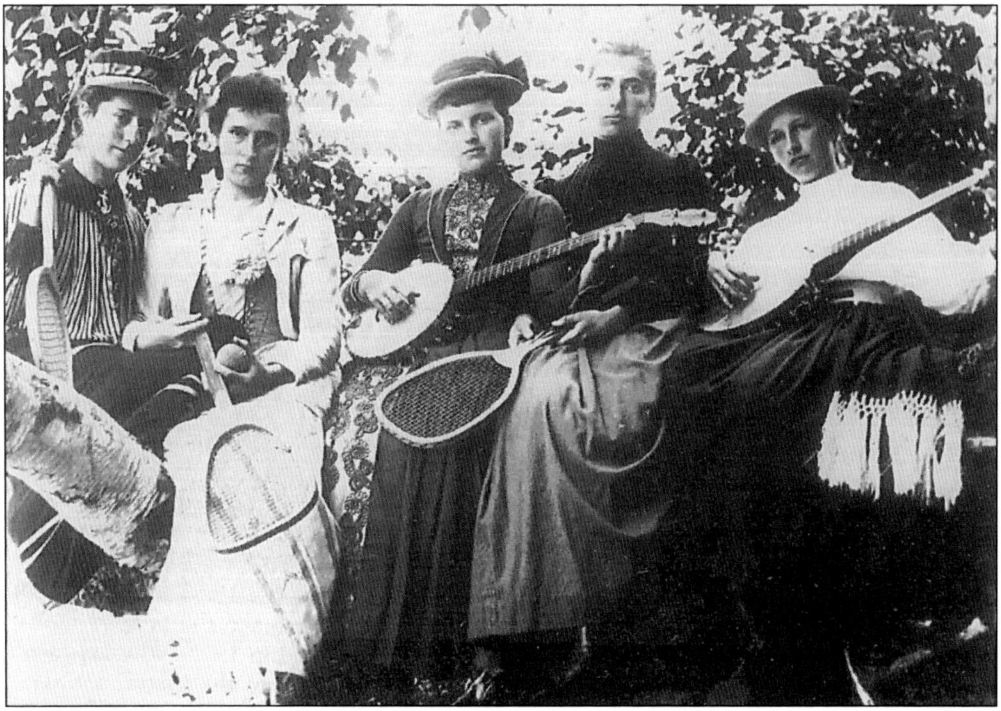

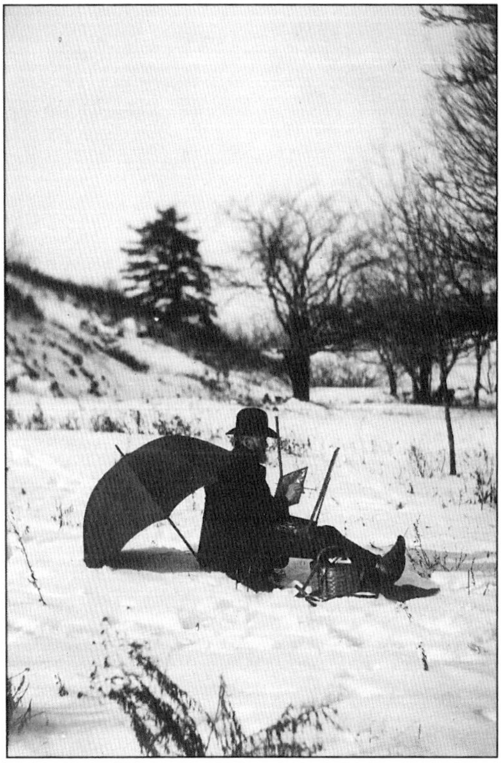

Taken in 1889, this photograph shows a group of women, outfitted in long-sleeved blouses, ankle-length skirts, and jackets. They look to be well prepared for some tennis on the Seaside Inn lawn in Seal Harbor, or perhaps a banjo recital in the hotel's music room, popular day and evening diversions. (Walter K. Shaw Sr).

George F. Morse takes advantage of a late fall snowfall to create a winter landscape at Delano Park in Cape Elizabeth, *c.* 1892. (Robert Shuman family).

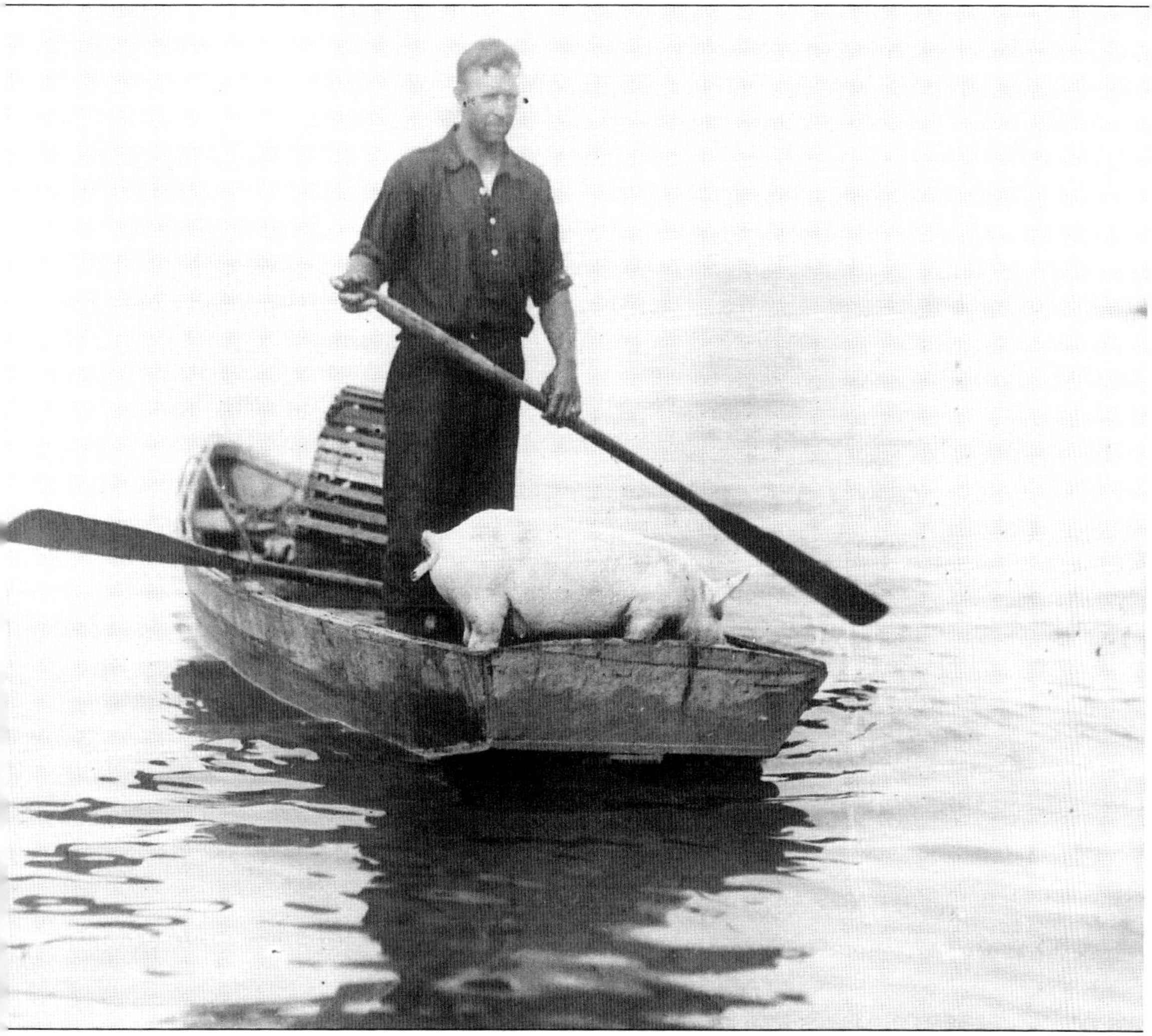

Frank Darling and the family's pet pig Suzie go lobstering off Broad Cove, Cape Elizabeth, *c.* 1920. A good swimmer, Suzie often went out lobstering and also enjoyed a good game of tag with the twelve Darling children. The Darlings rented the only home at Broad Cove and, when times were tough, were known to enjoy roast pig. (Ernest Darling).

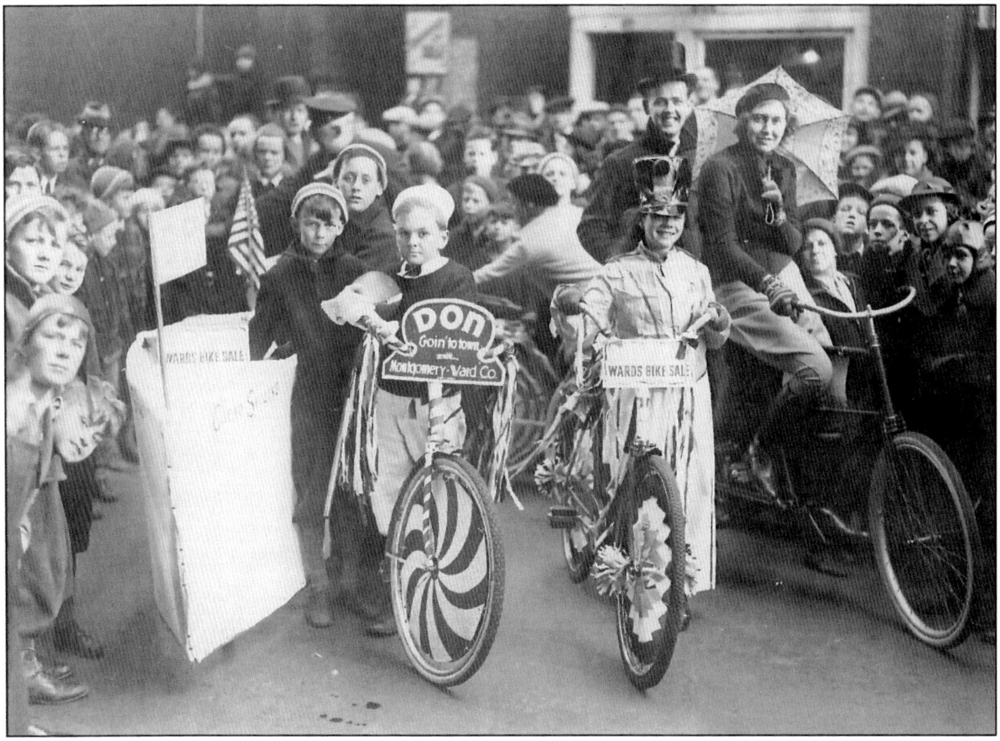

Montgomery Ward, once located on Congress Street in Portland, sponsored a bike parade in 1935 with prizes going to the best-decorated bikes. Twelve-year-old Harris Hinckley (to the left), of South Portland, was a winner with his entry, "Clear Sailing," though it was hard to keep his "boat" on course while parading down Congress Street in the wind. (Harris Hinckley, M.D.).

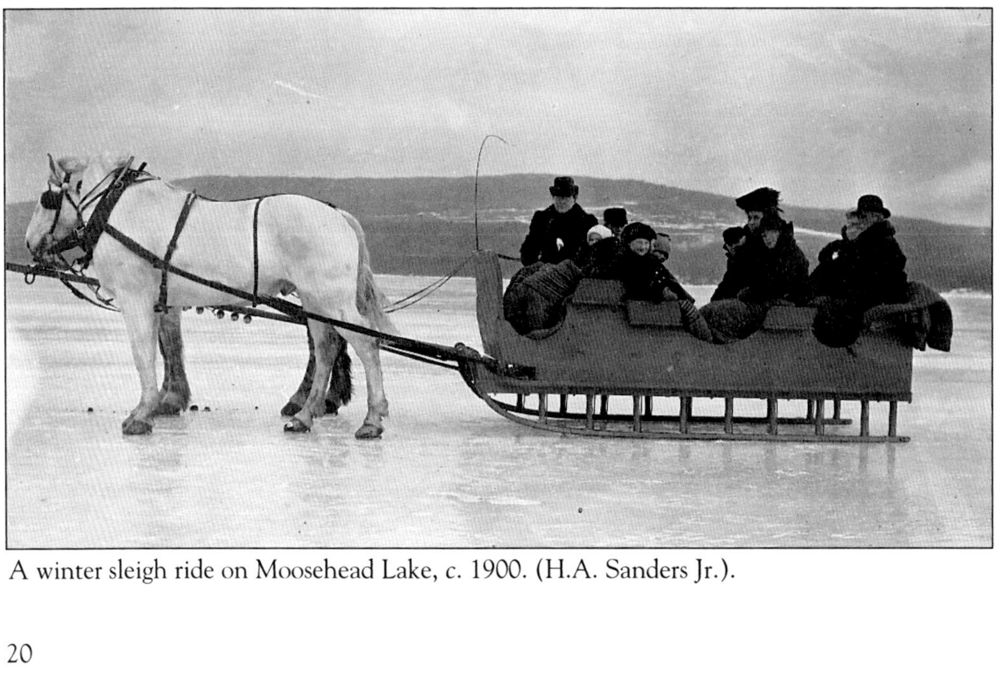

A winter sleigh ride on Moosehead Lake, *c*. 1900. (H.A. Sanders Jr.).

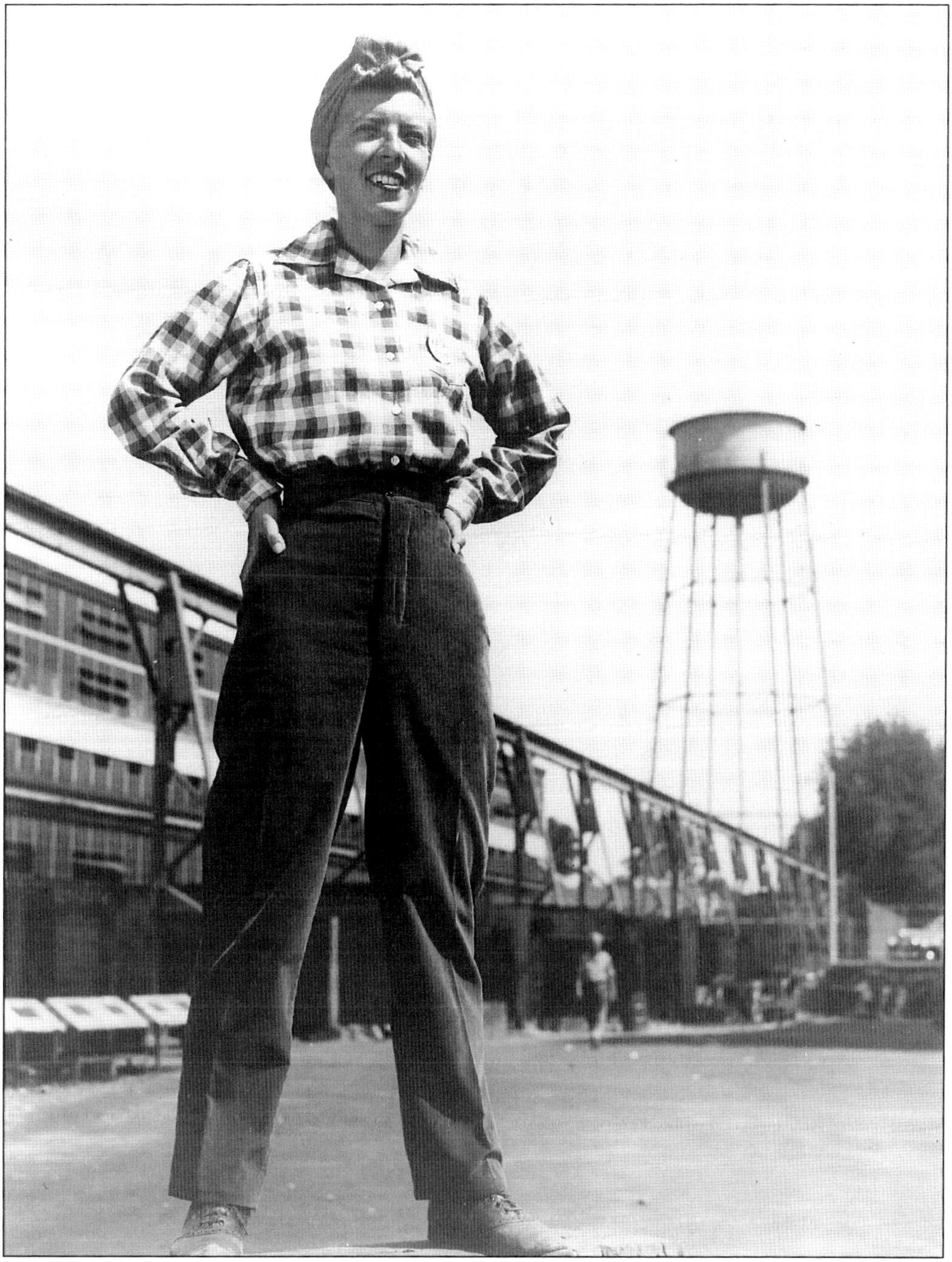

A "Wendy." Virginia Piston O'Toole of South Portland typifies the women who worked at the shipyards throughout America. The first non-clerical woman was hired in South Portland in 1942. Those assigned to the welding shop were known nationwide as "Wendy the Welder," a counterpart to "Rosie the Riviter." For most, it was their first taste of "men's work for men's wages," though they were handed pink slips when the men returned. (Edward Langlois).

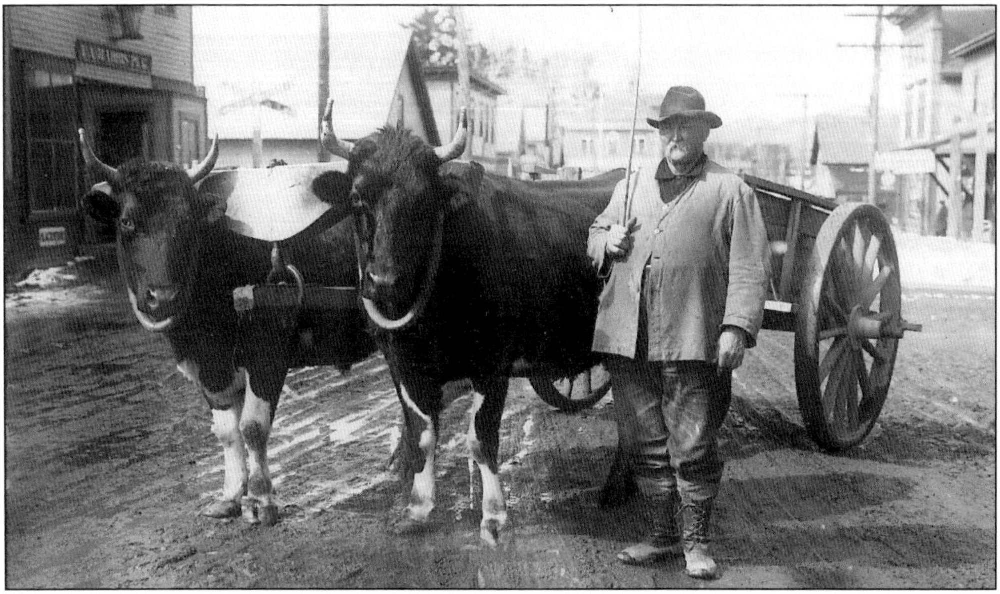

Two oxen and a cart in Greenville. The man with the team is Preo, who raised two enormous oxen: one was 7 feet 7 inches tall, and the other 7 feet 11 inches tall. (G.D. Hamilton).

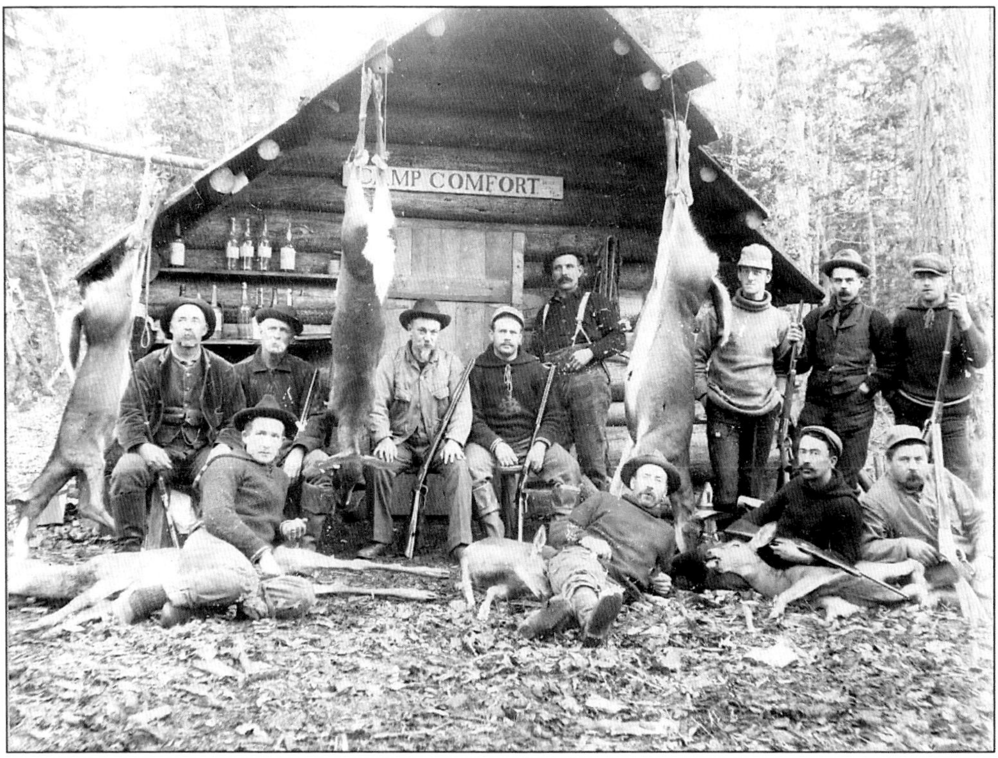

A deer hunting party at Camp Comfort on Moosehead Lake, 1890s. The party included twelve hunters, ten rifles, and twelve bottles of whiskey on the wall.

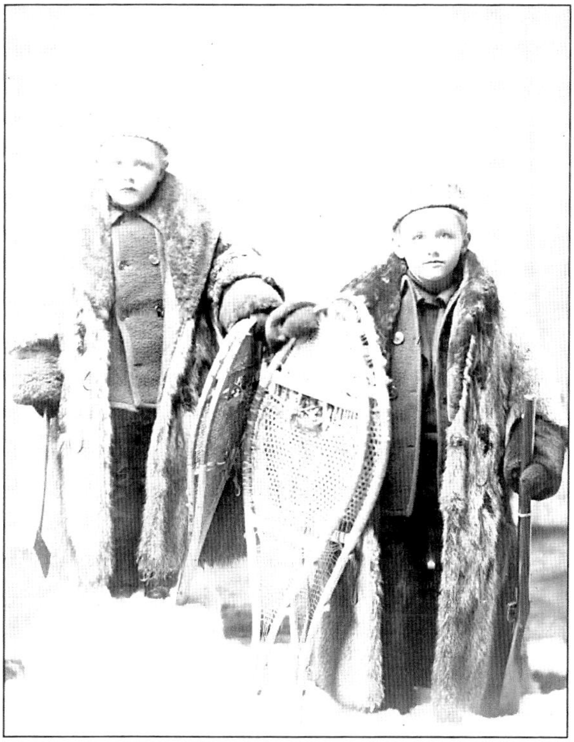

Harry A. and Paul B. Sanders of Greenville, Maine, c. 1890. This staged photograph depicts an outdoor scene complete with winter attire and snowshoes. (H.A. Sanders Jr.).

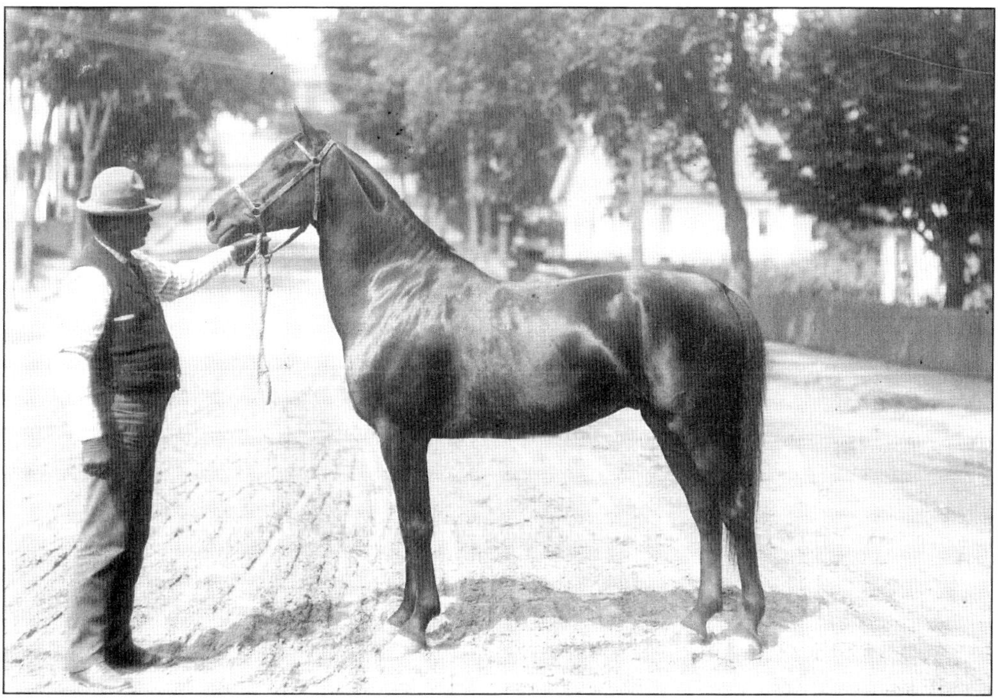

William Miller and steed were photographed in this view looking up Goff Hill in Auburn.

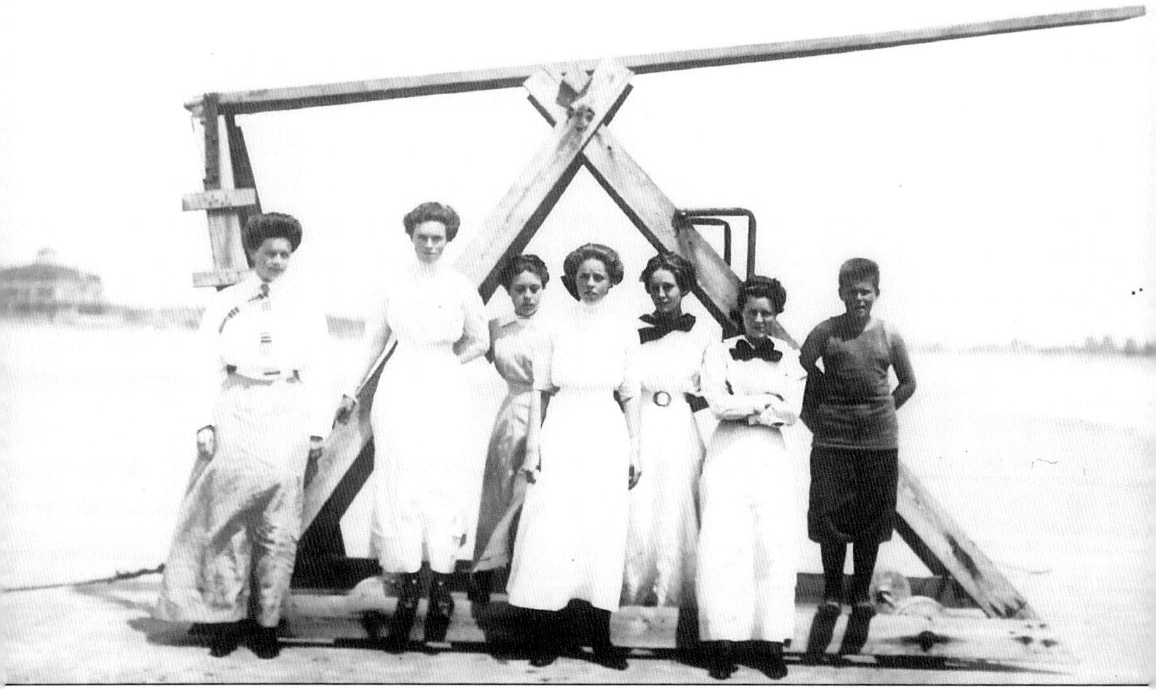

This diving platform was constructed for use at Long Beach. It had wheels that enabled the bathers to push it out beyond the breakers. A cable attached to a winch was used to pull the platform out of the water. A simple ladder provided access to the diving boards. The women are not dressed for swimming but their clothing is appropriate for walking on the beach.

The men in this photograph proudly display a 175 pound halibut caught on a hand line from Jack Young't Gay Day. The giant fish was caught off Boon Island by E.A. Clark on July 31, 1922.

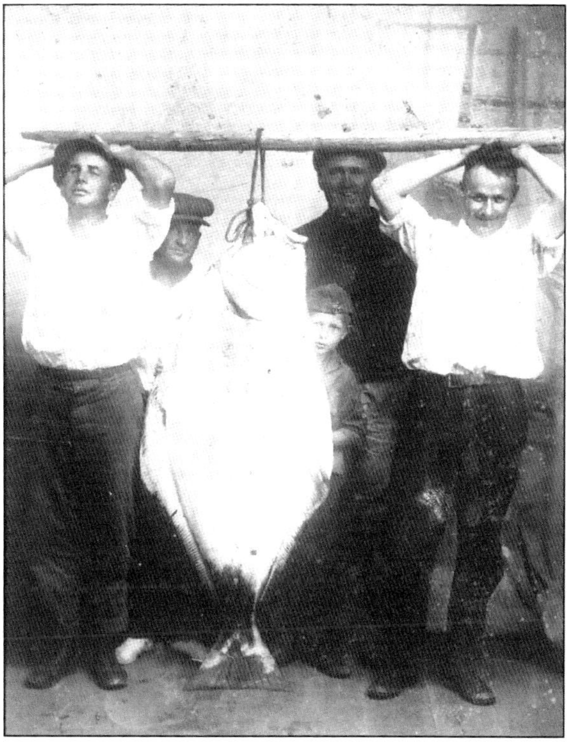

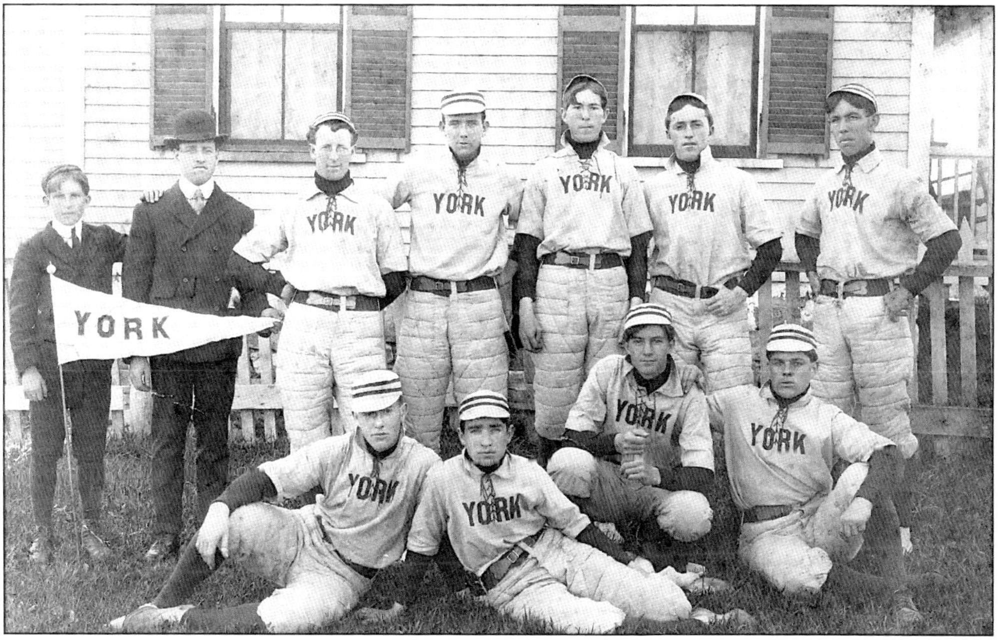

The 1910 York High School baseball team poses for a team picture. Seated, left to right: Ed Hawkes, Don Wakefield, Frewd Martin, and Bill Littlefield. Standing: Marshall Putnam, Harry Thompson, Same Moulton, Art Baker, John Ladd, Leslie Bragdon, and John Stover.

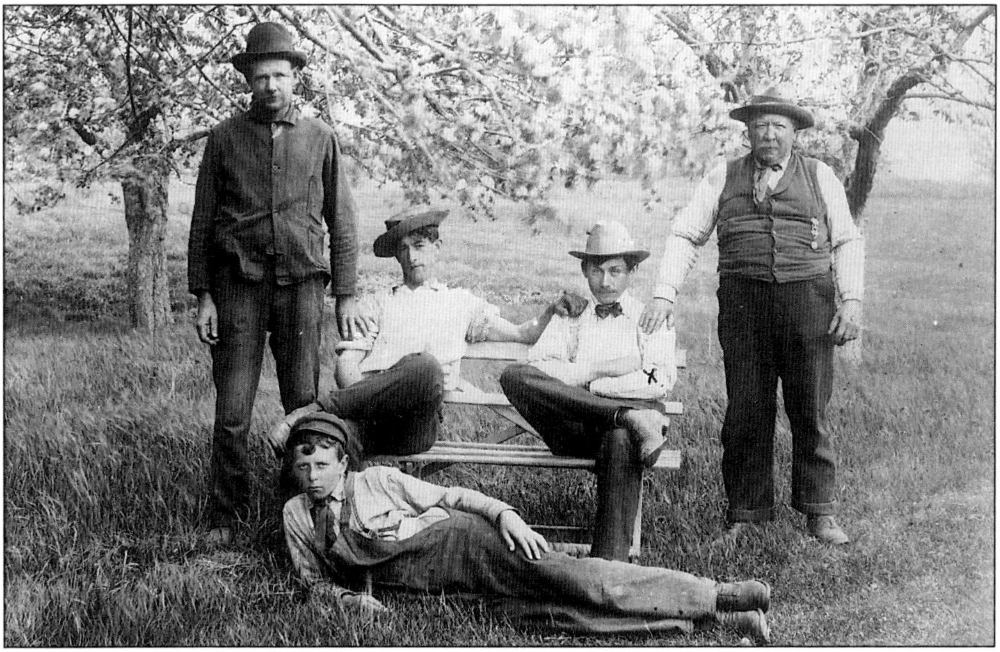

Pictured here are members of the gypsy moth crew that moved about the countryside destroying gypsy moth eggs. They wrapped tree trunks with burlap that had been soaked in creosote and removed rocks from stone walls in search of egg masses. This crew operated during the period 1912 to 1920.

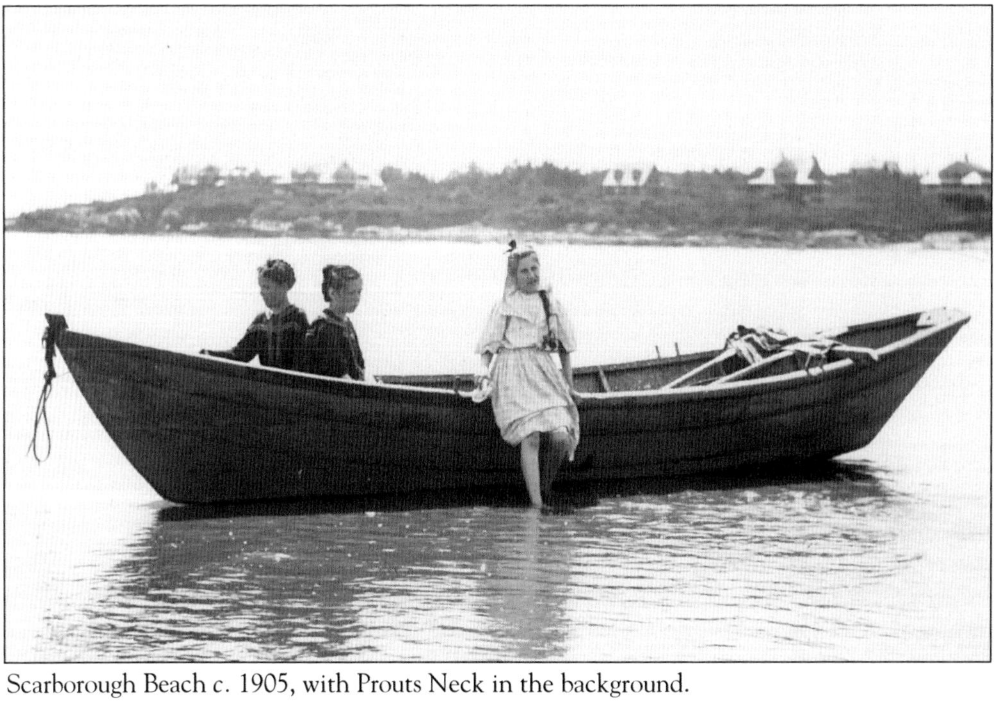

Scarborough Beach c. 1905, with Prouts Neck in the background.

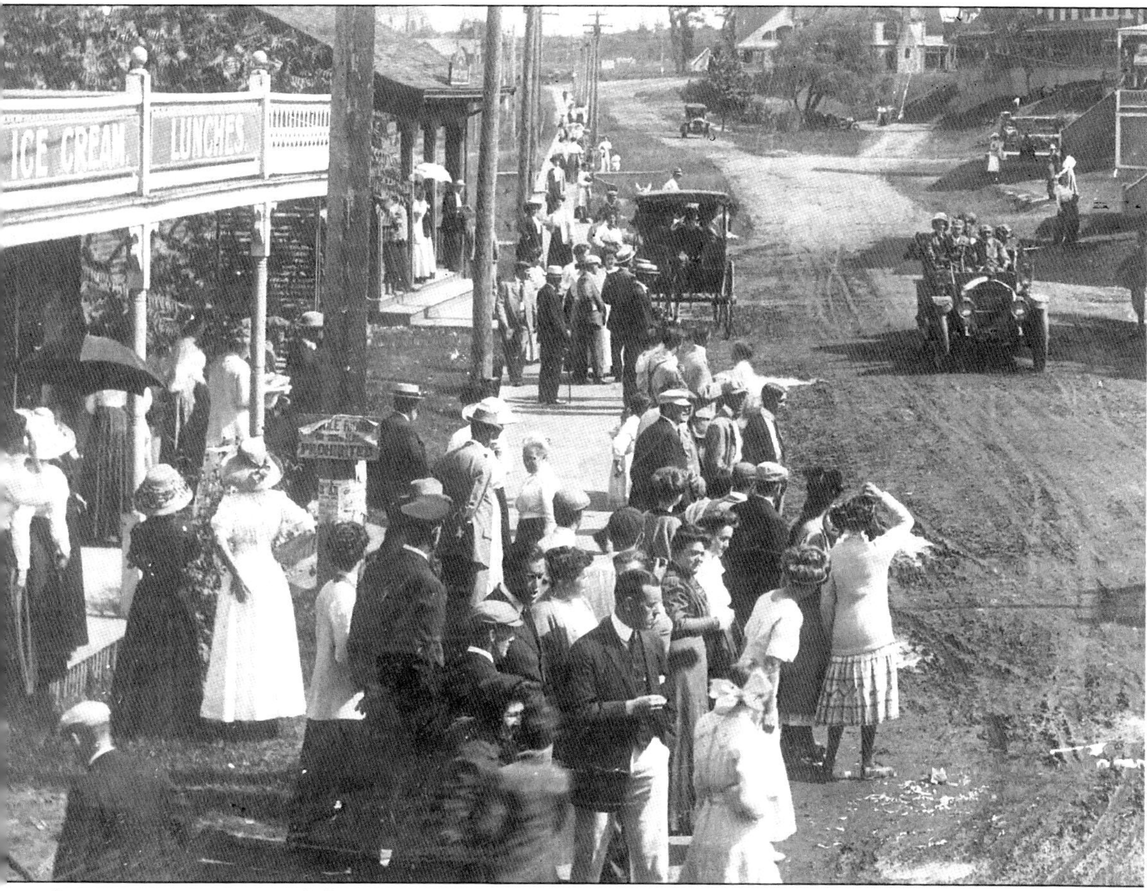

A cross-country automobile tour attracted a large crowd of spectators outside of Goldenrod Restaurant. At that time automobiles were so unusual that the curious gathered to watch the first of the touring cars arrive in York Beach.

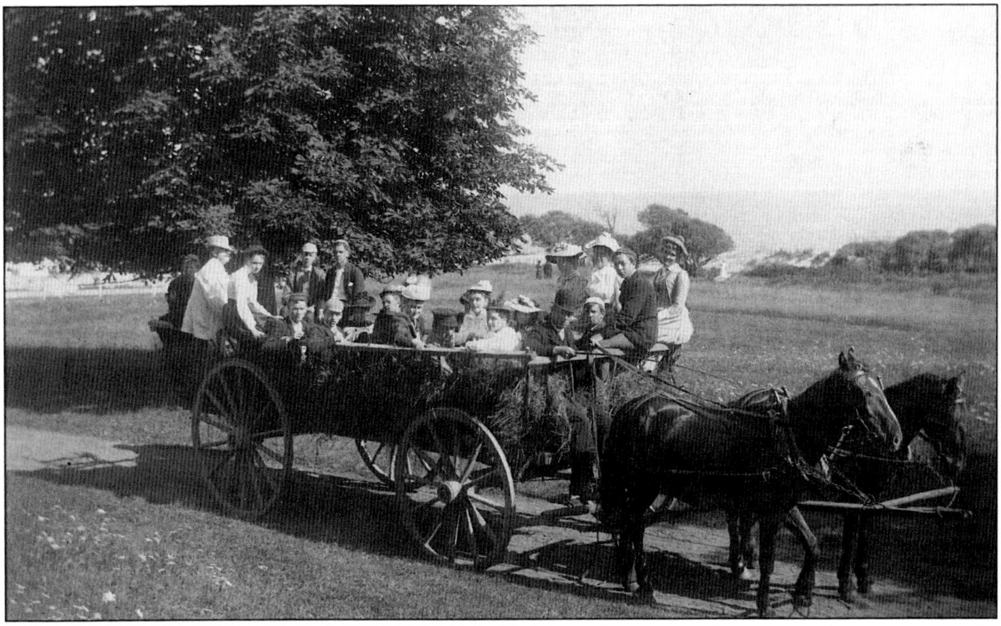

Hay wagon rides were a popular event in the summer. They would often take trips to such places as Mitchell's shore dinner house on the Spurwink River, or Two Lights in Cape Elizabeth. (Prouts Neck Historical Society).

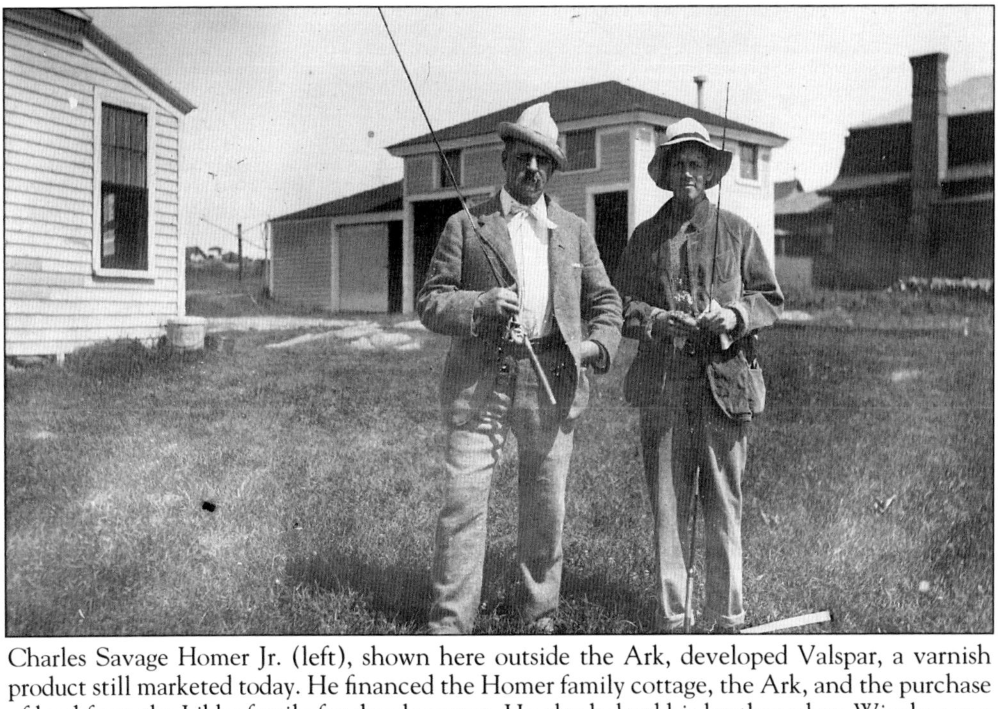

Charles Savage Homer Jr. (left), shown here outside the Ark, developed Valspar, a varnish product still marketed today. He financed the Homer family cottage, the Ark, and the purchase of land from the Libby family for development. He also helped his brother when Winslow was establishing himself as an independent artist. (Jane King).

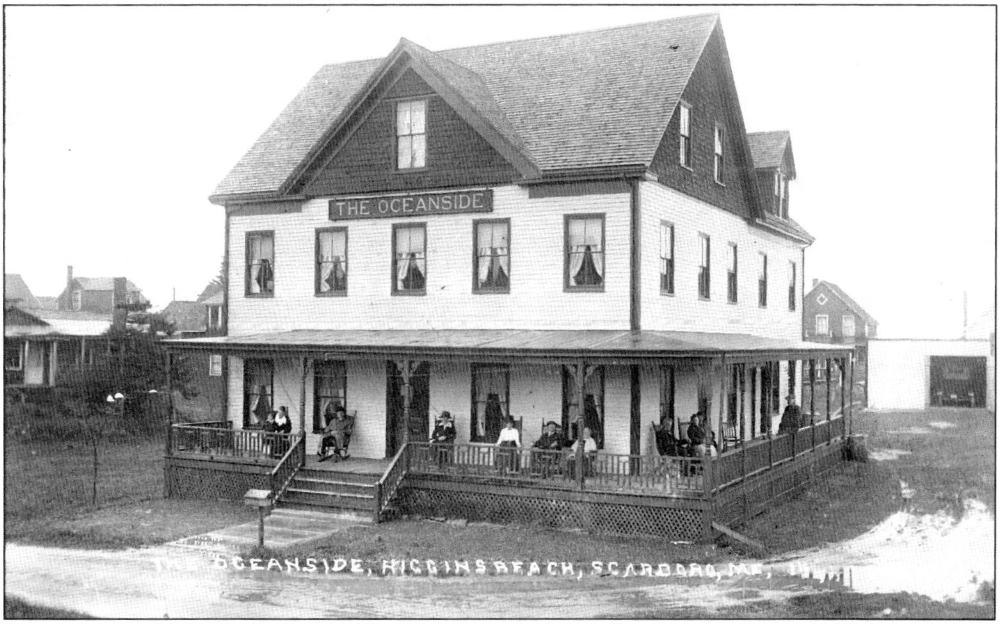

Built in 1897, the Oceanside was the first hotel at Higgins Beach. Located on Pearl Street, it was originally called the Lawson House, after the proprietor. It stands today as an apartment house.

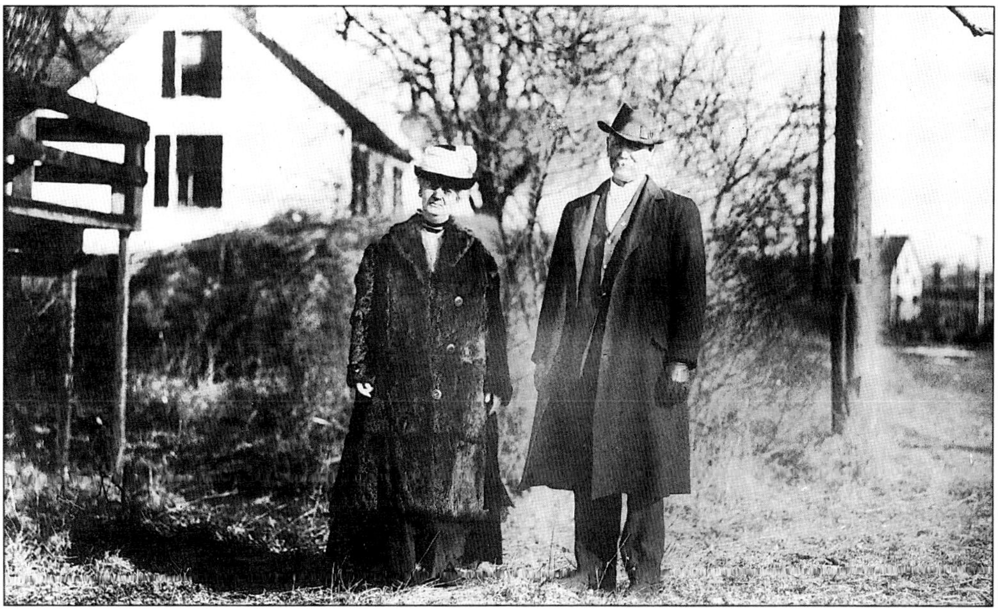

Carrie and Enoch Curtis head up Crow Hill, Cape Porpoise, where their home was located in the late 1800s. Some neighbors, preferring a more genteel address, claimed "Cape Porpoise Highlands" as their residence instead of Crow Hill, but the name never stuck. To their left was the Prospect House, a small summer hotel "only about four hours' ride from Boston." The Curtis house was lost in the 1947 fires. (Huff Family).

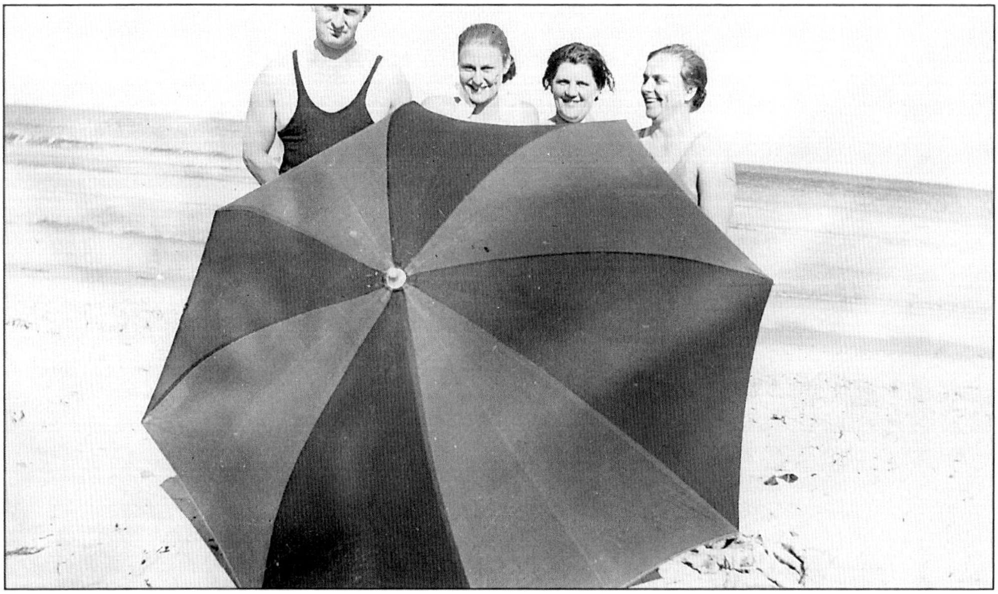

On a family outing at Goose Rocks Beach (also known as Beachwood) in the 1930s are, from left to right: Lyman Huff, Dot Huff, Ruby Shaeffer, and Goldie Huff. (Huff Family).

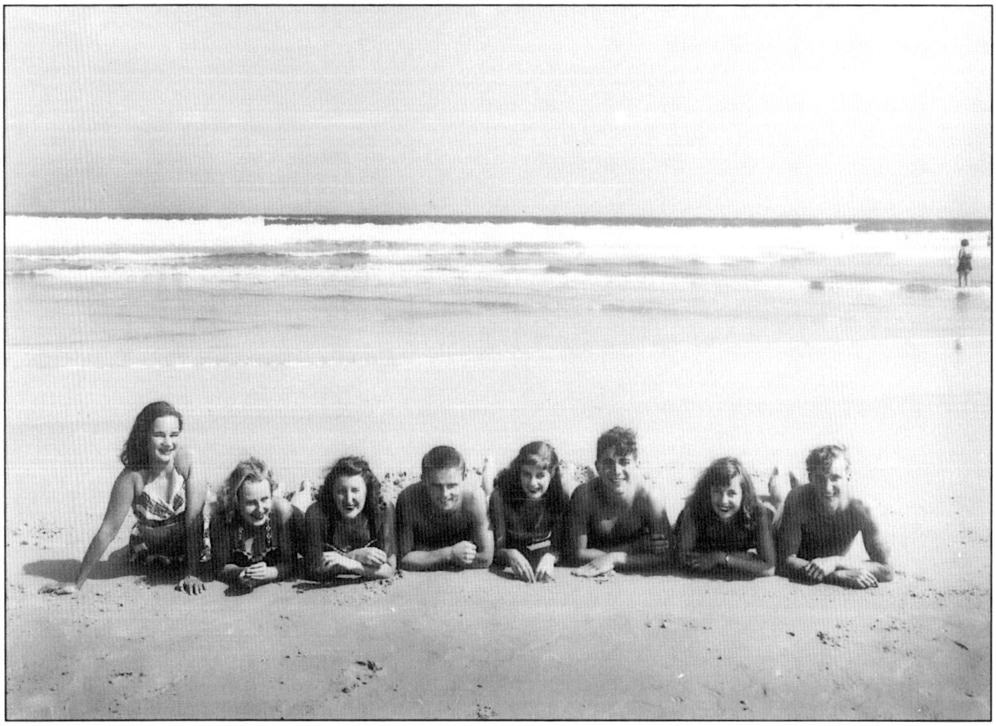

Young people out enjoying the summer of 1946 at Ogunqut Beach. Pictured from left to right: Mary Claire Kearns, Ann McAfee, Barbara Boston, Jack King, Sheila Lynch, unknown, Eleanor Holzborn, and Vernon Anderson.

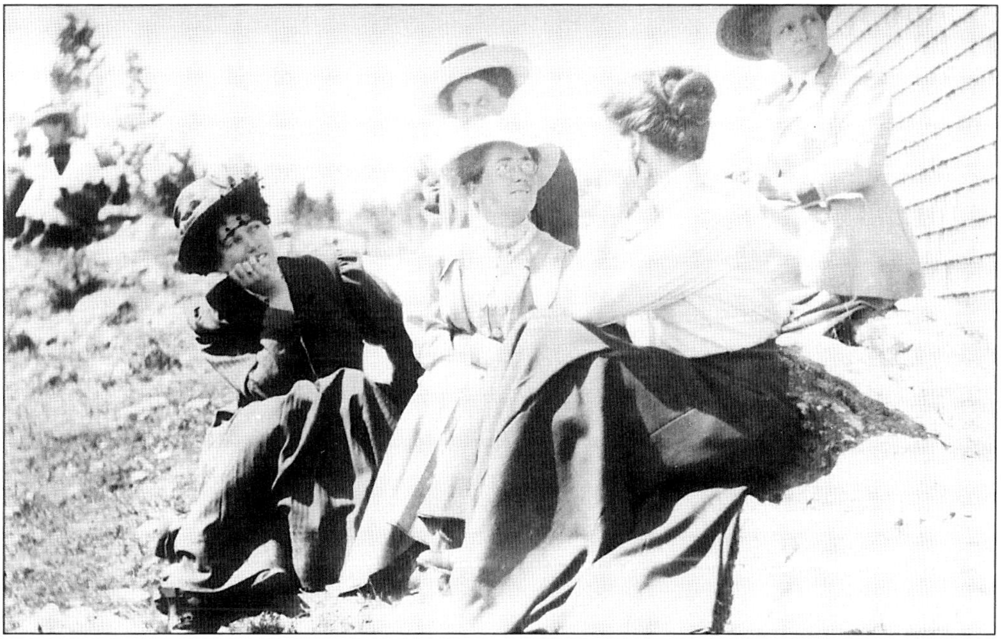

A group of well-to-do maiden ladies joined the art colony during the school's first nineteen years. Dressed in long skirts, high-collared blouses, and wide-brimmed straw hats, they were called the "virginal wayfarers" by locals who saw them painting along the Marginal Way.

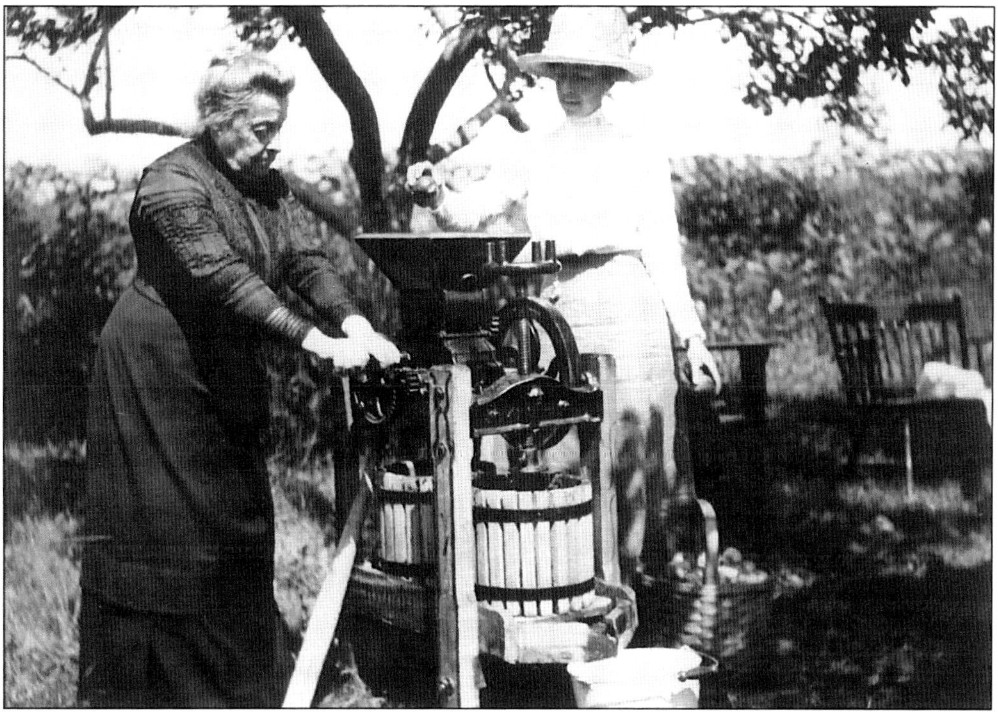

Painter Elinor Earle watching as her mother, Mrs. James M. Earle, makes cider.

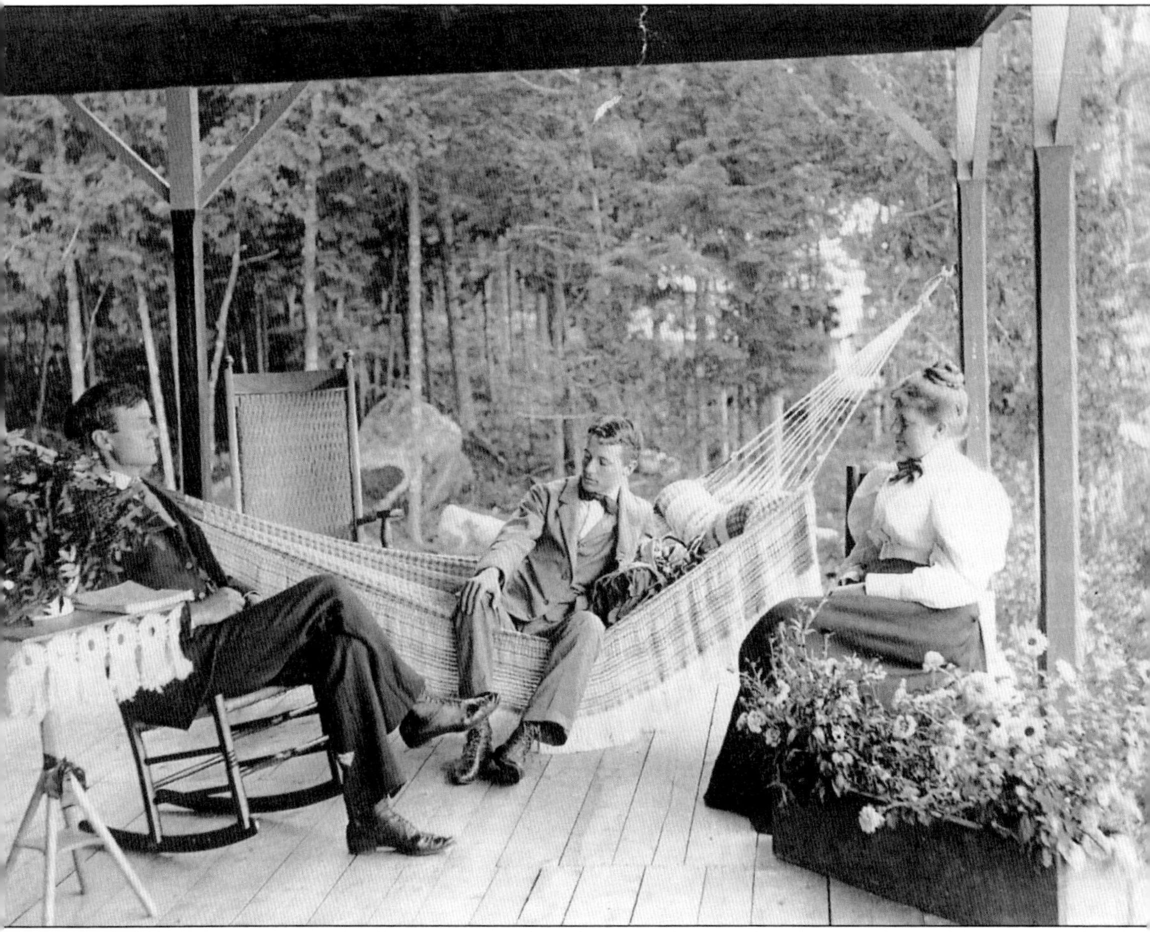

I love thy shores of forest green,
The birch, the fir, the pine;
Thy shaded groves, I rest serene
As neath them I recline.

Thy cooling wave, and gentle breeze
Are refuge from the heat;
And sunshine days beneath thy trees
Make summer joys complete . . .

From "Sebec in Summer," a poem written in 1926 by H.F. Huse, a Dover-Foxcroft clergyman. Photograph by Biri Fay.

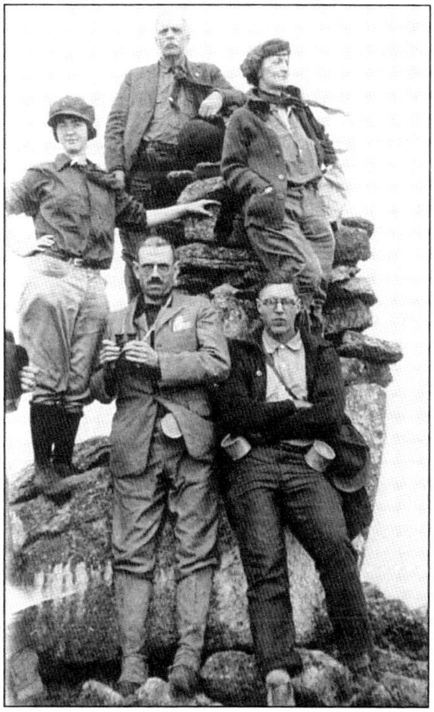

In this photograph, taken on Katahdin's summit c. 1929, Willis E. Parsons (top) stands with a group of hikers including his son, Willis G. (front with binoculars). The elder Mr. Parsons was Maine's first Commissioner of Inland Fisheries and Game, serving from 1918 to 1929. During his tenure he helped to establish several conservation measures designed to protect Maine's fish, game, and natural resources, including the single-deer-limit law, state fishing licenses, and the 90,000-acre Katahdin Game Sanctuary. (John Parsons).

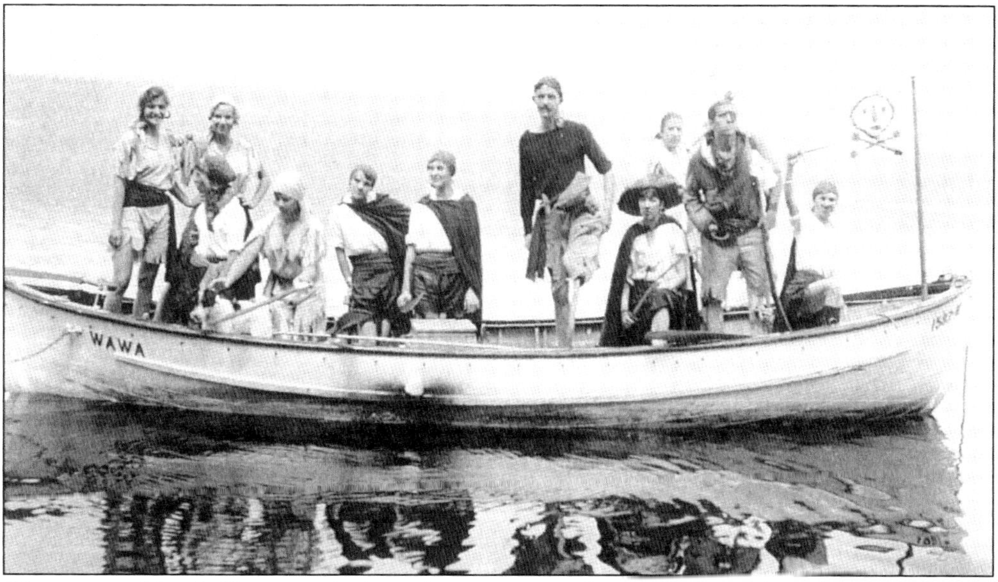

This group of South Shore youth dressed as pirates may have participated in a boat parade held during the Regatta at Greeley's Landing during the 1930s. From left to right are Betty Buck, Jane Hall, Dot Voorhis, Pat Hall, Betty Herley, Dot Kibbe, Bob Leavitt, Florence Redman, Lucy Barry, Ted Barry, and Betty Hall. Dr. C.C. Hall's boat, the *Wawa*, is not to be confused with another boat by the same name, owned by Dr. Hall's son, "Buzz." The second *Wawa* was a lifeboat from a U.S. Navy destroyer. (Gini Redman).

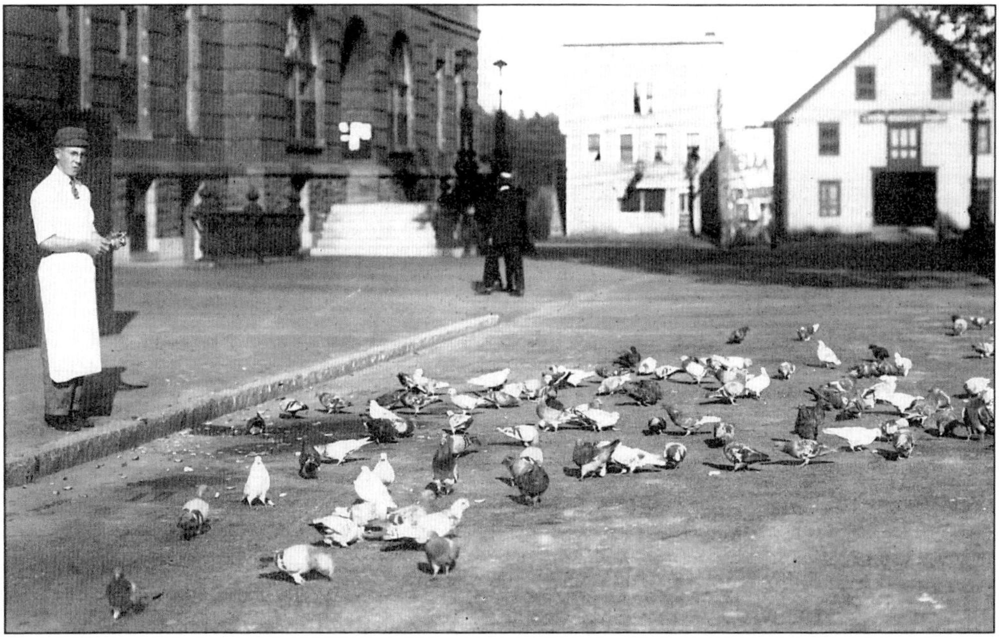

F. Harold Dubord feeds the pigeons in Waterville in the 1910s or 1920s. At this time he was an attorney, but he went on to become mayor and a Maine Supreme Court justice.

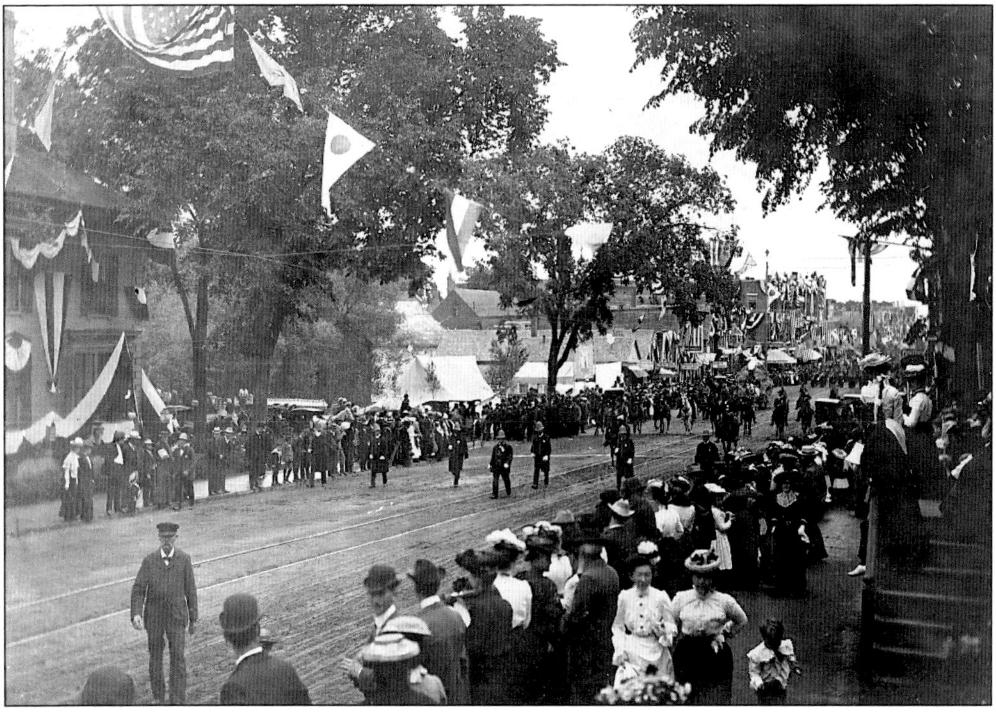

The 1920 Centennial Parade passing by the hordes of spectators as it heads north on Main Street.

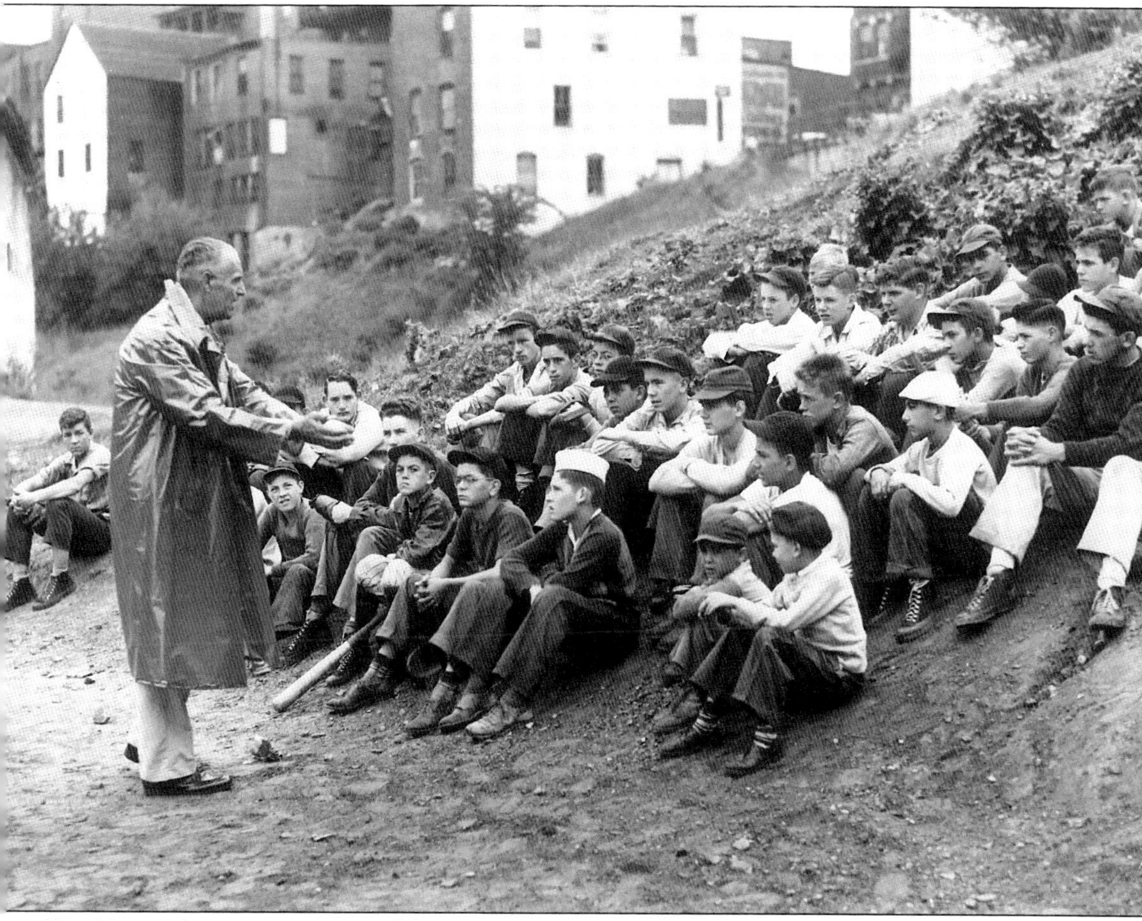

Ben Houser, longtime manager of the Augusta Millionaires and other Maine semi-pro baseball teams, gives pointers to a group of young players in Waterville in the late 1940s. The big boy on the right wearing a baseball cap, light-colored pants, and a dark sweatshirt is Robbie Mitchell, who became a banker. Mitchell was one of the elder brothers of future US Senate Majority Leader George J. Mitchell, who is two places left of his brother. Next to George Mitchell is Paul Paganucci, who became a leading economist, an investment analyst, and a Dartmouth College professor, and is now board chairman of Ledyard National Bank in Hanover, New Hampshire.

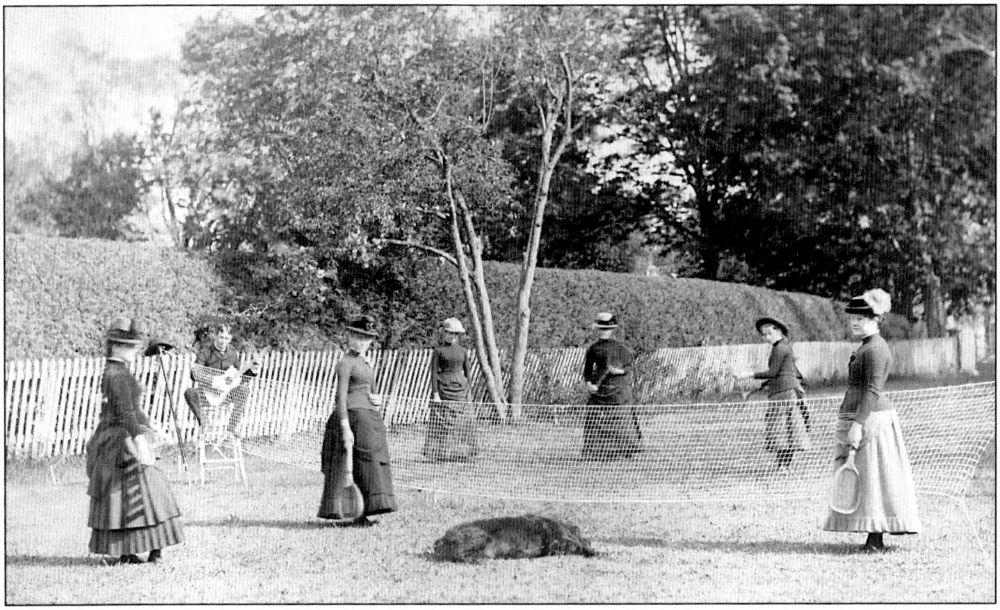

This grass tennis court was located north of Appleton Street behind the Elks Hall. The time is about 1885, and the players are, left to right: Annie Dorr, Sheridan Plaisted, Allein Foster (Arnold), Mary Elden (Mathews), Helen Plaisted, Daisy Plaisted (Bunker), and Carrie Kalloch (Cote).

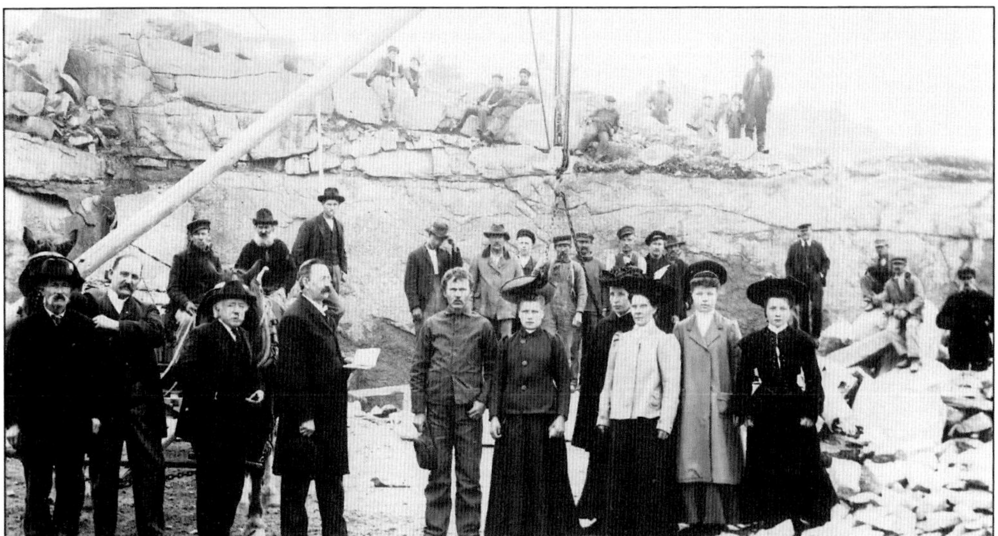

On April 21, 1905, Andrew Lakstrom and Alma Watame, natives of Finland, were married at the quarry on Armbrust Hill by Elder William Strout. Shown with the couple are James P. Armbrust (the owner and operator of the quarry), other quarry officials, quarry workers, friends, and curious bystanders.

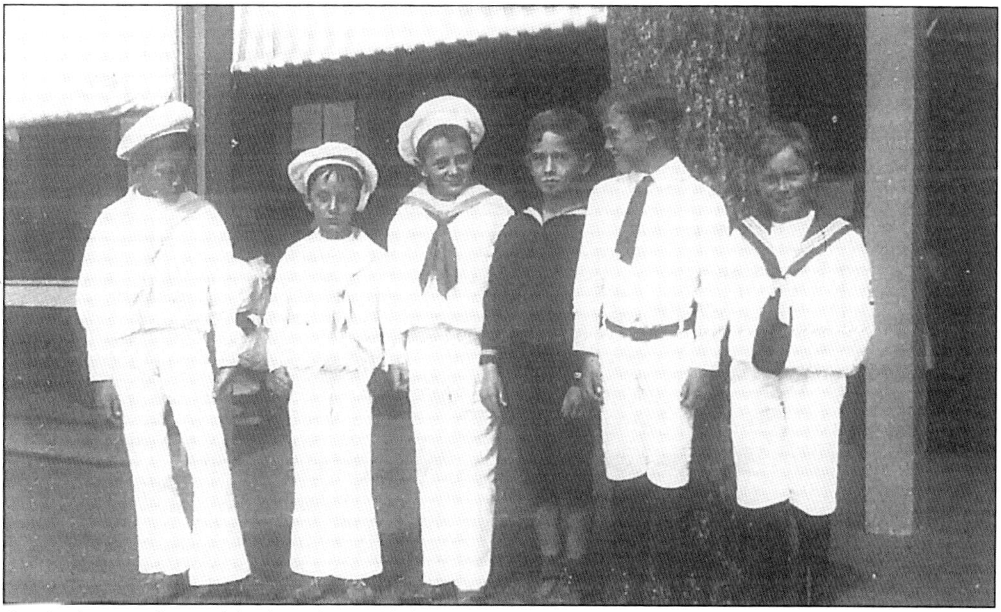

Six little rascals model what the well-dressed Shoaler was wearing at the turn of the century.

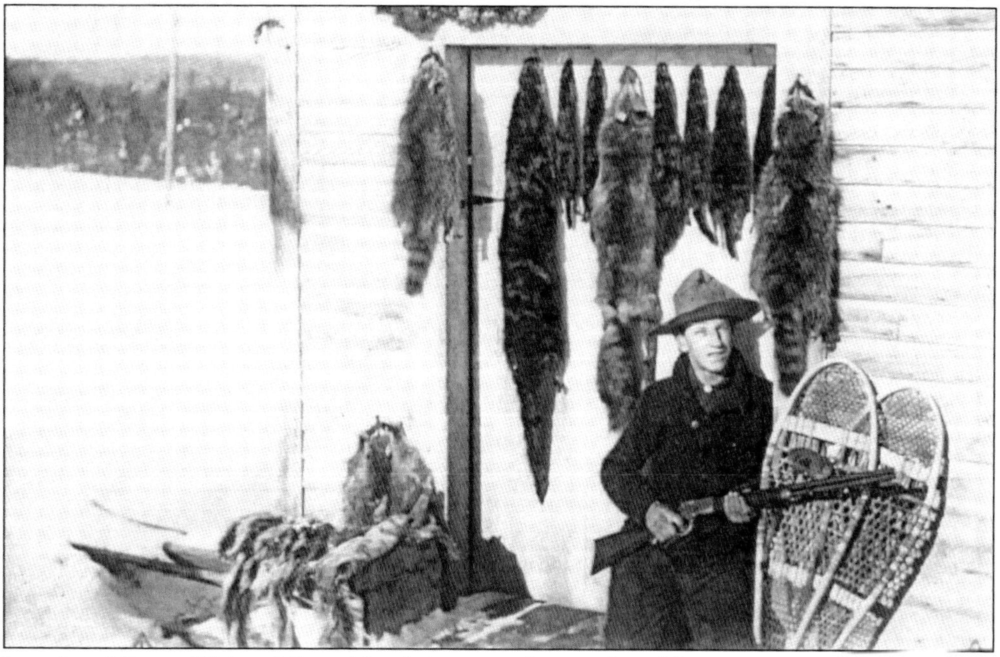

Lon Arnold's son Walter followed his father into the woods and began to earn a living trapping at an early age. Born and raised in the Willimantic back country, Walter Arnold became one of Maine's most famous trappers and guides. He was the author of several books and manuals on trapping, and was a mail-order dealer in trappers' supplies and scents. A familiar figure at sportsman's shows and trappers' conventions, Walter Arnold became the subject of many articles written about his profession and lifestyle in the Maine woods. (Beth Cawley).

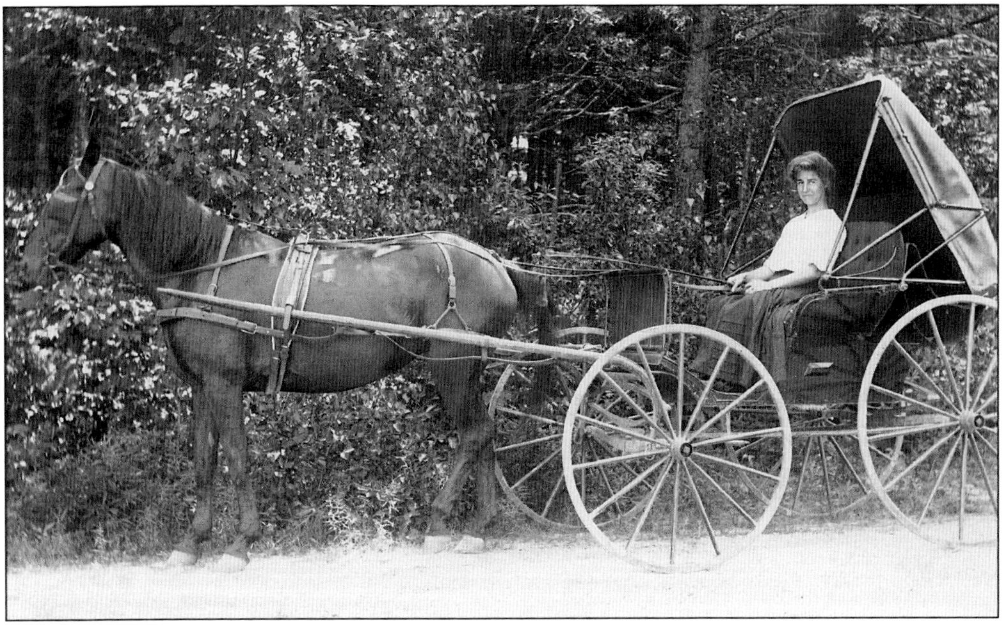

Ms. Effie Fife of Boston enjoying a summer ride. This photograph dates from her 1905 visit with relatives on Phipps Point, Woolwich.

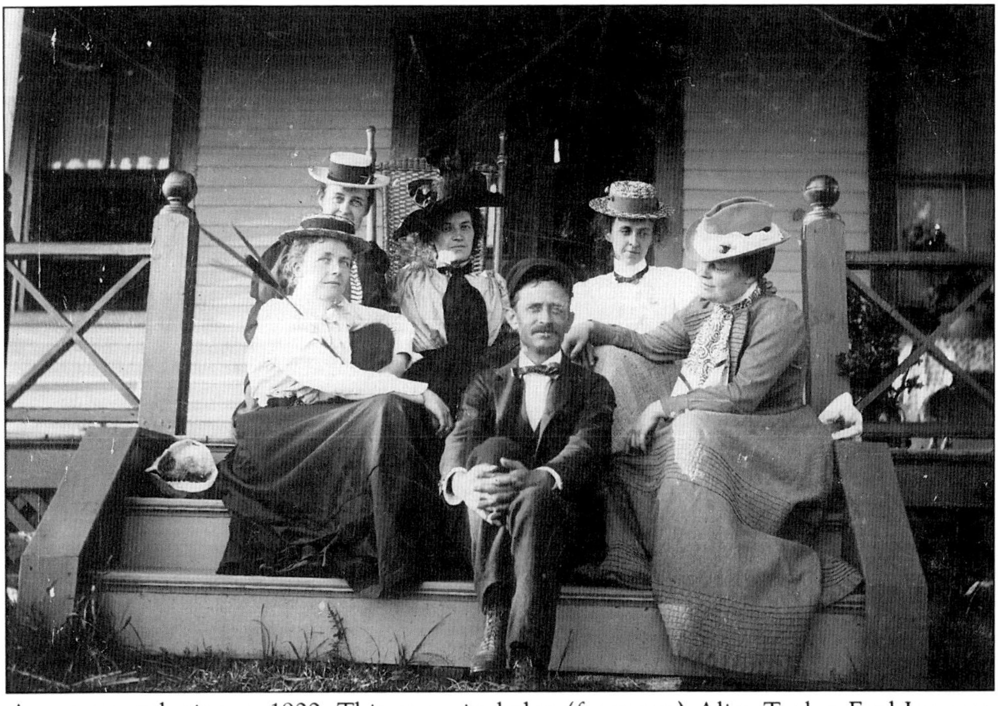

A summer gathering, *c.* 1900. This group includes: (front row) Alice Taylor, Fred Lennox, and Anna Brown; (back row) Nina Rundlett Lennox, Elizabeth Neal Tucker, and Helen Lennox McLaughlin.

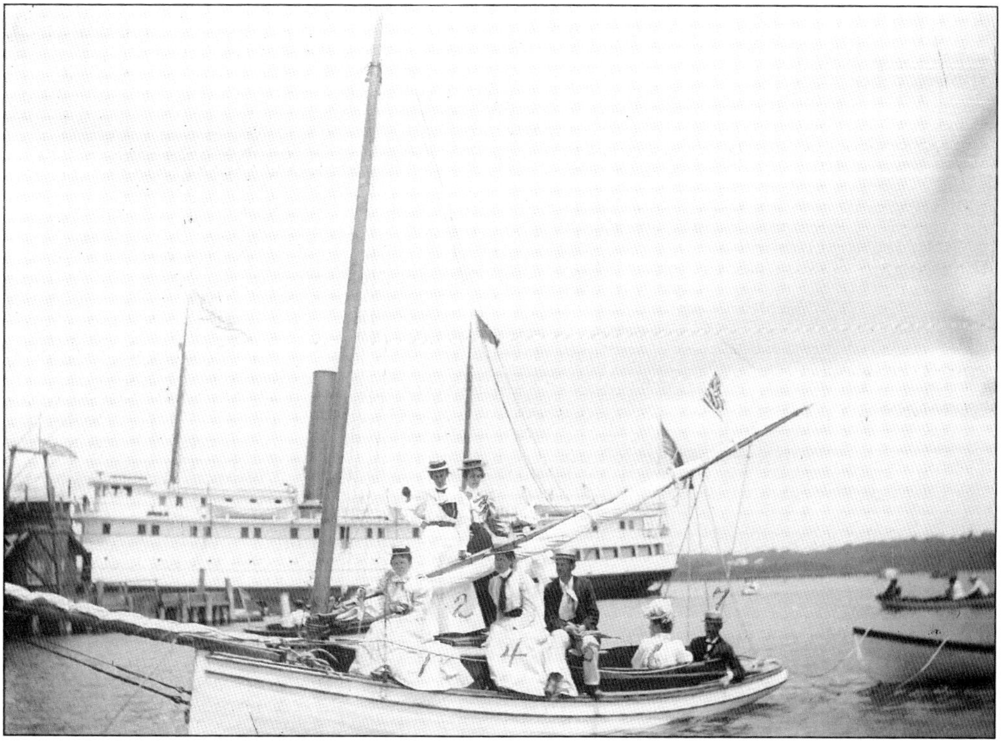

A yachting party during the summer of 1900, near Whaleship Wharf, Wiscasset Harbor. The party included: Mrs. Sol Holbrook, Helen McLaughlin, Mamie Taylor Hubbard, Nina Rundlett, Fred Lennox, Elizabeth Neal Tucker, and Joe Tucker.

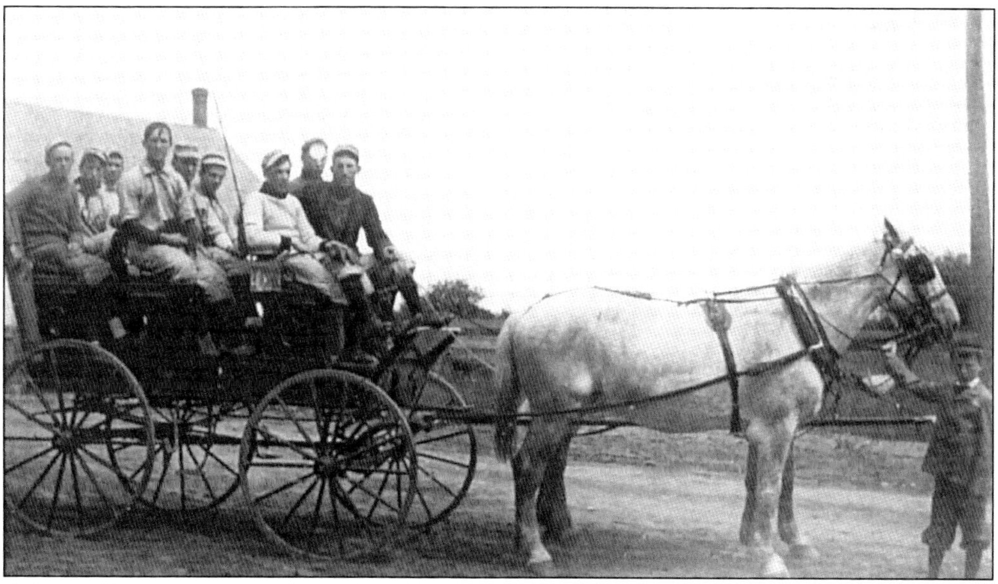

A baseball team *en route* to York. In 1897, horse-drawn buggies were the the most popular mode of transportation.

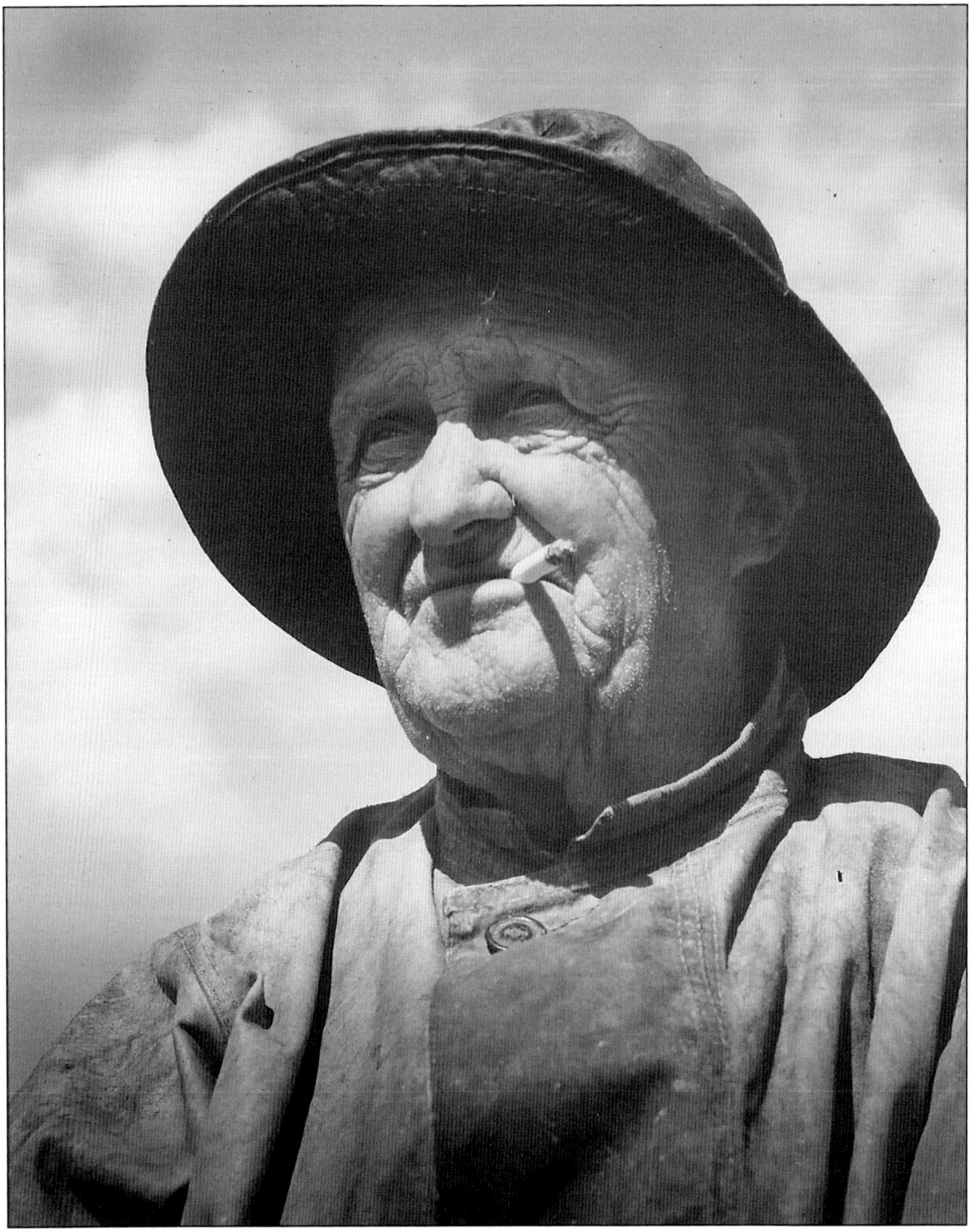

The quintessential New England fisherman, Winkie (Elwyn) Perry was a colorful presence in the Kennebunkport area in his latter years, until his death in August 1961. Once a city boy residing in Boston and New York, he retired to the Cape and set up housekeeping in a fishhouse on the Langsford Road. If you come across a painting of a two-dormered fishing shack on the water's edge, with brightly painted lobster buoys dangling from the eaves and lobster traps piled around, it may be the "Perrywinkle," Winkie's home and fishhouse which was a favorite subject for artists. (Fred & Harriett Eaton).

Two

TO SERVE AND PROTECT

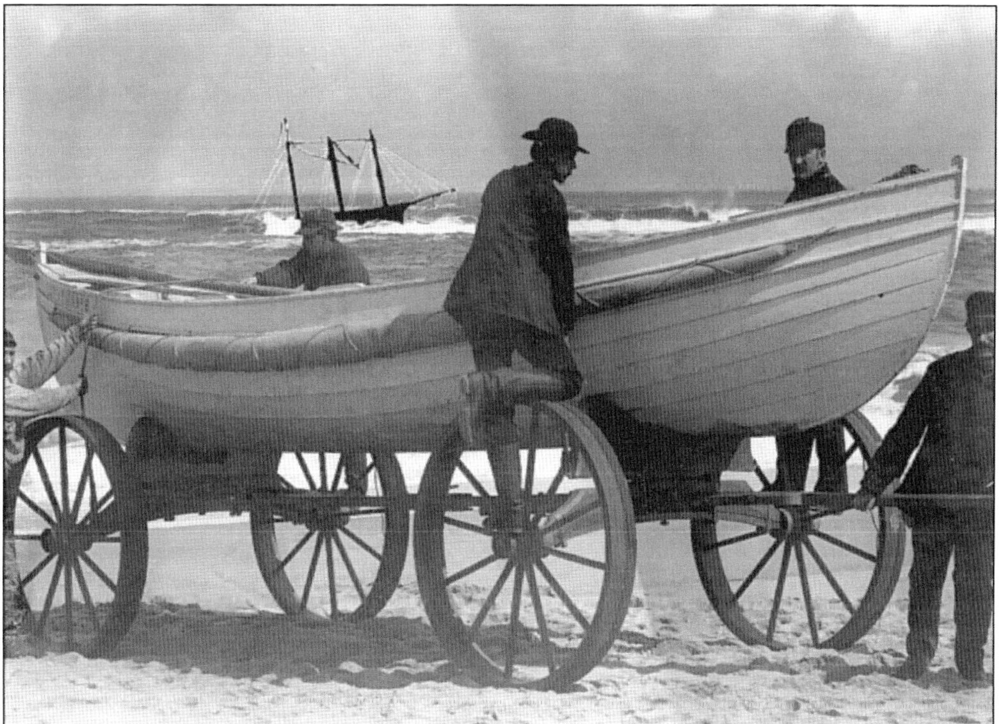

Upon being alerted to a vessel in distress, the station keeper would decide how best to make the rescue, which would usually depend on the distance of the wreck from the beach. The three methods of rescue at the keeper's disposal would usually be breeches buoy, life-car, or rescue by surfboat. Breeches buoy and life-car were used when the vessel was within 600 yards from the beach.

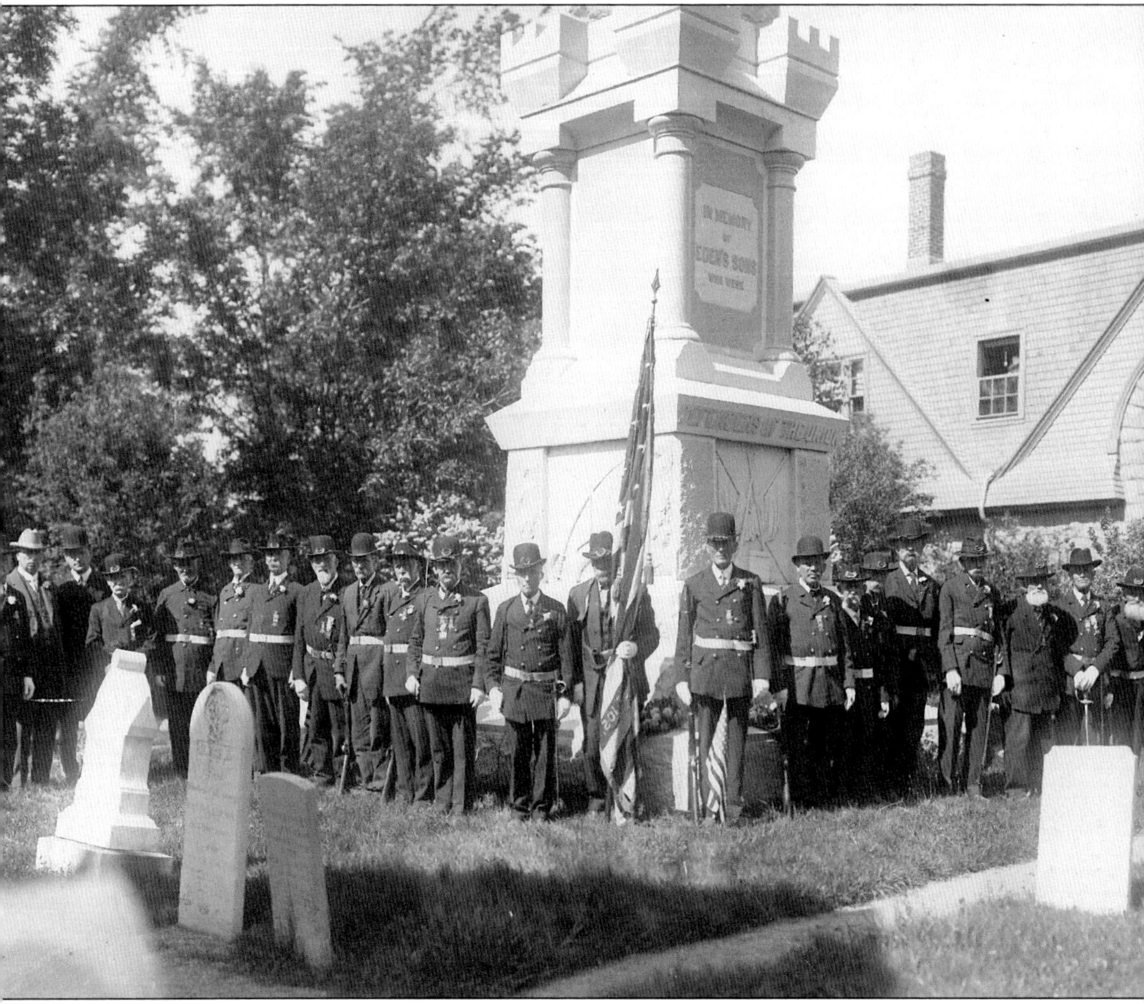

The dedication of this war monument to local men and boys who served in the Civil War ("In Memory of Eden's Sons Who Were Defenders of the Union") took place on Mt. Desert Street, next to the Congregational Church. (Robert Dolliver).

Surfmen were quite proud of their profession. The men constantly repaired and painted where needed and were always ready to pose for the camera. Here, life savers take a break from their duties to pose in their white summer uniforms at a New England station in the 1890s. Just behind can be seen the station's cistern, which was used to collect and store rain runoff from the station roof to serve the station's needs.

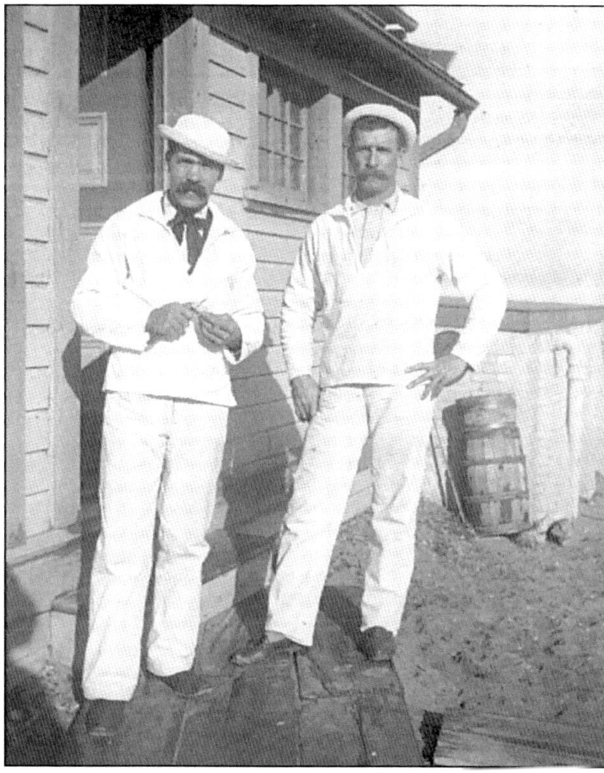

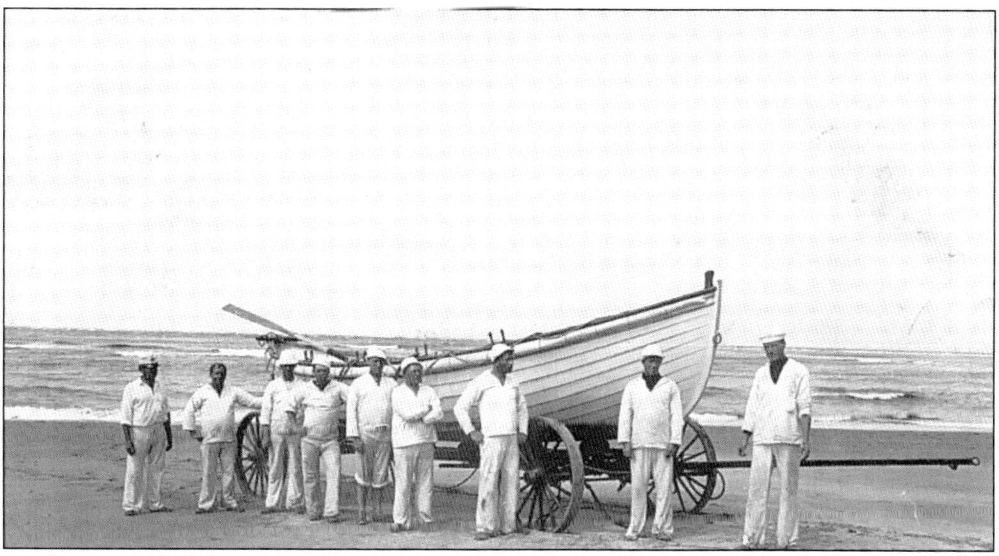

Surfboats used by life savers were designed to be smaller and lighter than the lifeboats of the day in order to enable the men to haul them the long distances down the rocky or sandy beaches to a wreck. Boats were manned by six surfmen with six oars and the keeper with a long steering oar at the stern. Here, the life-saving crew prepares to launch their surfboat during a drill. Note the canvas bumpers used to prevent damage when alongside a wreck.

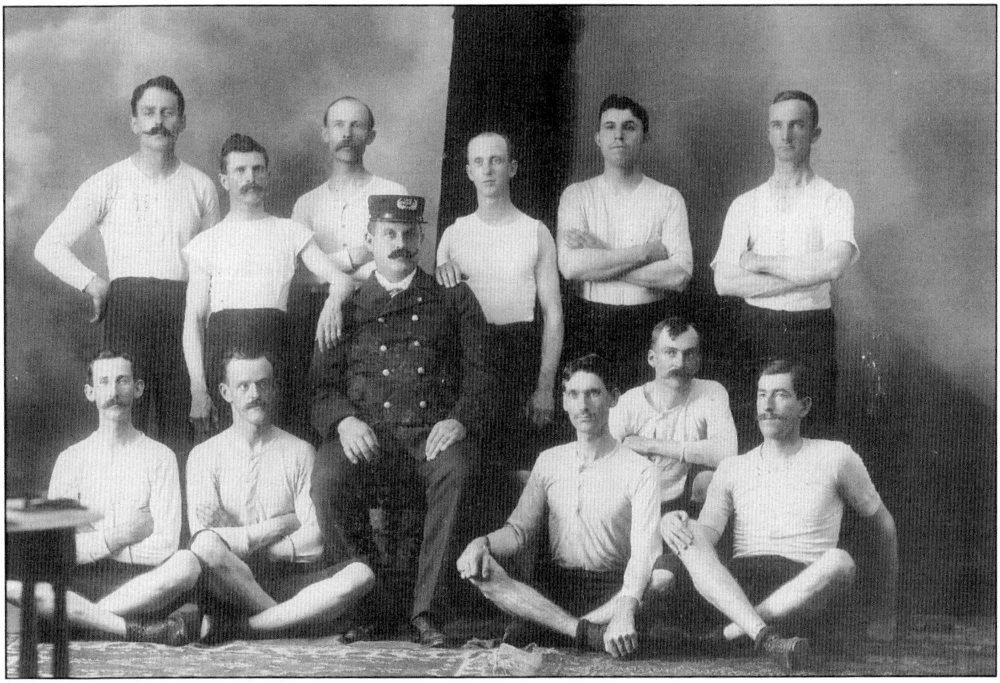

The Auburn Fire Department posed at the "Muster" at Bath in 1898.

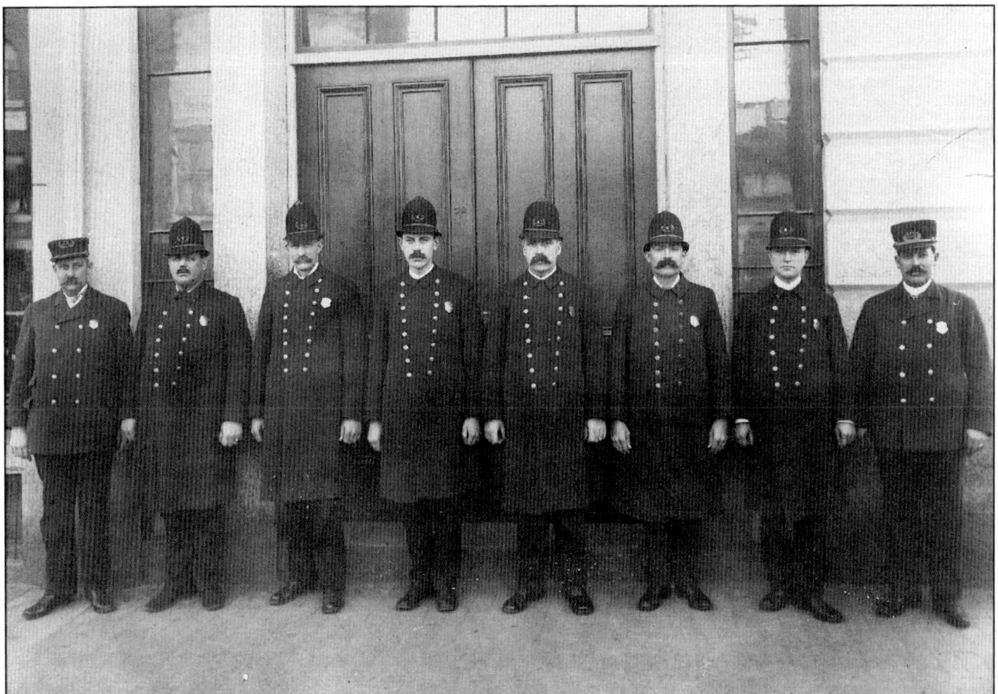

The Auburn Police show off their finest uniforms in this official portrait.

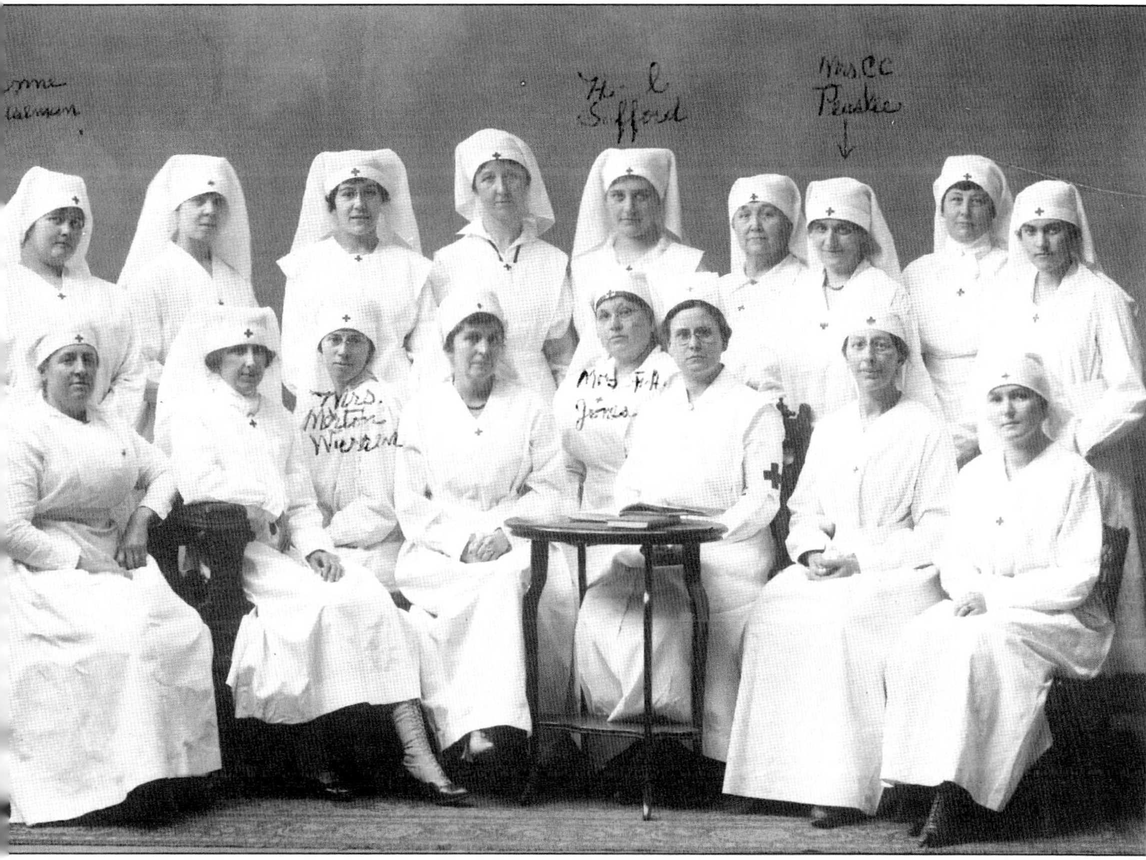

This is a 1918 photograph of the first Red Cross volunteers of Auburn and Lewiston. From left to right are: (front row) Miss Annia Wiseman, Mrs. C.W. Lawlor, Miss Hazel Mitchell, Miss Annia Brawshaw, Mrs. Iva Safford, Mrs. F.H. Packard, Mrs. C.C. Peaslee, Mrs. Hattie Allen, and Miss Therma Hicks; (back row) Mrs. Charles Bosehby, Mrs. Ashely Thurston, Mrs. Merton Warren, Mrs. John McMurrey, Mrs. F.A. Jones, Miss Lorena A. Chaplin, Mrs. A.W. Auehowy, and Miss Helen McCaretry.

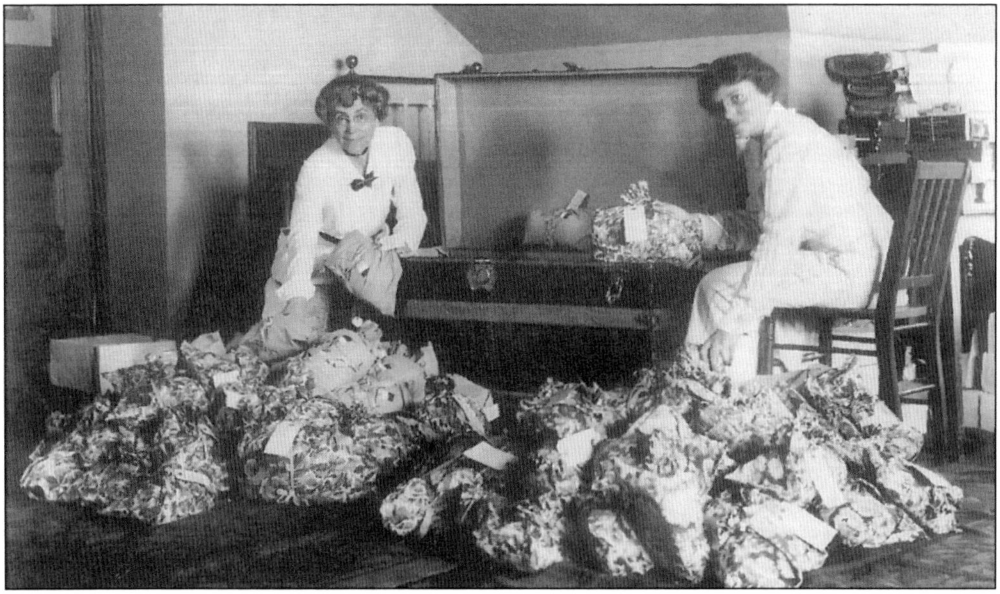

Once Seal Harbor's American Fund for French Wounded volunteers had collected their donations, the bundles were packed in trunks and shipped to Paris, where they were distributed to small hospitals. Theodora Dunham, busily packing beside her mother, would volunteer overseas during the war. At the age of 21, she drove on the Fund's supply trucks and saw first-hand that the donations, carefully prepared by her fellow Seal Harbor residents, reached their intended destinations. (Dunham Family Collection).

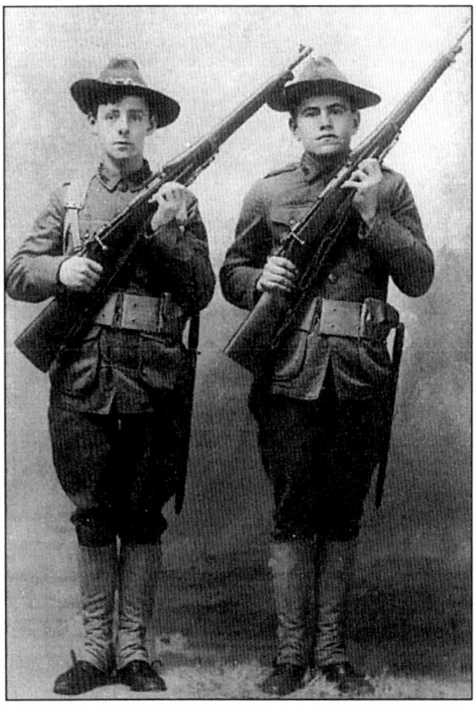

Two young soldiers from Skowhegan are shown in this 1915 photograph. The soldier on the left is unidentified. The soldier on the right is William Demo. Both were part of Skowhegan's Company E that served both at the Mexican border (1916) and in France (1917–1919). (Bernice Laney Collection.)

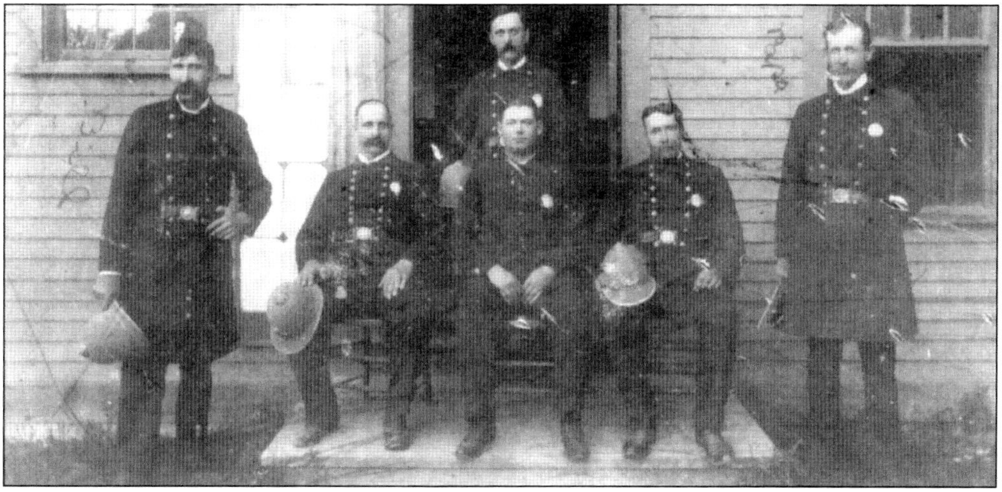

The local constabulary posed for this photograph, c. 1900. From left to right are: (standing) G.H. Hamor, Everet Brewer, and Frank I. Leland; (seated) Frank Higgins, Frank Holden (chief), and Gilman Rich. (Raymond Strout).

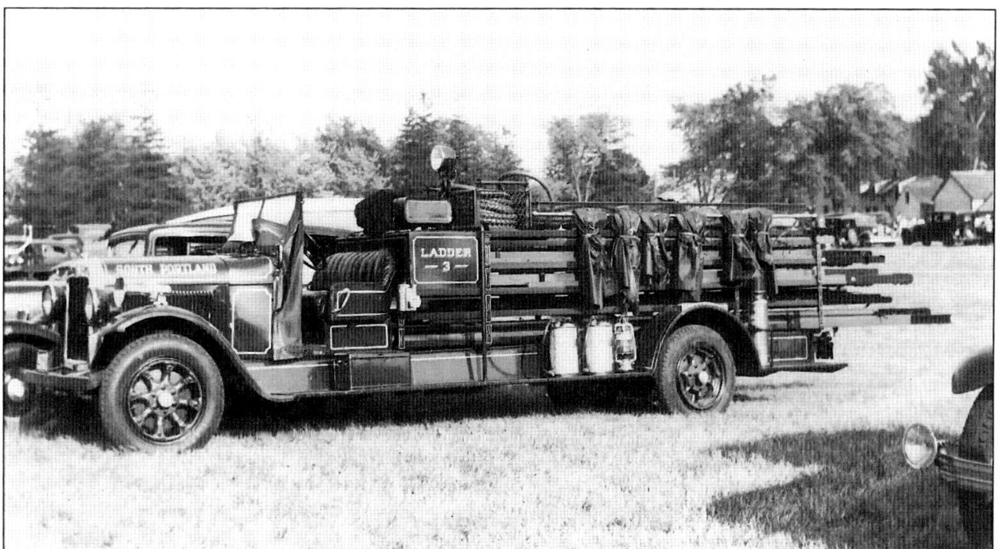

On display at a South Portland field day in the late 1920s is Pleasantdale Hose Co.'s new Dodge chassis truck. Hose No. 3 was organized in 1893. (Tom Heseltine).

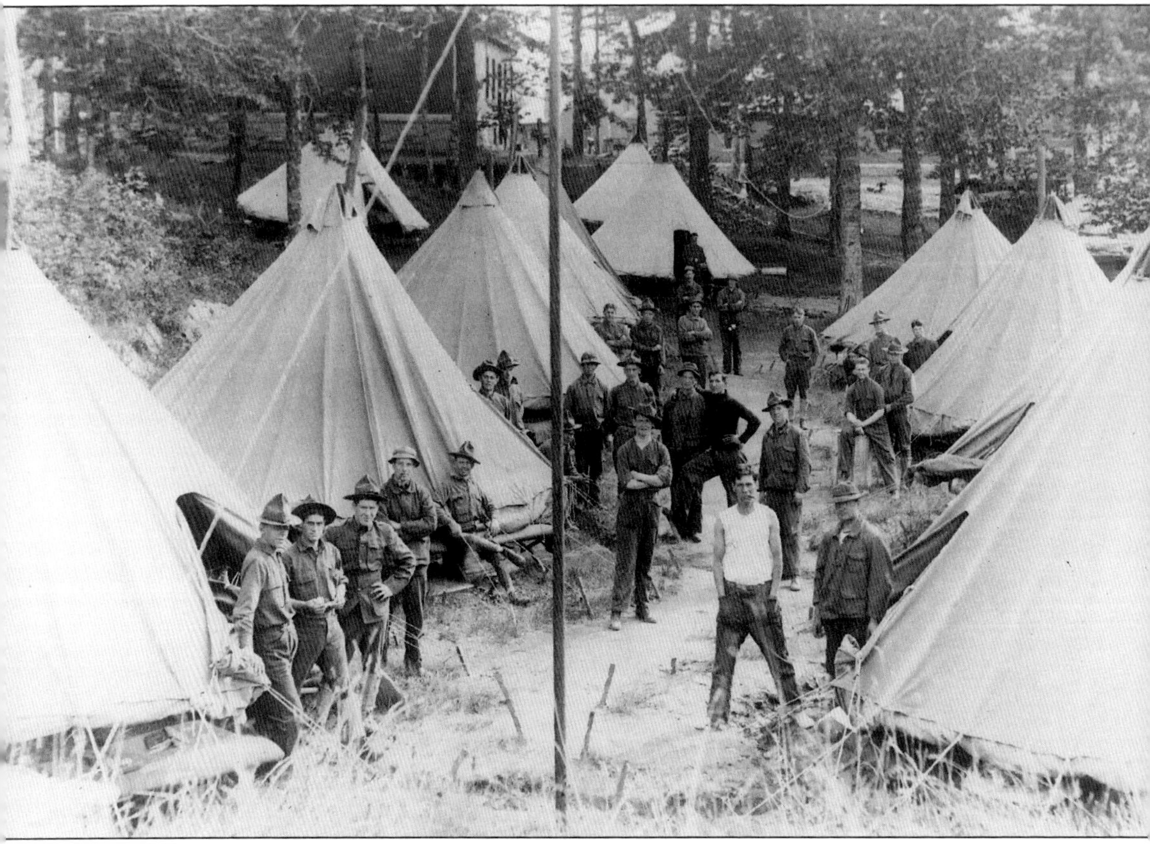

Militiamen join regular forces at Cape Elizabeth in defense of the coast at the turn of the century. (Sullivan Photo Collection).

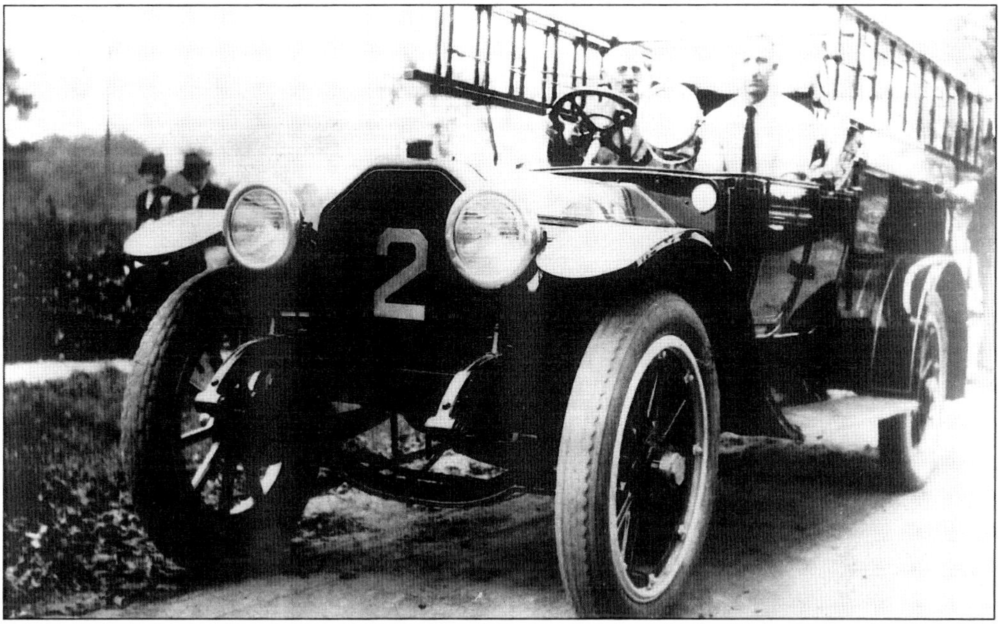

In 1923, Willis Strout, the first president of the Willard Hose Co., and Daniel Strout rode in one of the company's first motorized fire trucks, a converted Peerless sedan. Willard's Hose No. 2 was organized in October 1892, and was preceded by Ferry Village's Hose No. 1 in September. Cape Elizabeth's first municipal fire department was established in the 1920s. (Tom Heseltine).

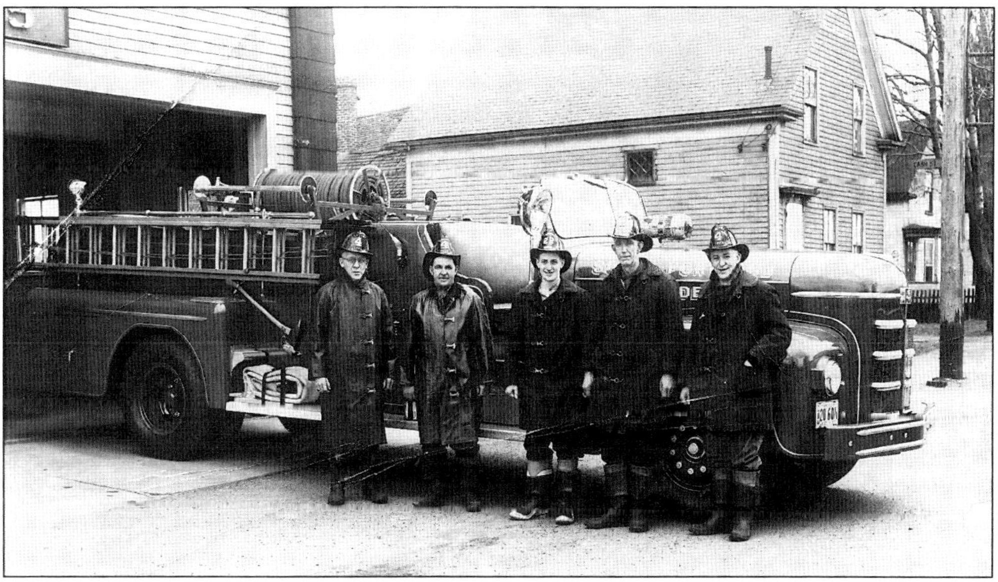

An Ahrens Fox truck, with a pumping capability of 1,000 gallons of water per minute, is displayed at the Cash Corner station in South Portland in 1950. From left to right are Ralph F. Thompson (driver), Albert Nugent, Norman Cribby, Captain Raymond W. Smith, and Charles. (Tom Heseltine).

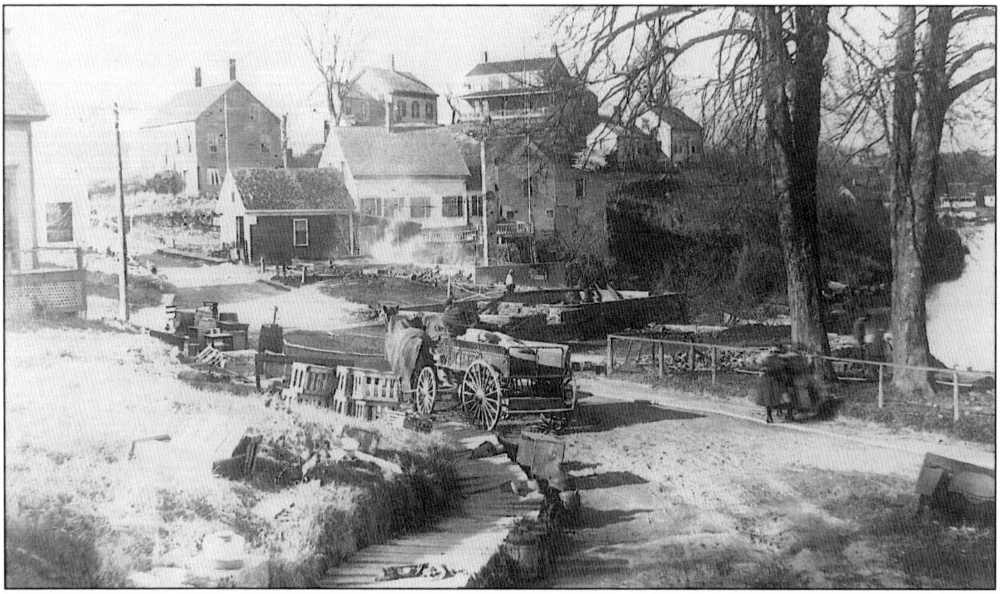

In 1917 a major fire destroyed three establishments in Parker Head Village. Foundations and smoldering embers were all that remained of Lizzie Harrington's boardinghouse, Duley's Store and home, and the Ed Wyman homestead. Situated to the left of the fire-burned buildings, the Parker Head Post Office survived. The horse-drawn vehicle seen here is the fire truck. The crates and barrels on the opposite side of the road were presumably removed from the burning buildings. The wooden sidewalks were clearly in need of repair.

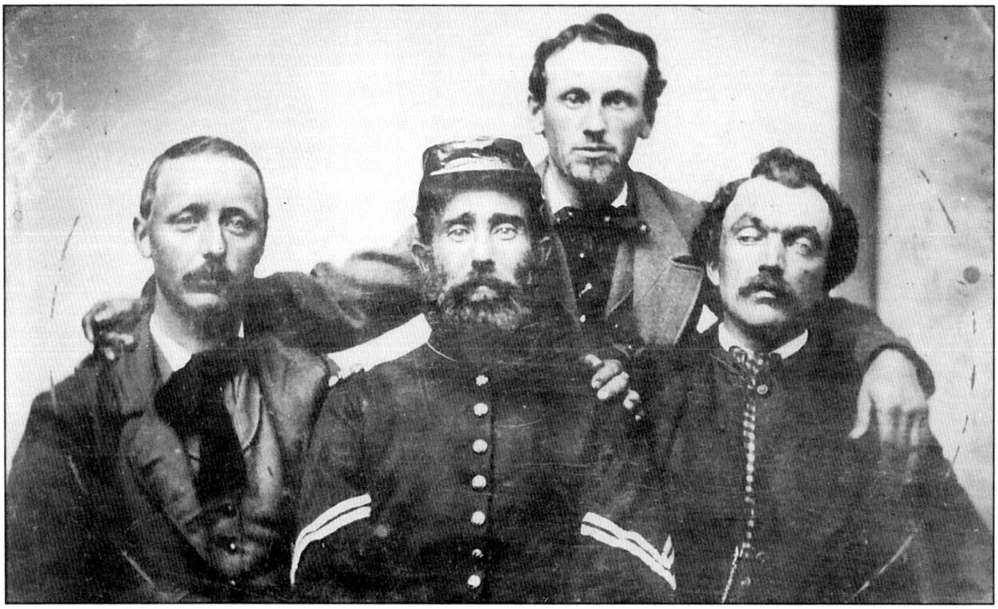

"Returned from the war" was written on the back of this picture. These Civil War soldiers are, left to right: Joseph Howard Preble, Jeremiah Linscott McIntire, Andrew Jackson McIntire and Hiram Hobbs Thompson.

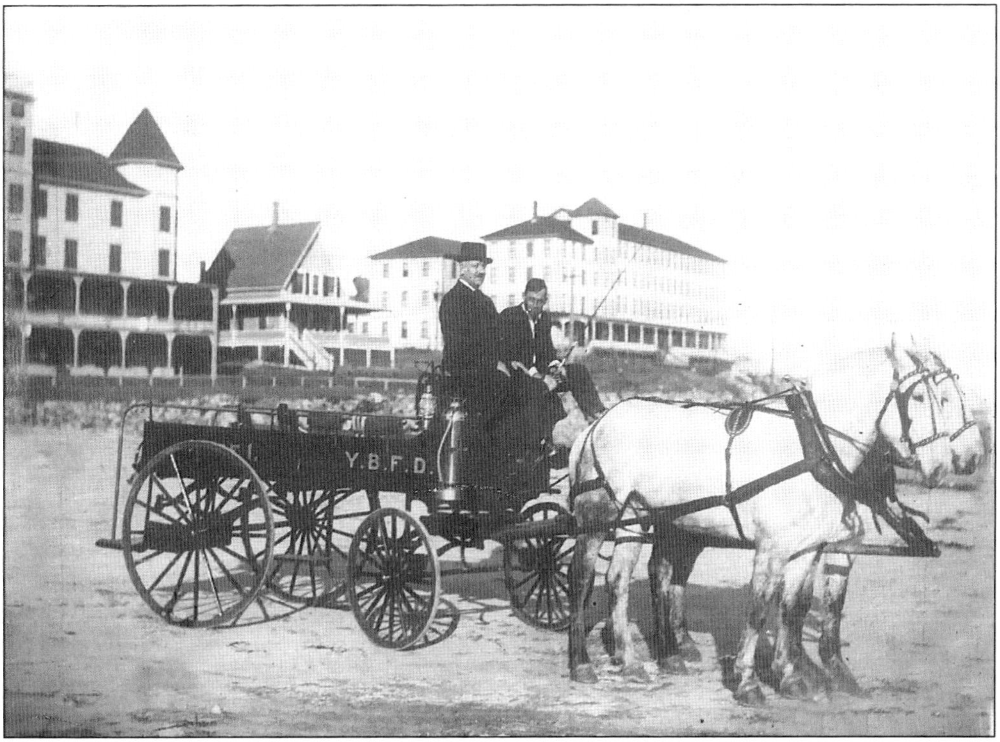

The York Beach social club raised $235 in 1890. They purchased a used horse-drawn hook and ladder wagon in Dover, New Hampshire, and 12 leather fire buckets from the Portsmouth Navy Yard. The York Beach Fire Department was organized in that year.

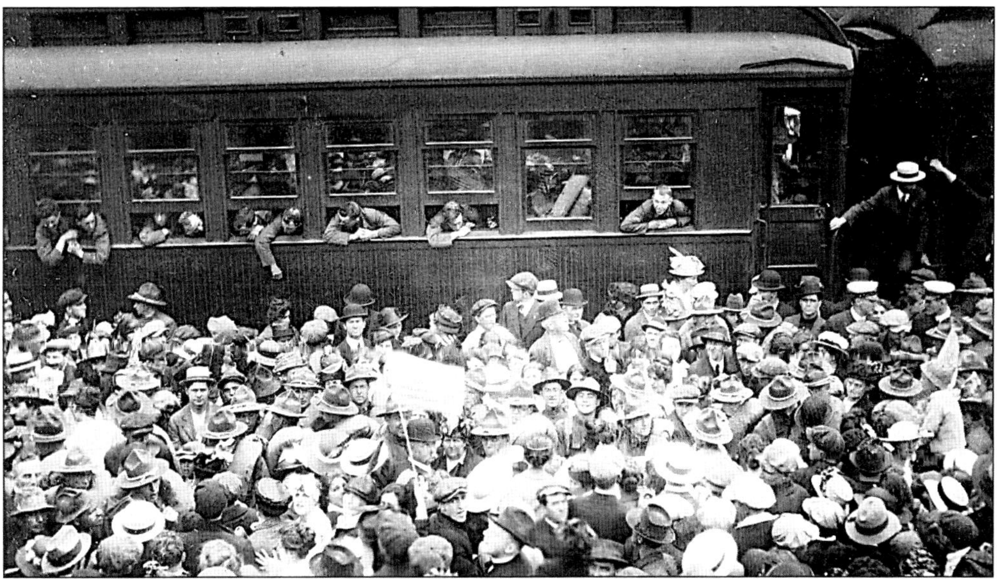

It is 1917 and the boys are leaving from the Waterville Railroad Station to fight in World War I. When the boys returned in 1918, politics changed quite dramatically.

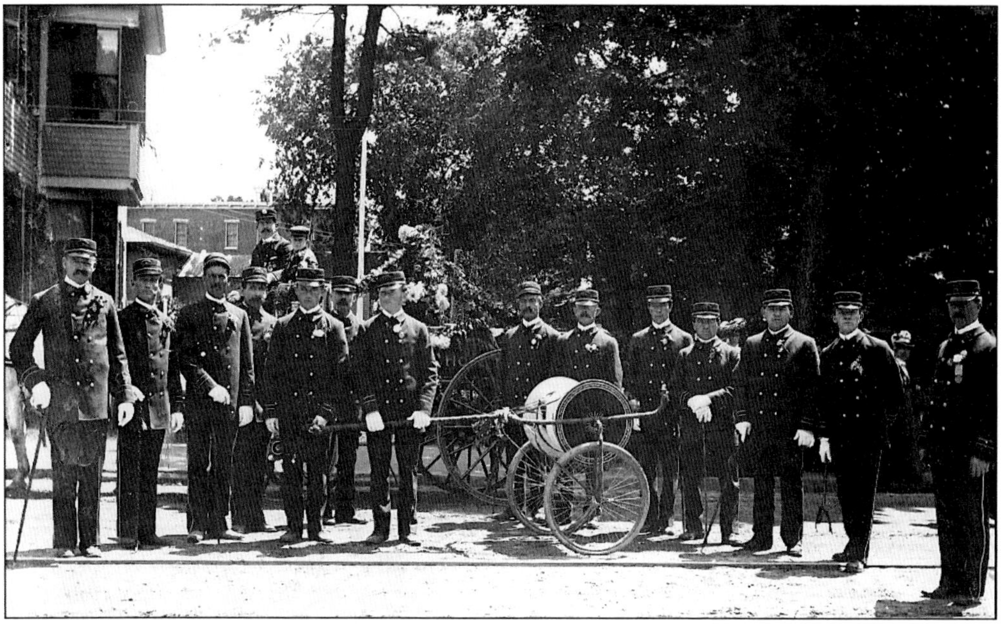

This is the Columbia Reel Team in Waterville on June 24, 1902.

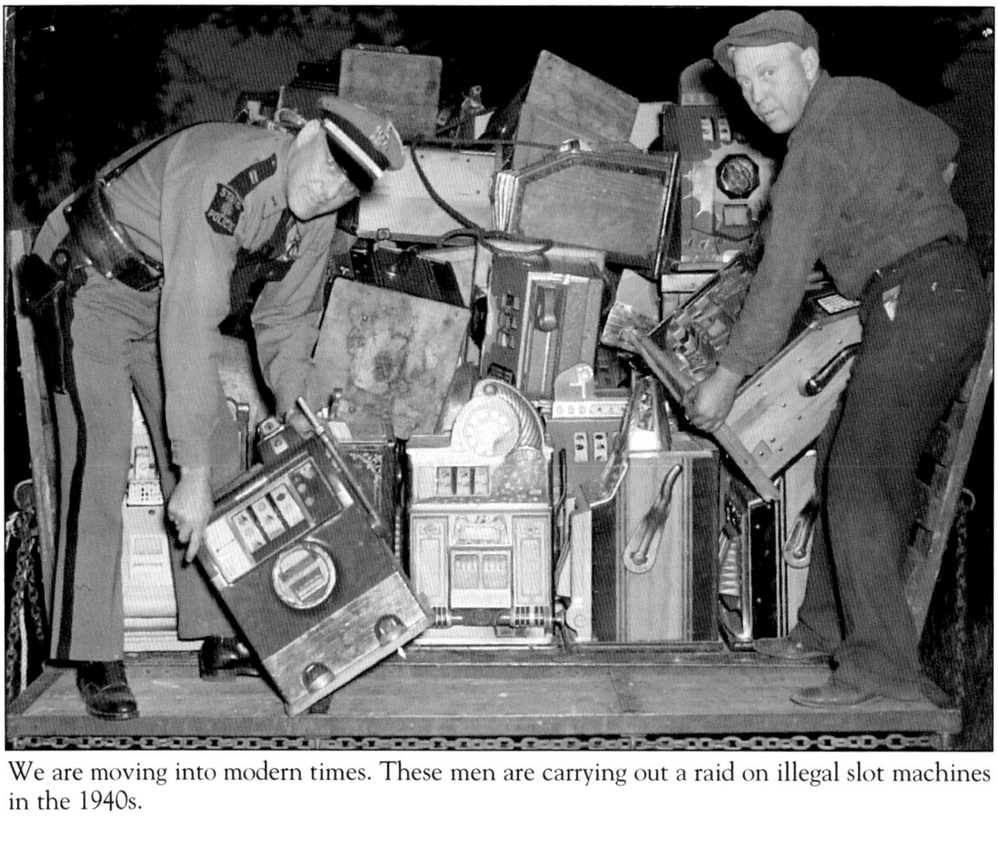

We are moving into modern times. These men are carrying out a raid on illegal slot machines in the 1940s.

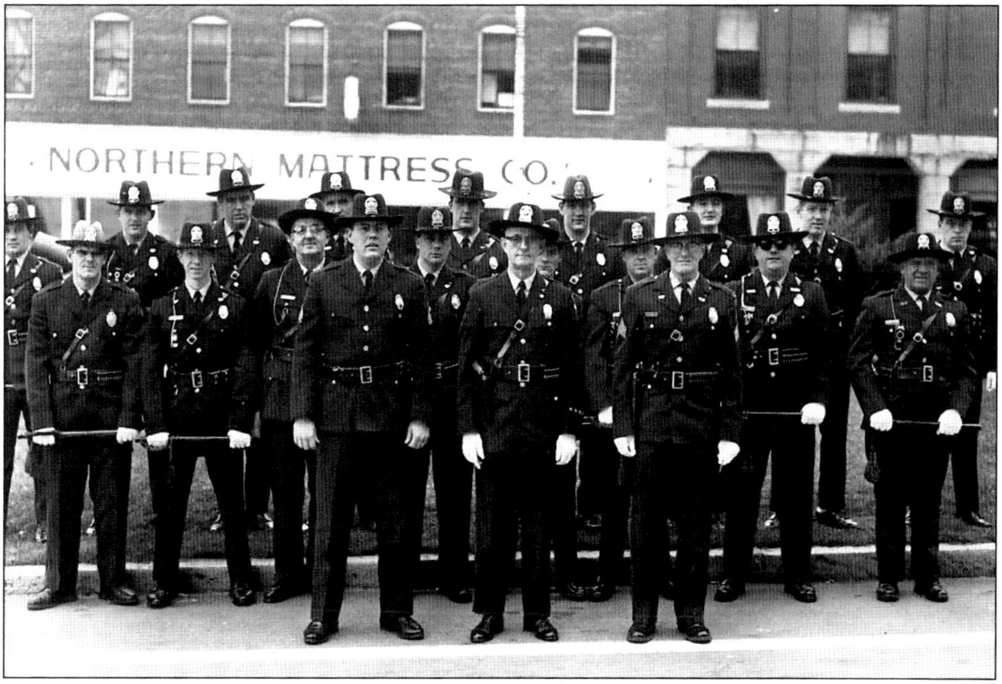

Waterville Police Department in the 1950s. Alton Laliberte, John D. MacIntyre, and Sergeant Glenwood Kierstead are the men pictured in the front in this photograph.

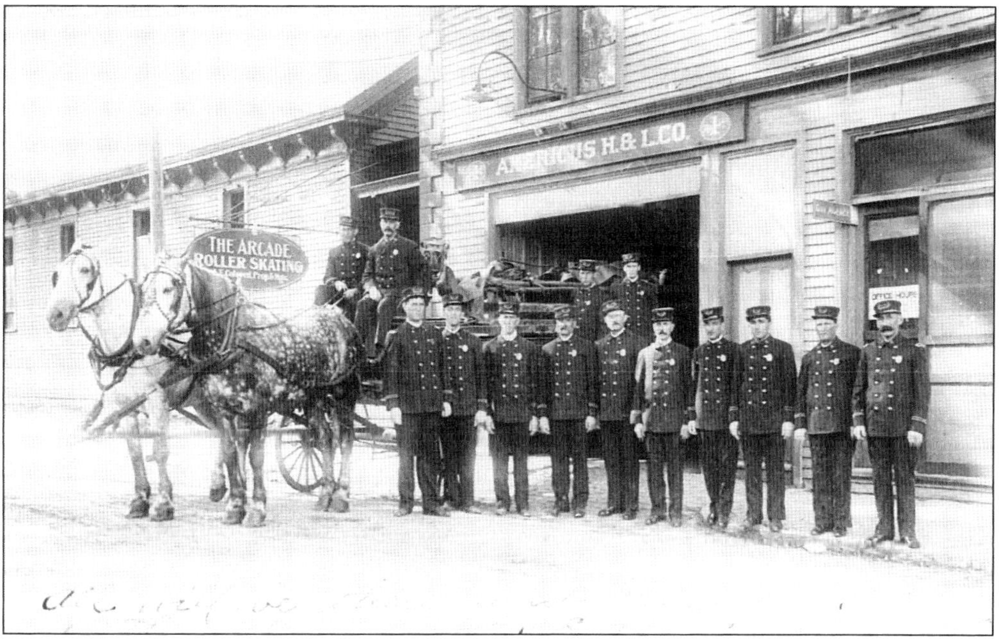

The Americus Hook and Ladder Company, shown here in 1905 in front of the old armory. To the left is the Arcade, a large one-story building used for food fairs and other Rockland area community events.

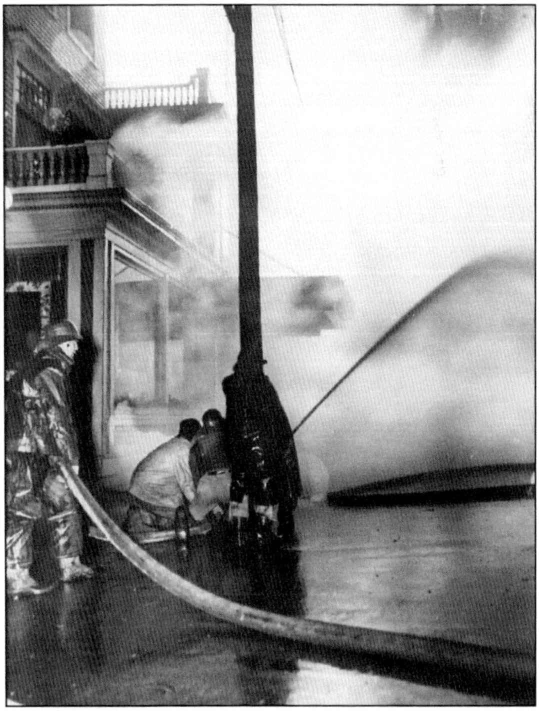

A view showing the Hotel Rockland's porch engulfed in flames as fire moved from the Sutdley Furniture Company through the hotel.

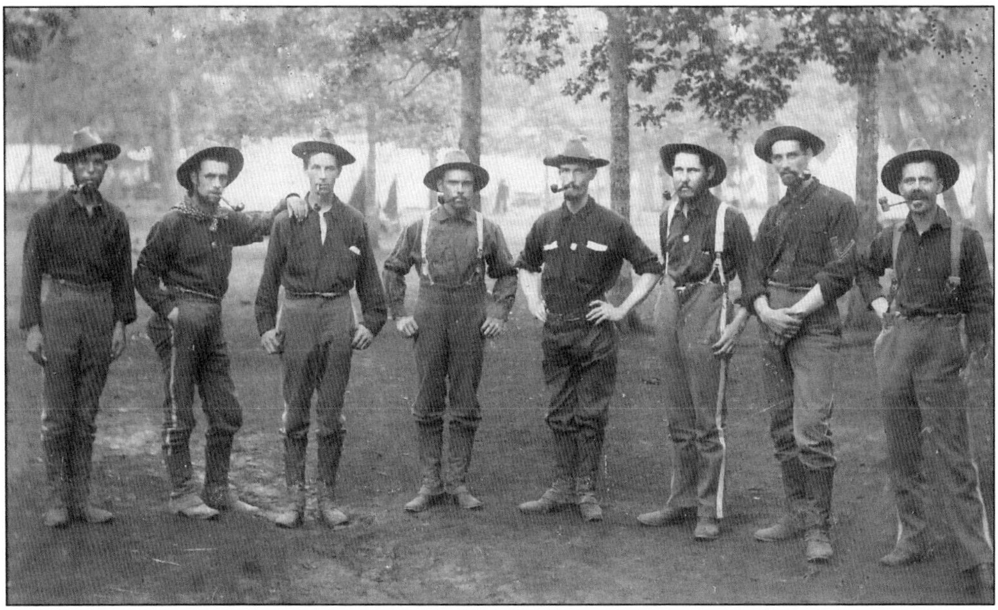

Members of Tillson's Light Infantry stationed at Chickamauga Park, Tennessee, in 1898. Shown here are, from left to right: Albert Hastings, Arthur Doherty, William Glover, Phillip Howard, William Graves, ? Pillsbury, Alton Small, and Herbert Thorndike. These men found themselves fighting typhoid fever and malaria instead of Spanish regulars and Filipino guerrillas. They were hit hard enough by disease that they were shipped home, not to battle.

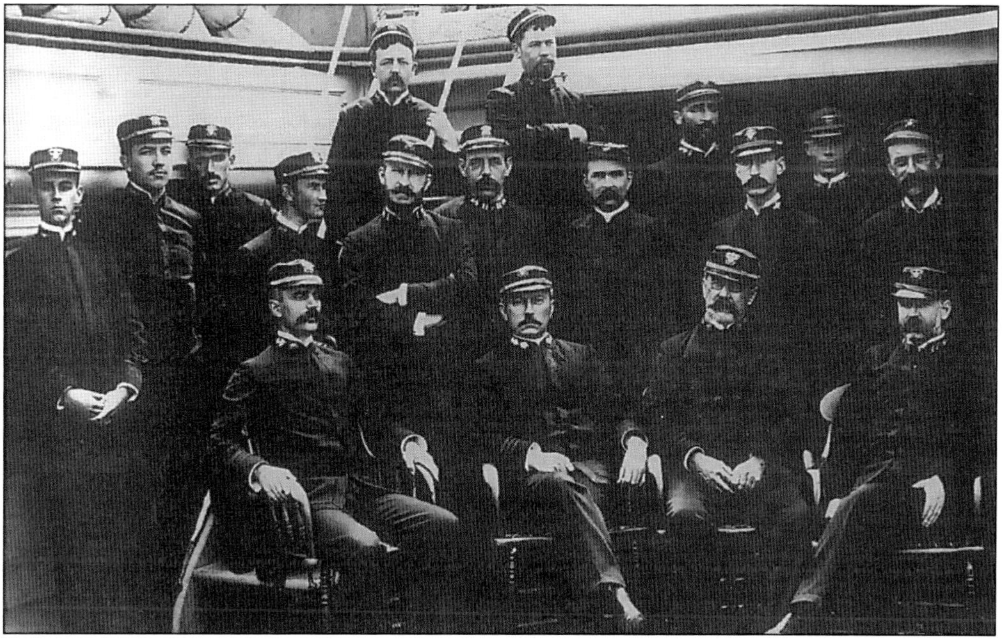

The *Kearsrge* engaged the Confederate raider *Alabama* off the coast of Cherbourg, France, in June 1864. The *Alabama* had been at sea for 22 months and had destroyed 65 Union vessels. Many others had been captured and released under bond.

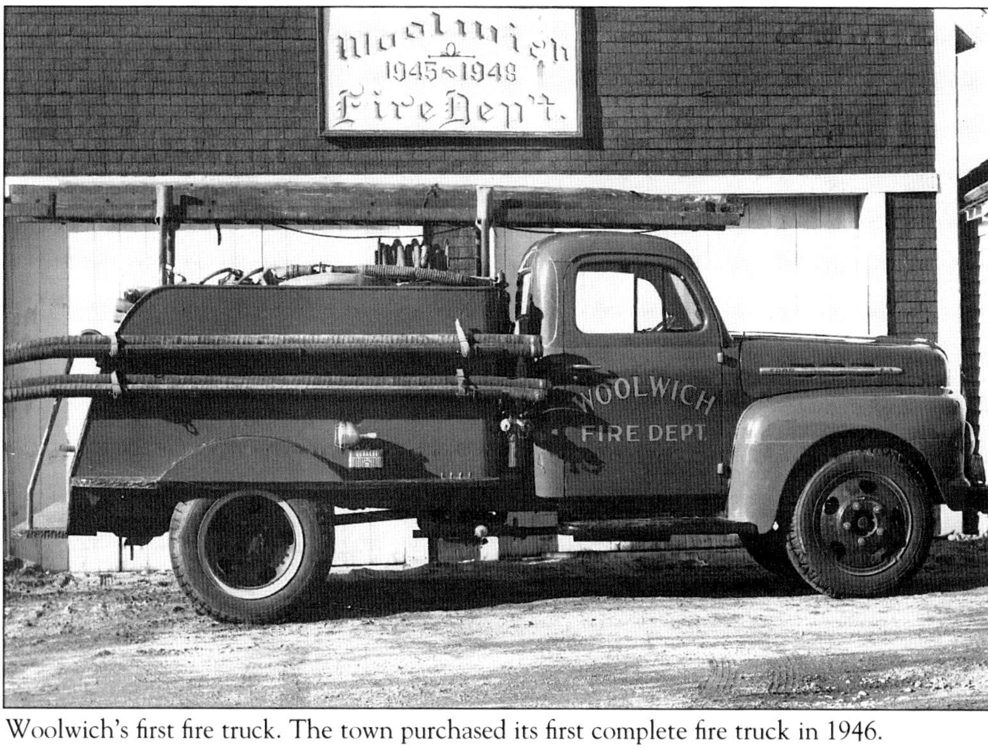

Woolwich's first fire truck. The town purchased its first complete fire truck in 1946.

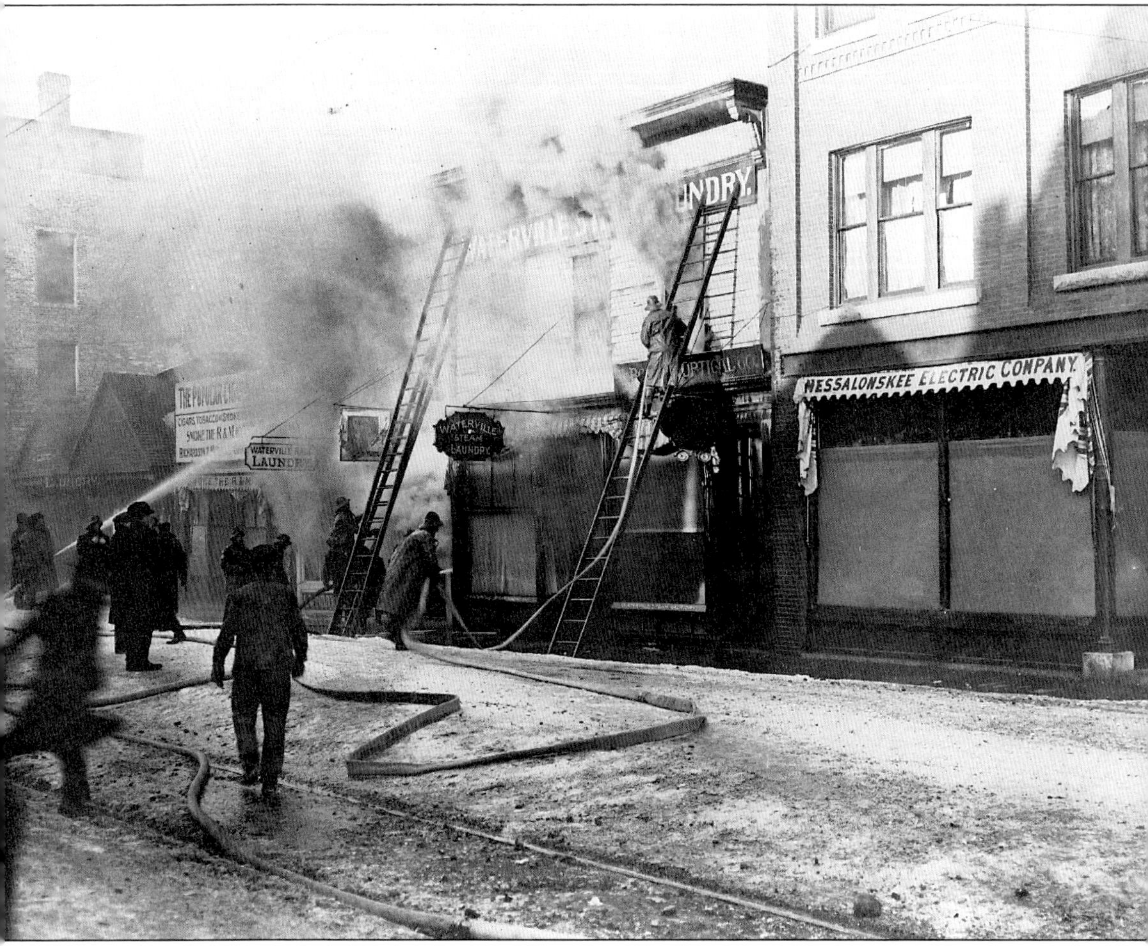

These brave firefighters battle the blaze outside the Waterville Steam Laundry in the early 1900s.

Three

At Work

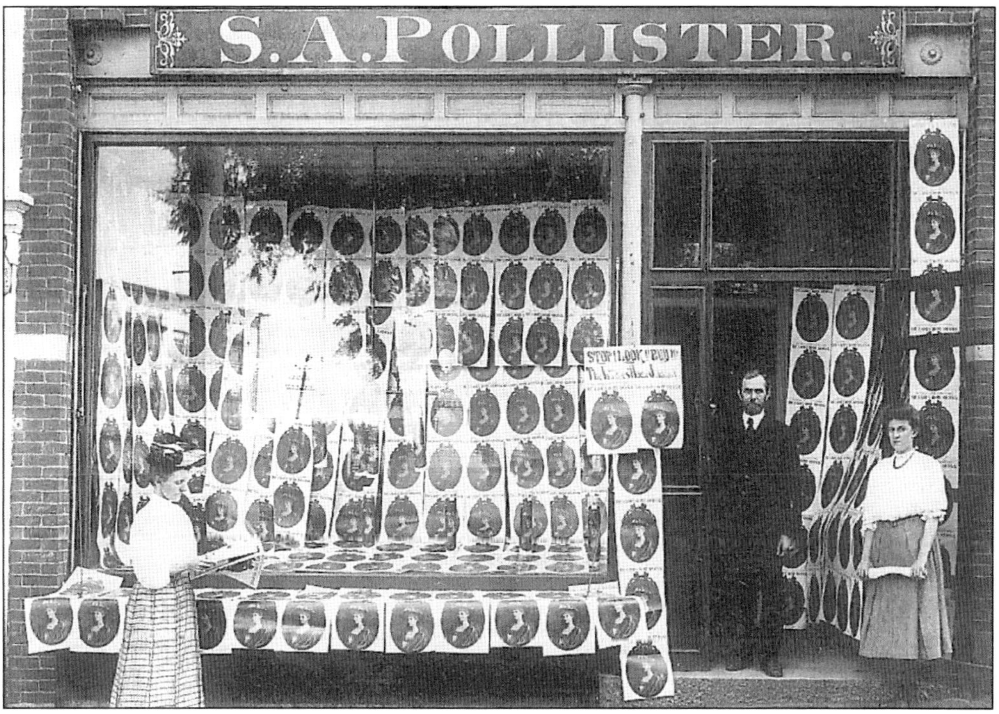

The S.A. Pollister Store on 88 Court Street, Auburn. A sign near the door says "STOP! LOOK! BUT! The Ladies Home Journal." Sewall Pollister founded the store to sell rubber stamps, office supplies, newspapers, books, and magazines. S.A. Pollister was near the site of the new Orphan Annie's Store.

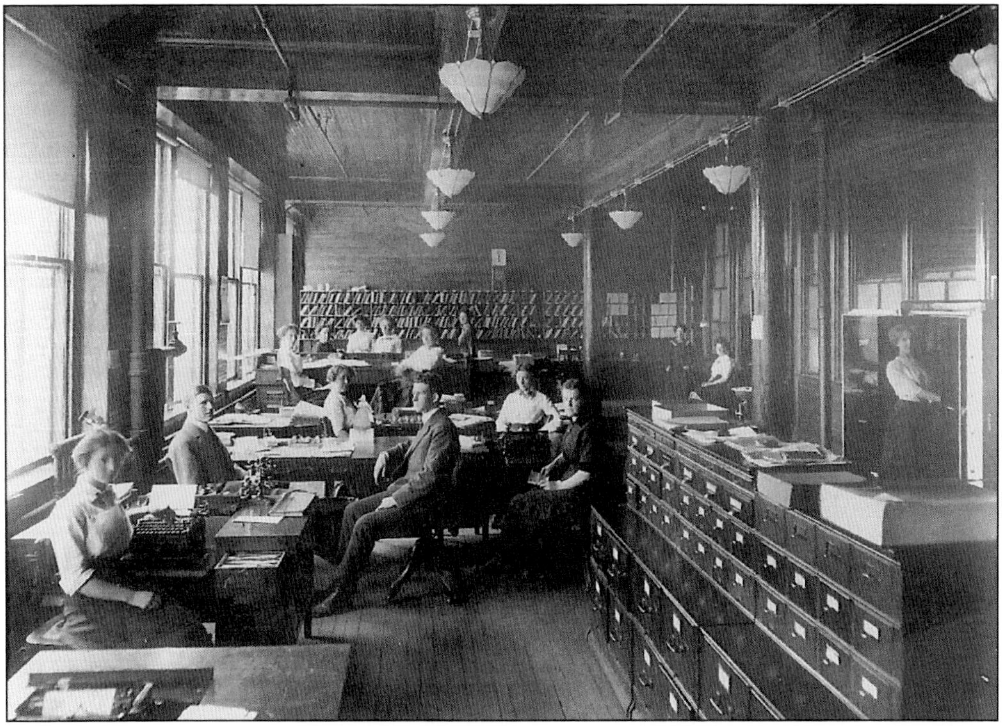

The Lunn and Sweet Shoe Shop, Minot Avenue, Auburn. This was the location of the offices.

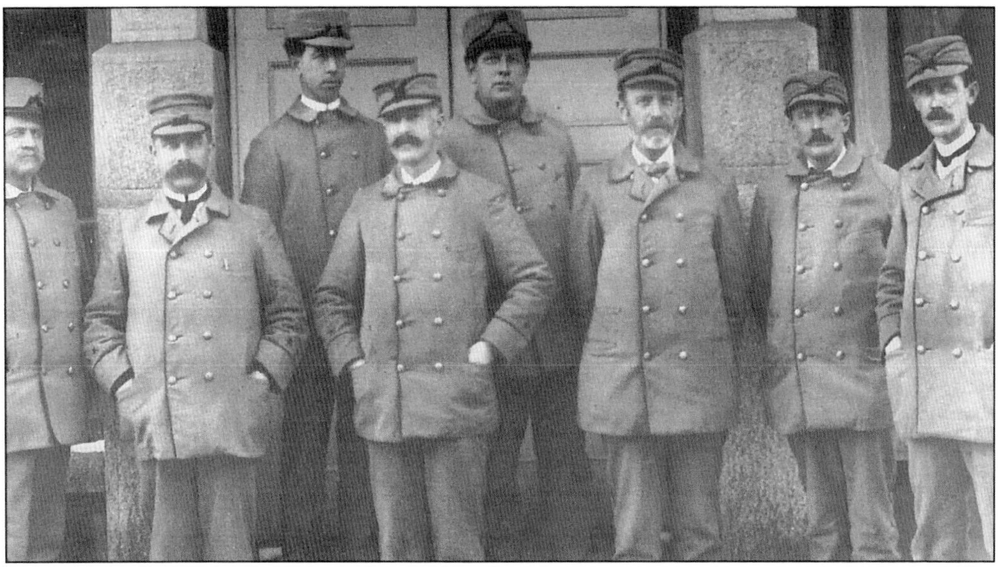

The city of Auburn's mail carriers. The post office was located at the Morrill-Webber Building. The year is uncertain, but there is a date of 1911 on the back of the photograph. In 1887 Auburn numbered the houses and started home delivery. In the 1830s a letter cost $2 to be mailed from Augusta to Lewiston, and Edward Little of Auburn owned this route for a period of time. On July 15, 1799, Lewiston became the second city in the area to establish a post office.

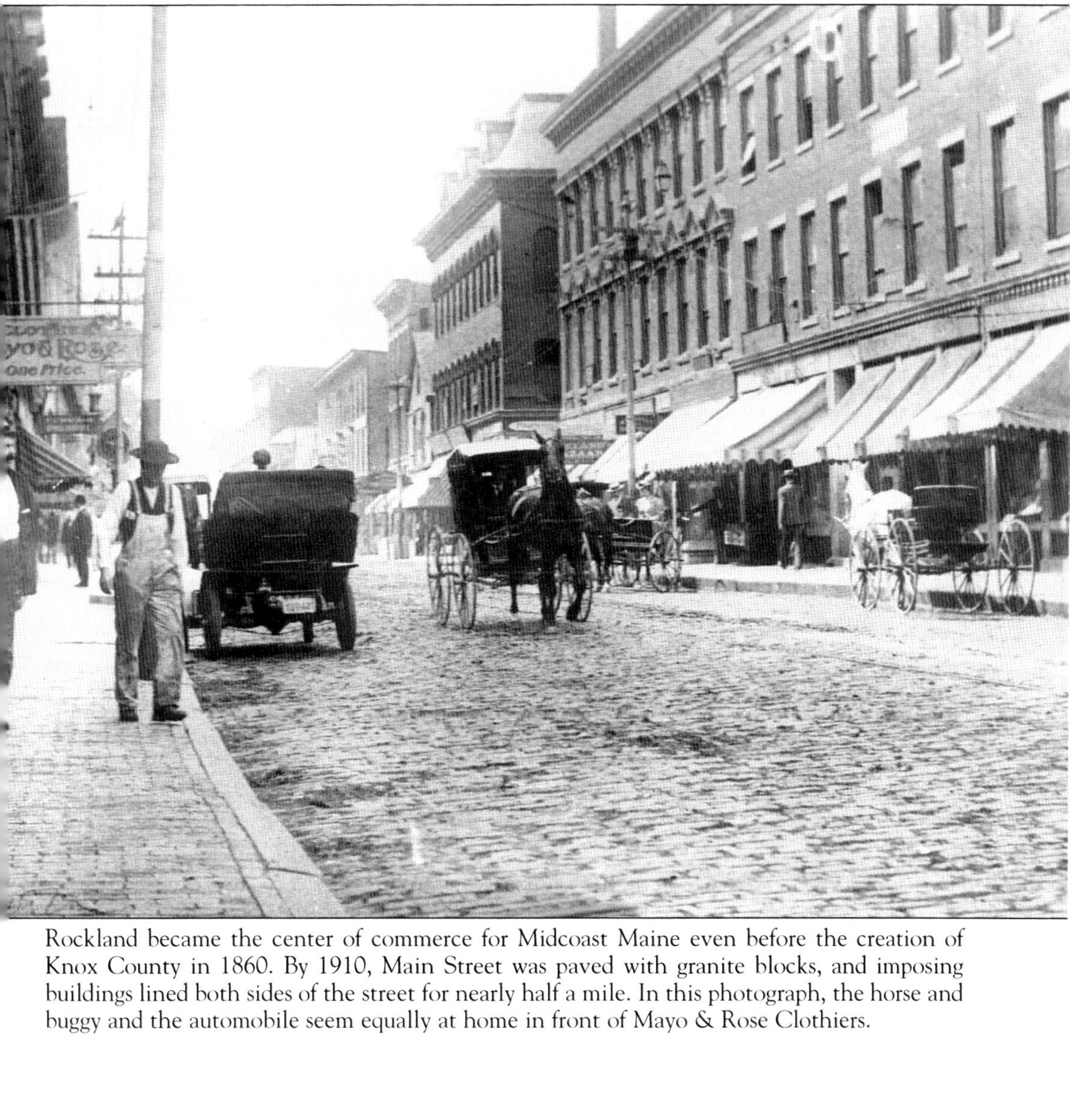

Rockland became the center of commerce for Midcoast Maine even before the creation of Knox County in 1860. By 1910, Main Street was paved with granite blocks, and imposing buildings lined both sides of the street for nearly half a mile. In this photograph, the horse and buggy and the automobile seem equally at home in front of Mayo & Rose Clothiers.

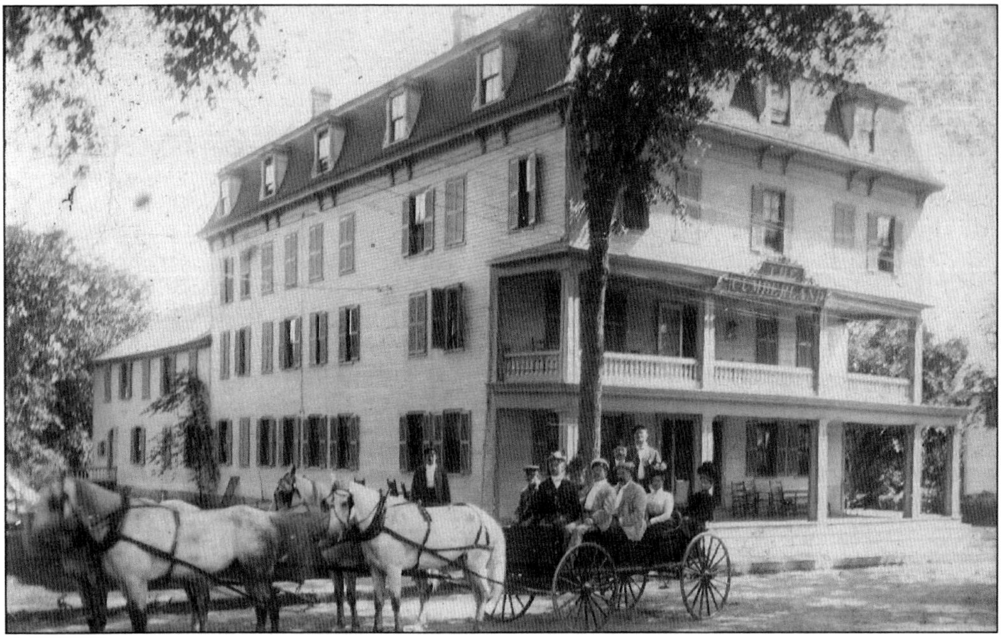

Located on the corner of Main and Bacon, The Cumberland Hotel was a popular place for guests to repose and dine, especially during the many years it was operated by Marshal and Joshia Bacon (and later by Marshal's three children). Marshal purchased the hotel in 1858 from Rufus Chase and greatly expanded it over the years. Very likely those in the open wagon are guests either headed out on an excursion or to the railroad station. The building was demolished in 1970.

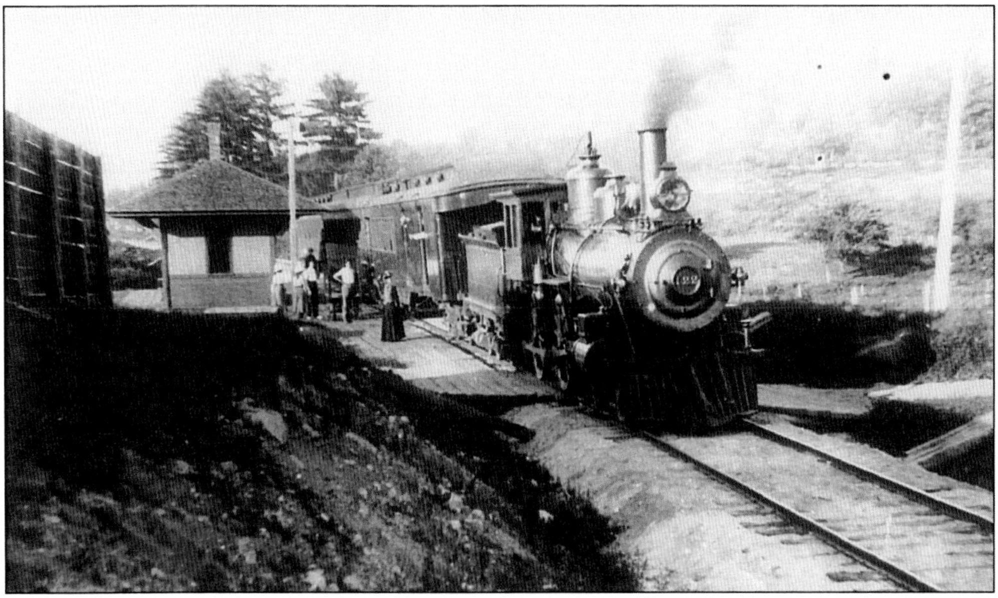

The steam train No. 122 of the Lake Shore Railroad at the Glendale Station in the summer of 1897. The railroad ended its service in 1930. In 1933 the tracks were removed.

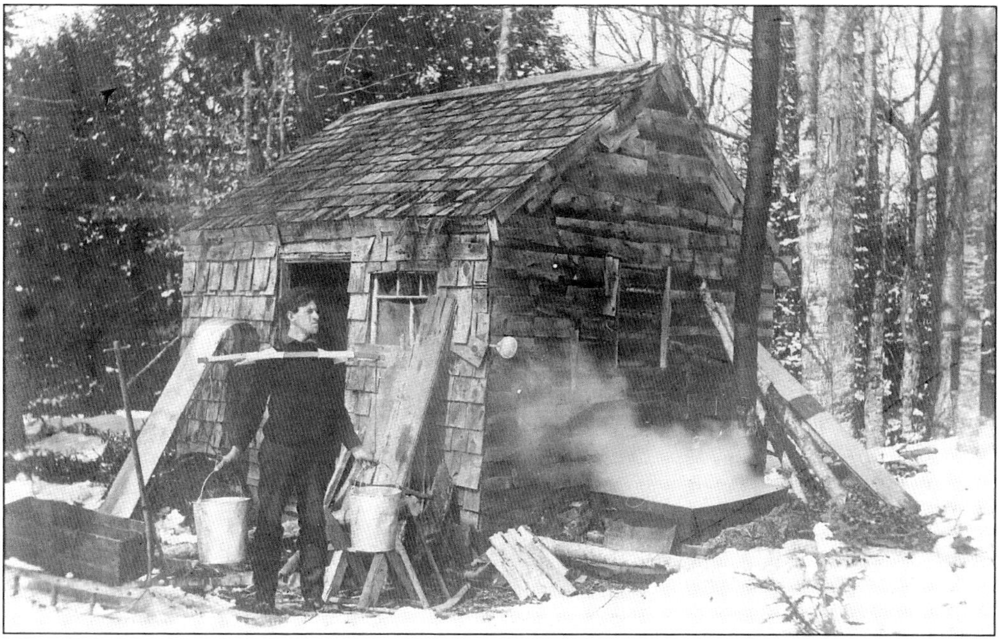

In early March, as rural Maine began to awaken from its long winter hiatus, farmers such as Fred Johnson began tapping sugar maples and gathering the sap to be boiled down to syrup (and in some instances, sugar) at sugar houses such as this one.

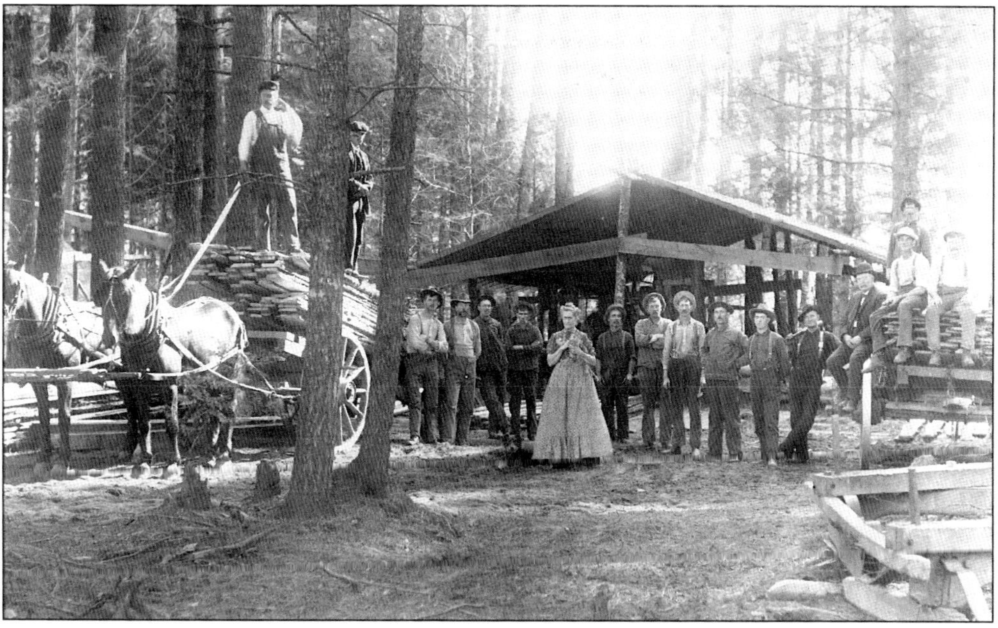

Until after World War II at least, portable sawmills such as this one were operating on logging sites throughout Maine. The bulky logs were sawed into tough lumber, and then the lighter boards were transported to planing mills located on permanent sites. This is one of Lewis Knight's portable mills. He obviously employed a sizeable crew of cutters, sawyers, and teamsters.

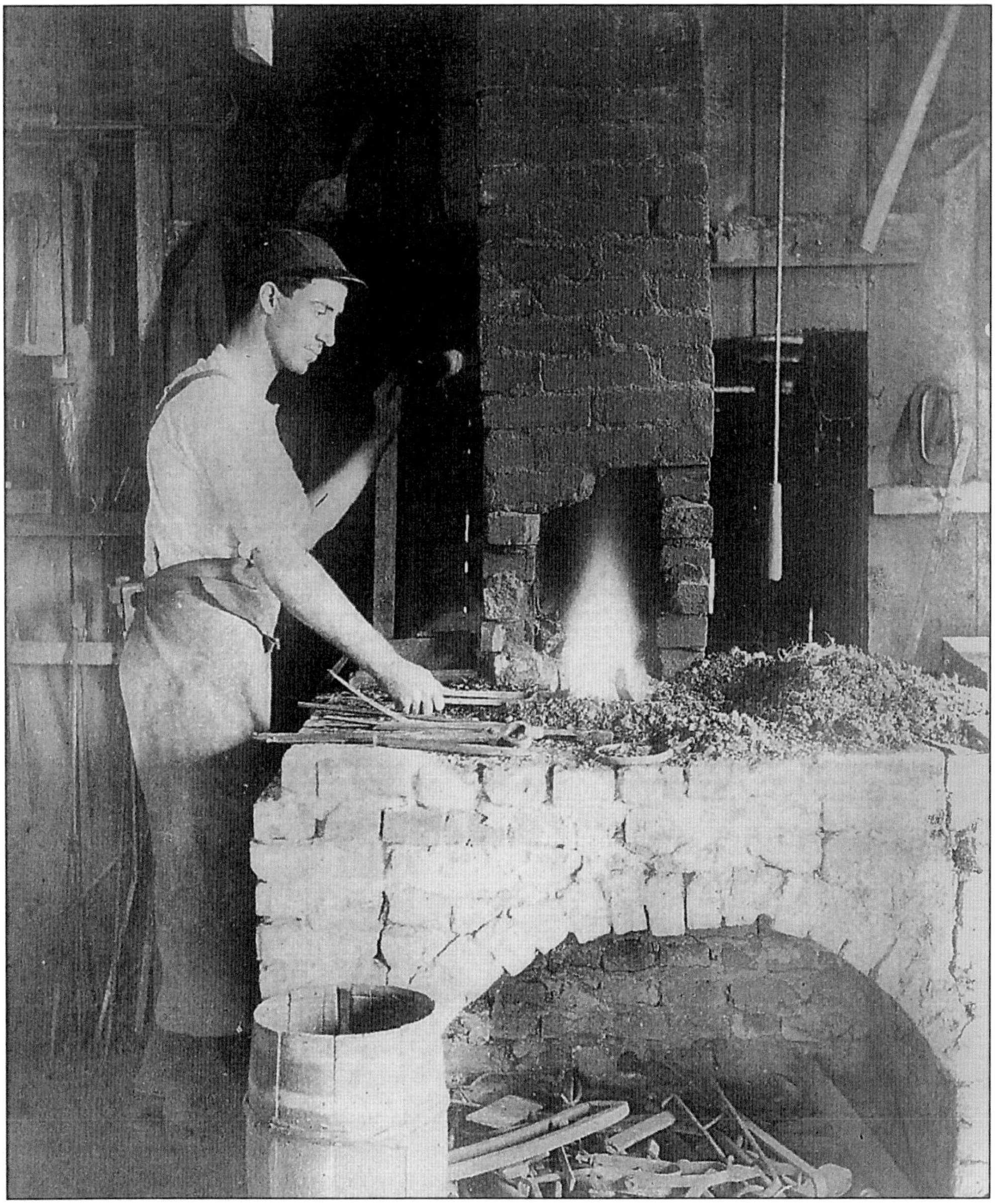

This photograph of an unidentified blacksmith working at his forge, thought to have been located in East Bethel, is an outstanding example of Nettie Cumming Maxim's ability to use both artificial and natural light in her photography.

A working blacksmith is very challenging to photograph, for he toils only by the light of the fire. Since he monitors the temperature of the metal by the subtle changes in color, working in a dark space is essential.

The blacksmith was indispensable to every town and hamlet throughout rural Maine at the turn of the century. Many farmers who lived in isolated areas such as Bird Hill learned the basics of blacksmithing in order to keep their farms functioning.

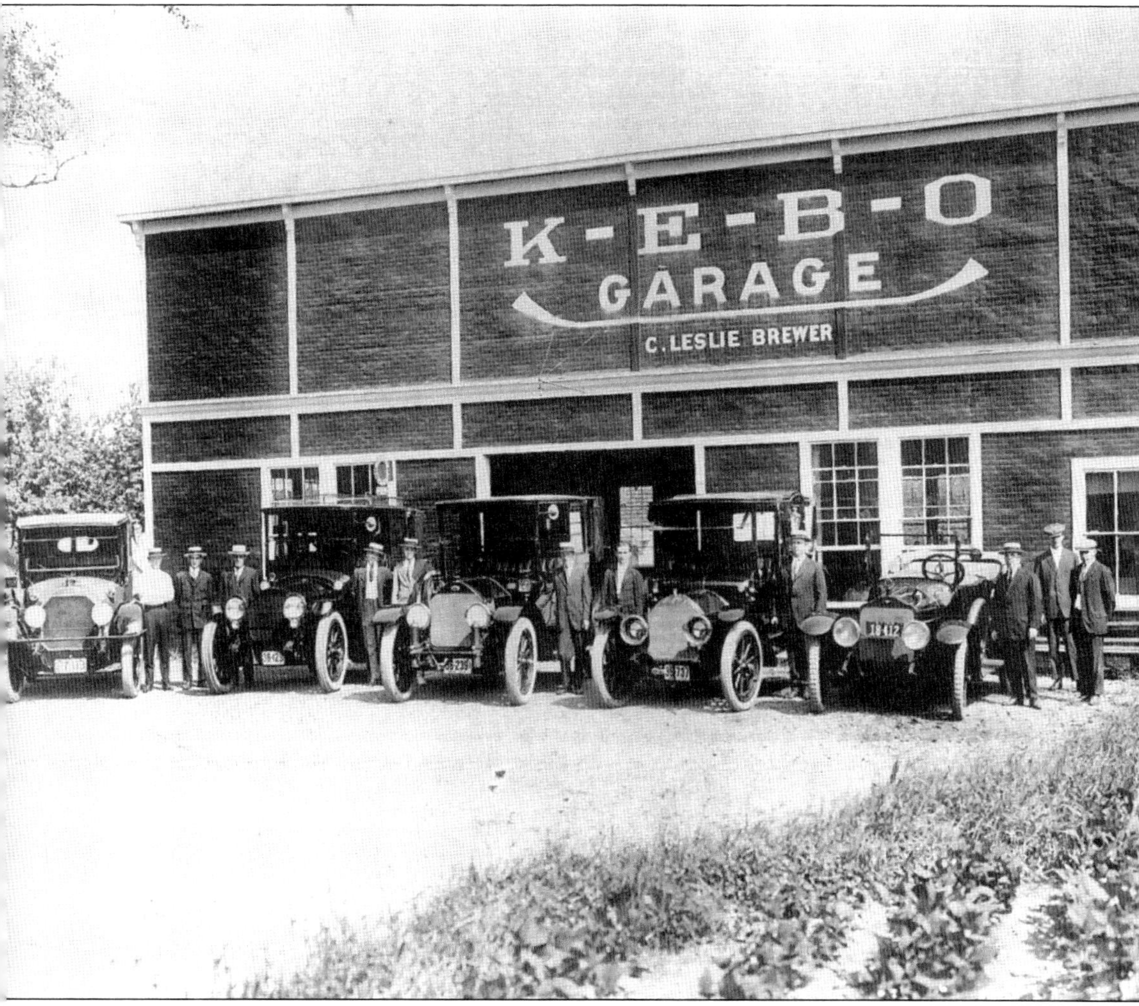

Groups of men pose with the fashionable automobiles of the day at C. Leslie Brewer's Kebo Garage in Bar Harbor. (Raymond Strout).

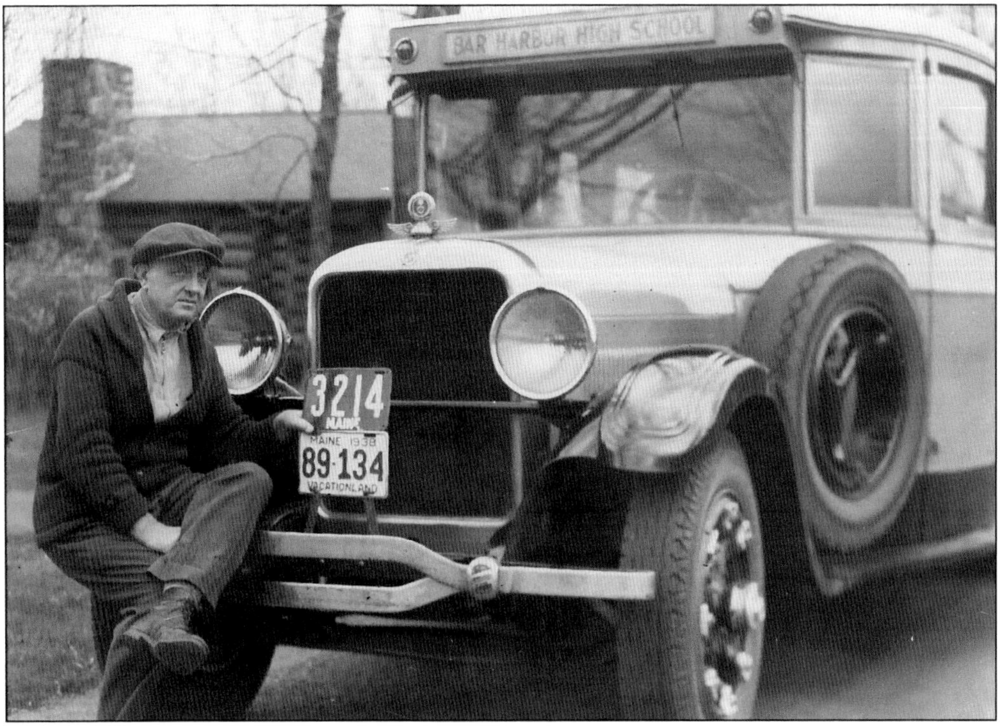

William Dolliver started the first school bus service and drove the first bus on the Island. (Robert Dolliver).

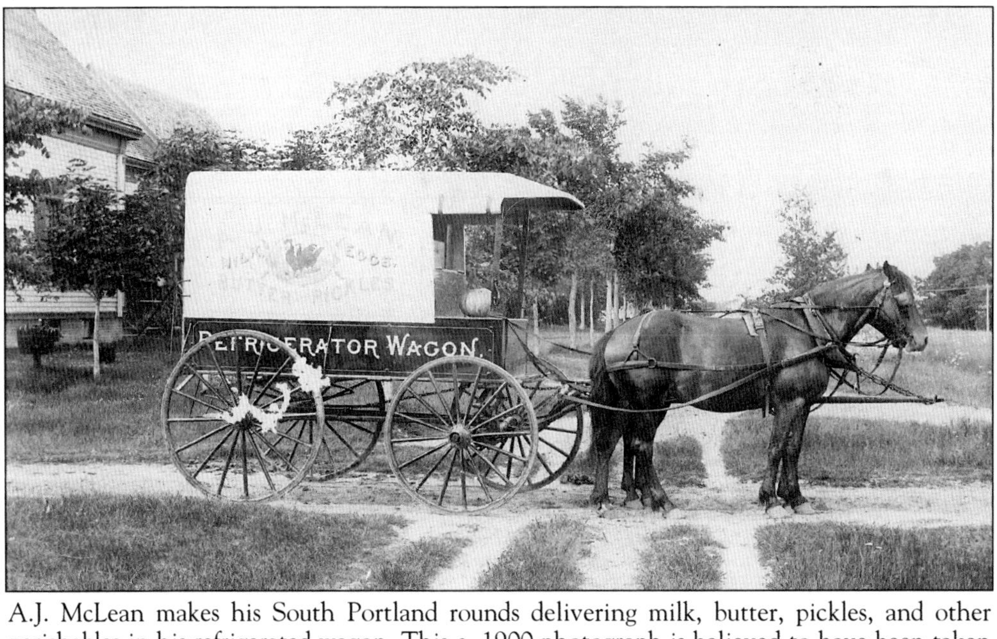

A.J. McLean makes his South Portland rounds delivering milk, butter, pickles, and other perishables in his refrigerated wagon. This *c.* 1900 photograph is believed to have been taken in the Parrott Street area. (Dorothy M. Wilkes).

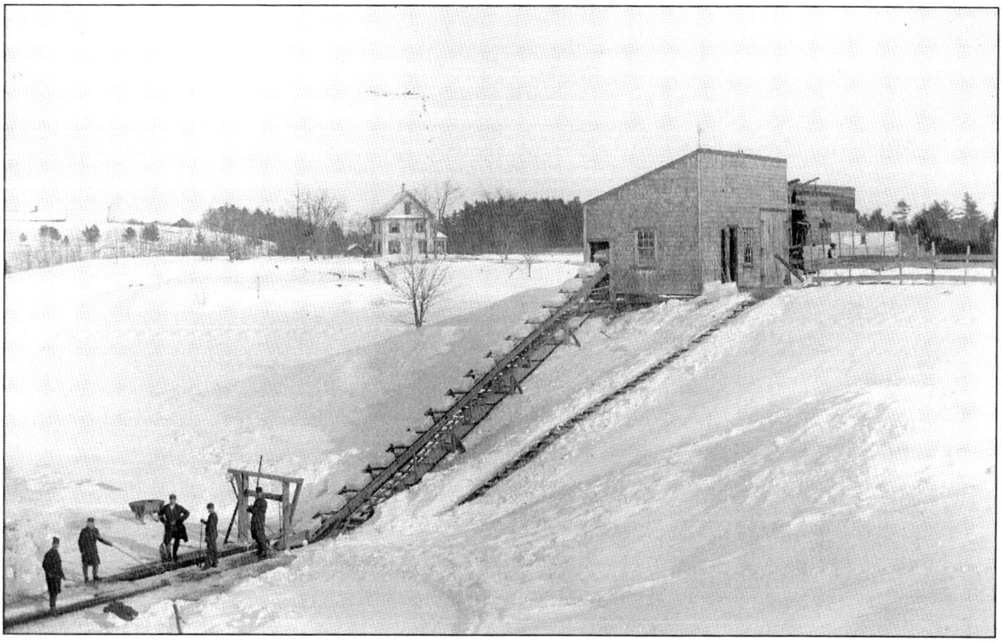

Ice is harvested in the Pleasantdale area for storage in D.W. Clark's ice house, c. 1900. Another ice house was located at Clark's Pond at Long Creek. In 1946 the pond was stocked with fish and the city's first fishing derby was held there. (Ray Taylor).

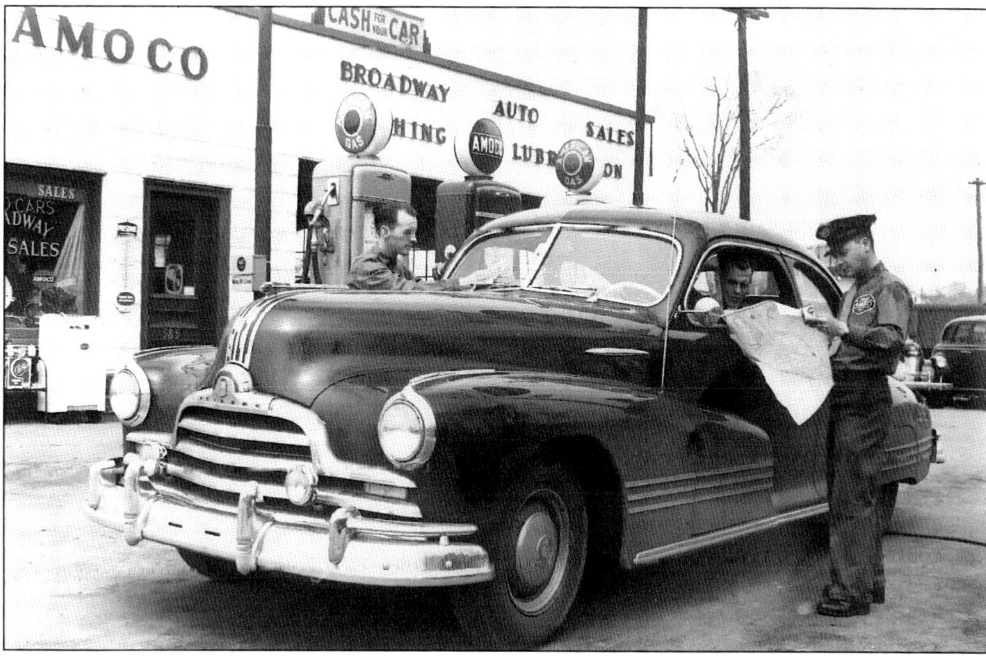

A filling station attendant, attired in the company's uniform, gives directions to a motorist at Broadway Auto Sales in South Portland, while another attendant washes the windows, c. 1948. (Sullivan Photo Collection).

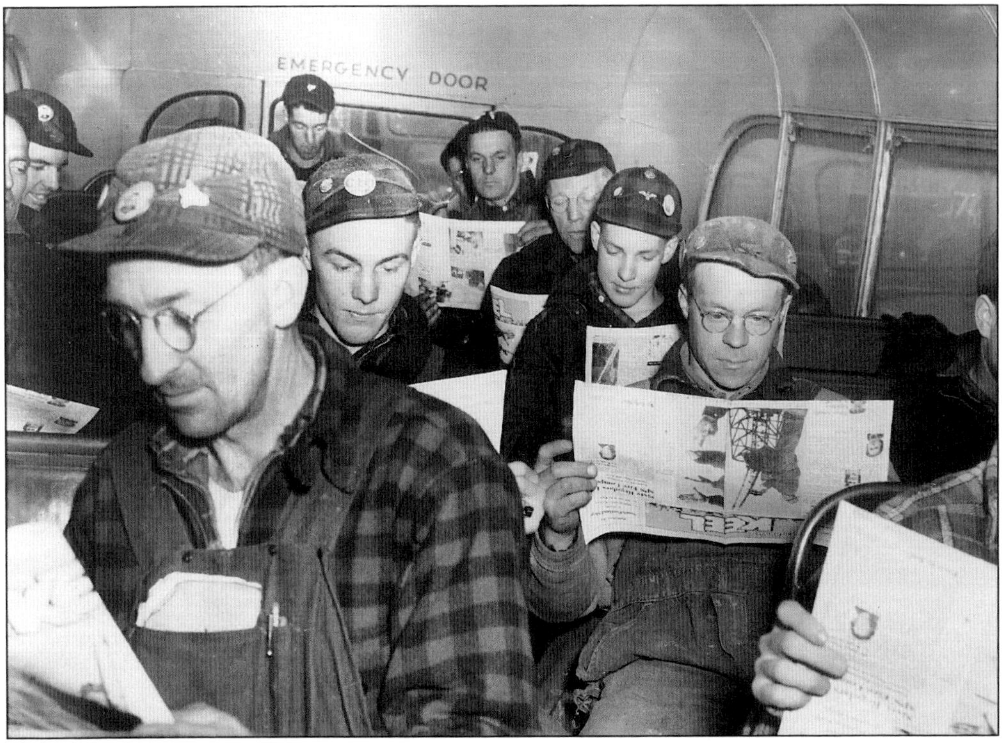

Workers keep up with shipyard happenings via the *KEEL*, a weekly newspaper published at the West Yard "for the men and women workers of New England Ship, So. Portland, Me." (Edward Langlois).

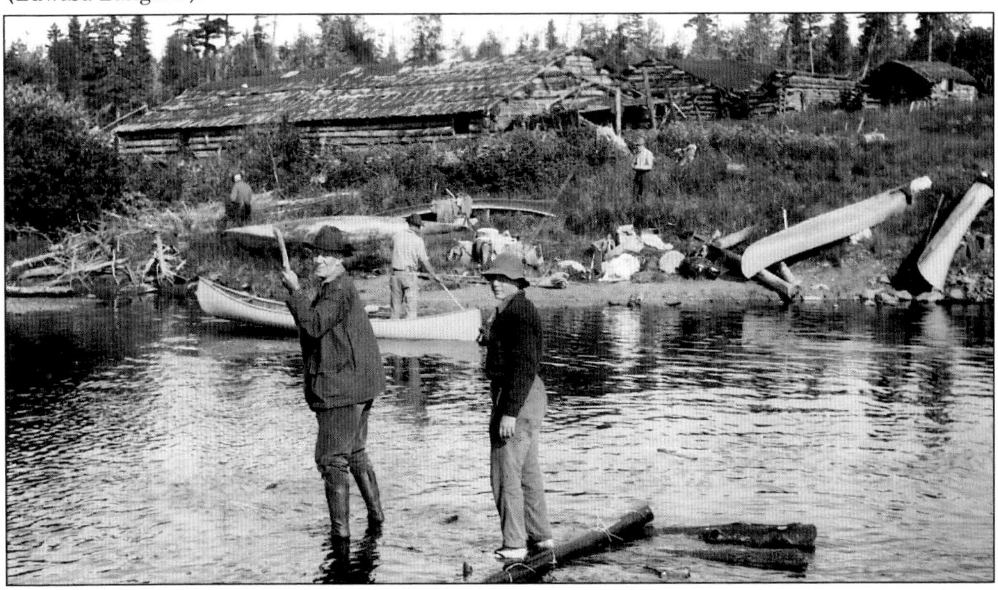

On a raft and in a canoe in front of Sanders and Cullen's winter lumber camp, Moosehead Lake, 1920s. (H.A. Sanders Jr.).

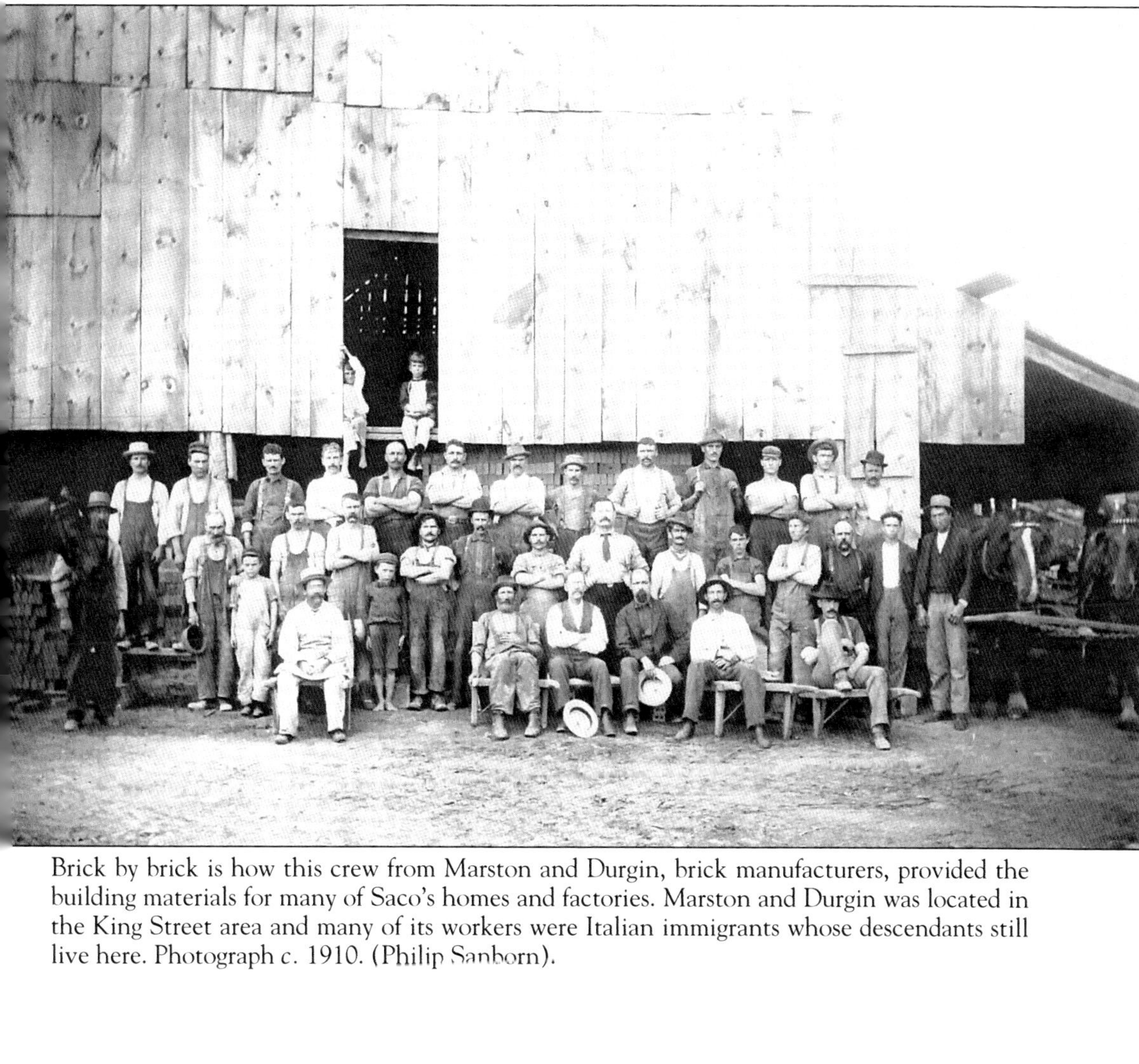

Brick by brick is how this crew from Marston and Durgin, brick manufacturers, provided the building materials for many of Saco's homes and factories. Marston and Durgin was located in the King Street area and many of its workers were Italian immigrants whose descendants still live here. Photograph c. 1910. (Philip Sanborn).

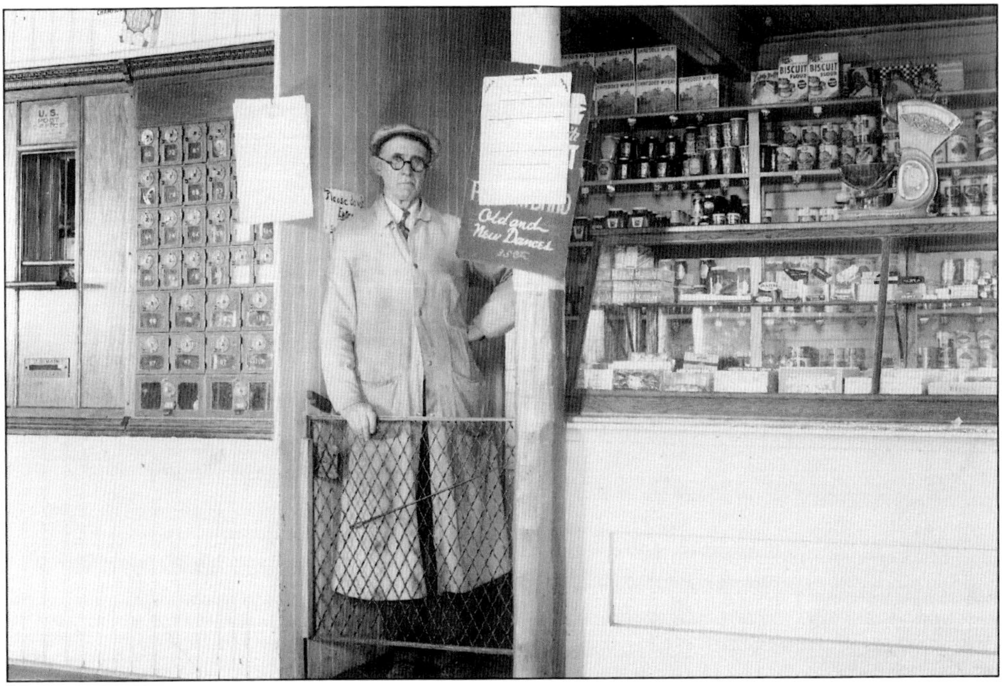

James C. Gilman, postmaster and store owner, stands inside his store at Sebasco Estates in the early 1930s. He had been postmaster for 33 years when he retired in 1946. Combining stores and post offices was a typical practice; the post office sometimes moved from one store to another, depending on the political party of the administration.

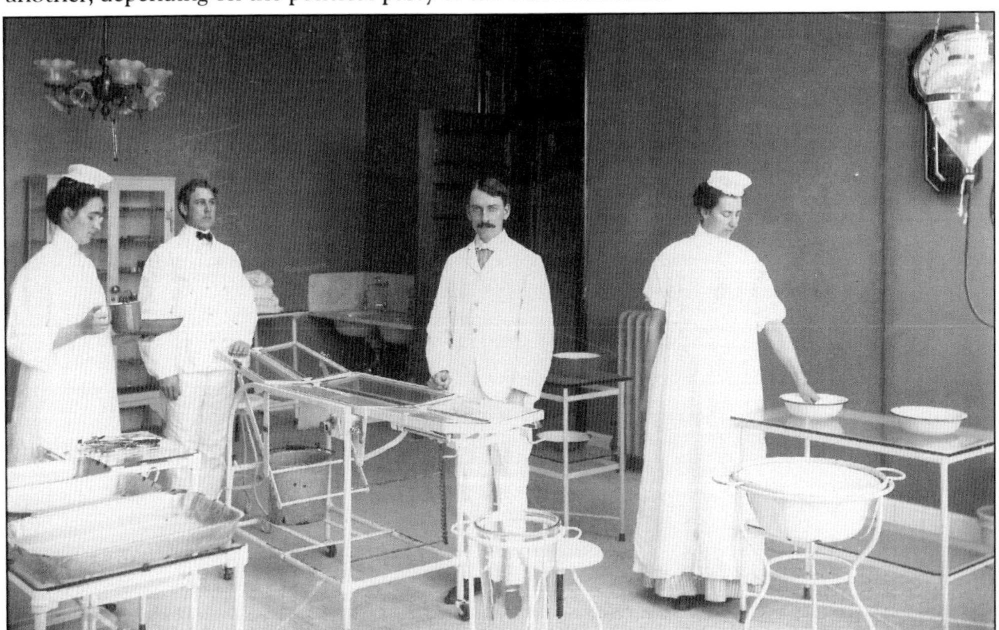

This early photograph shows doctors and nurses in the operating room in Auburn.

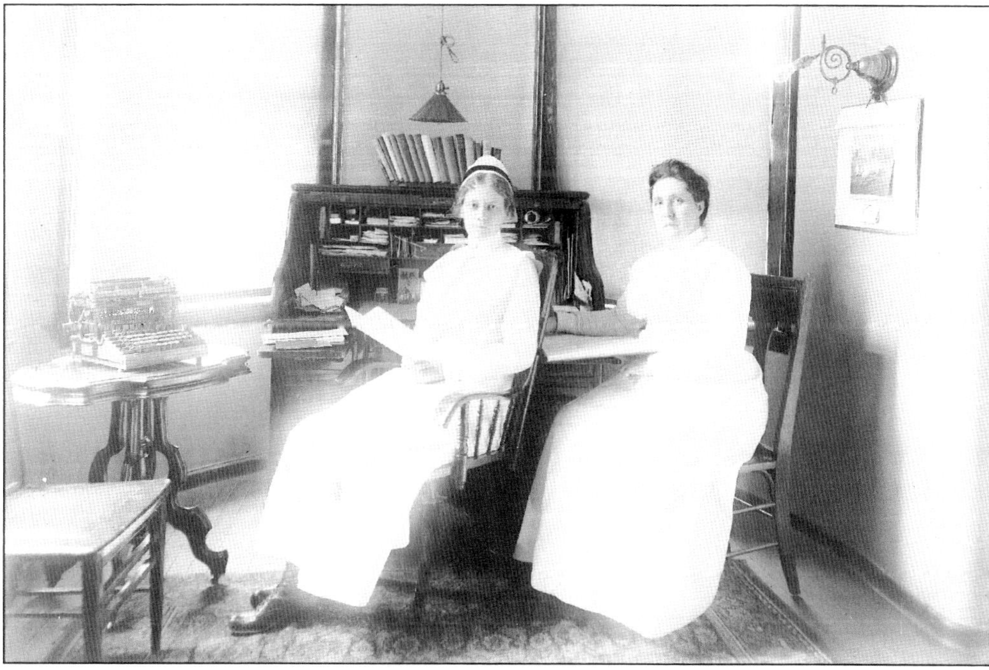

Miss Lamberson and Miss R. Metcalf posed at the Central Maine General Hospital in 1912.

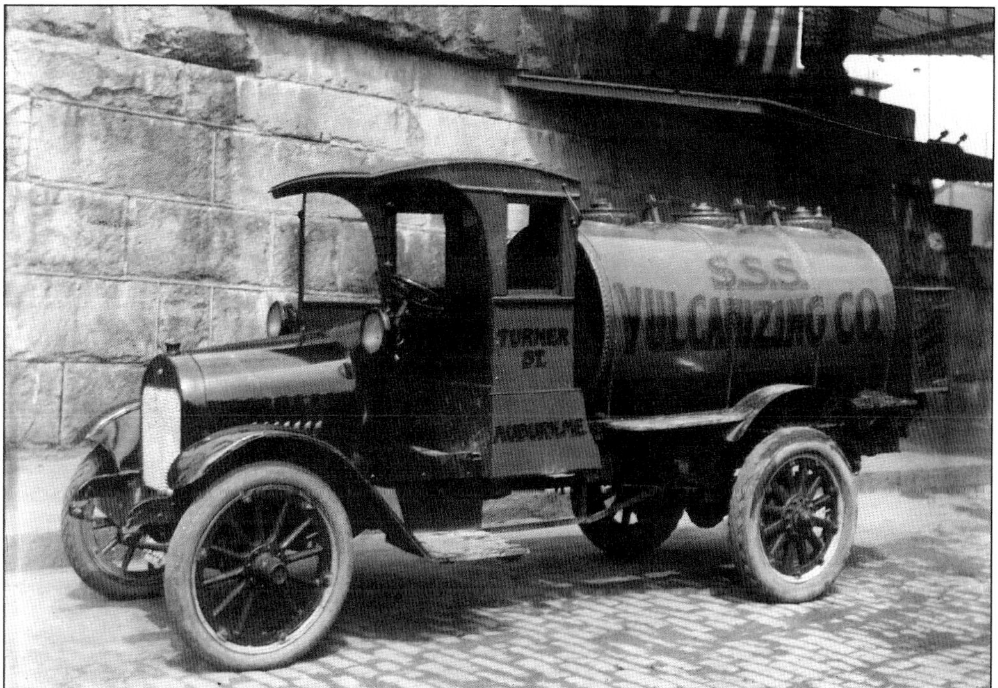

One of the first oil-delivery trucks in the Auburn area, owned by Fred McKenny, was photographed under the Turner Street underpass.

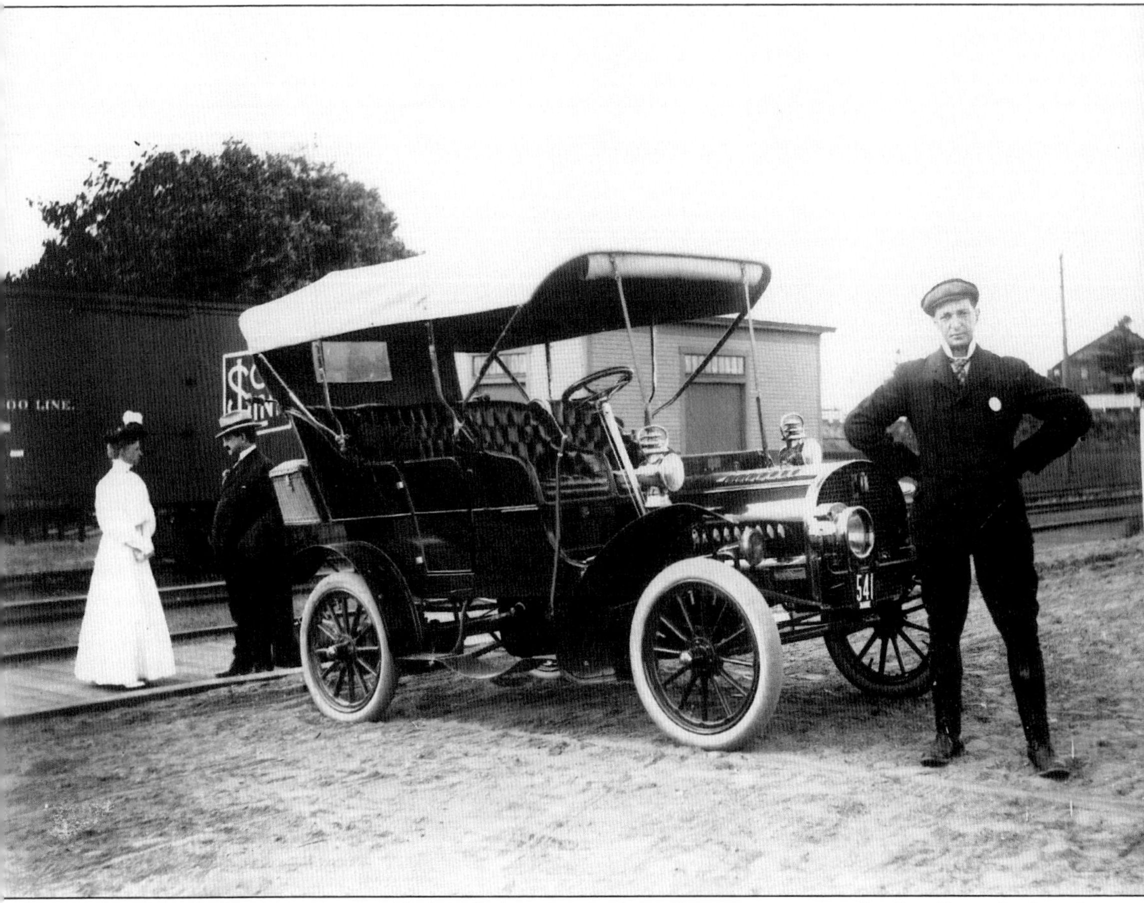

This chauffeur poses proudly beside his automobile. During this period, chauffeurs had to be registered in Massachusetts (but not in Maine). Identification was issued in the form of a badge, which this driver is wearing on the left side of his jacket.

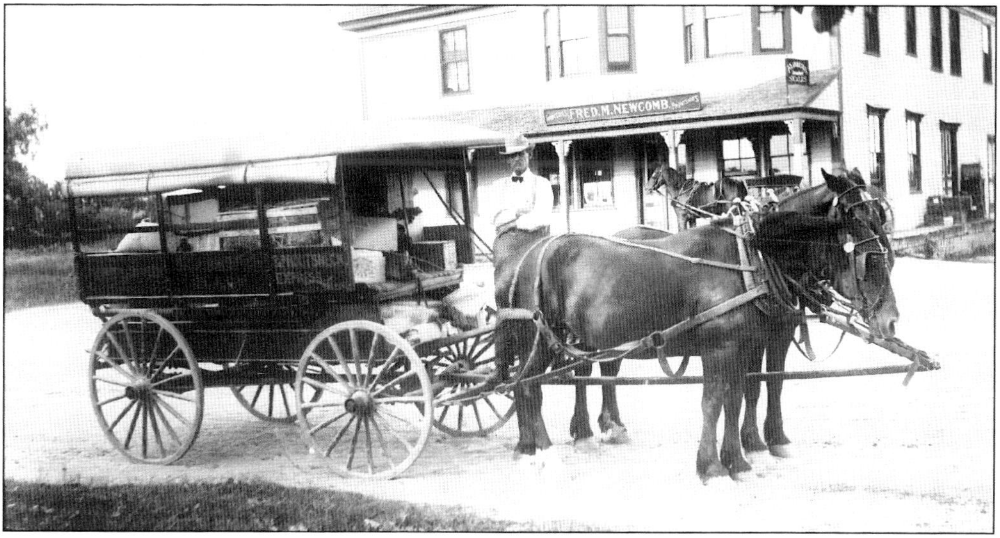

Mr. Newcomb and V.T. Shaw kept stores in the area of Black Point Road because of the proximity to the train station. The building looks the same today as it did when this photograph was taken. Along the side of the delivery wagon is printed "Portland, Prouts Neck and Scarboro Beach Express." The wagon and team were the equivalent of the private parcel delivery companies of today.

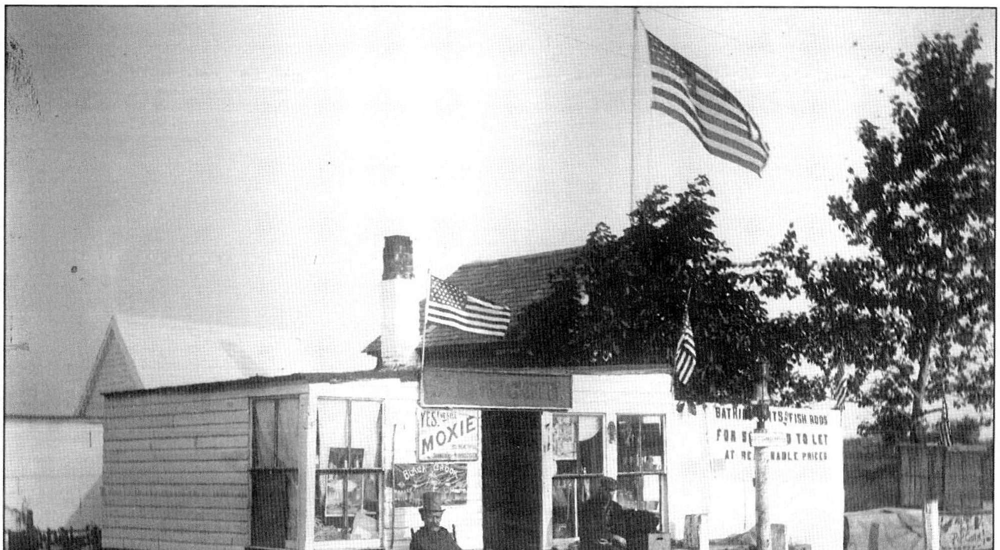

Captain John Wiggin was the proprietor of a small store located on the shore across from the entrance to the Southgate Hotel. A local character, he was a favorite of many visitors to this area one hundred years ago. Wiggin was described as eccentric, and the "captain" in his name stood only for "captain of his domain." Wiggin catered to the needs of the growing summer colony at Prouts Neck. He supplied everything from soft drinks and ice cream to clams and lobster. It was from him that you could rent a dory, bicycle, fishing pole, or clam digger. (Courtesy Jane King).

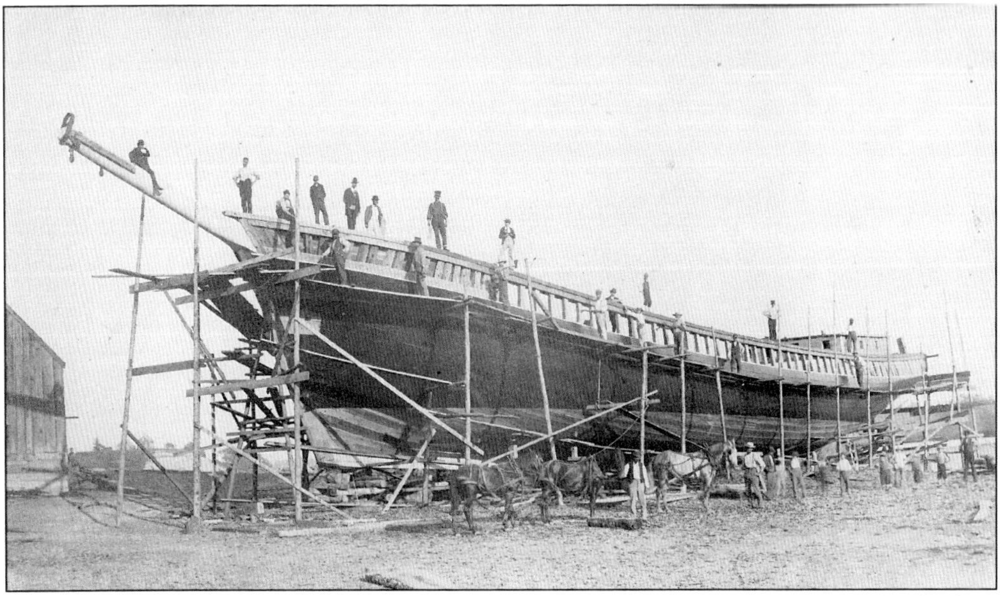

The *Delia Chapin* was constructed at Dunstan Landing in 1847. The area around the landing was called the Ship Yard. It was not uncommon for there to be one or more vessels under construction there at a time. Timber which was cut on the interior of southwestern Maine, was exported from the landing. Flood gates, built on the Dunstan River in 1877, severely restricted the flow of water. The change was so dramatic that today it seems hard to believe that a thriving port ever existed there. (Scarborough Historical Society).

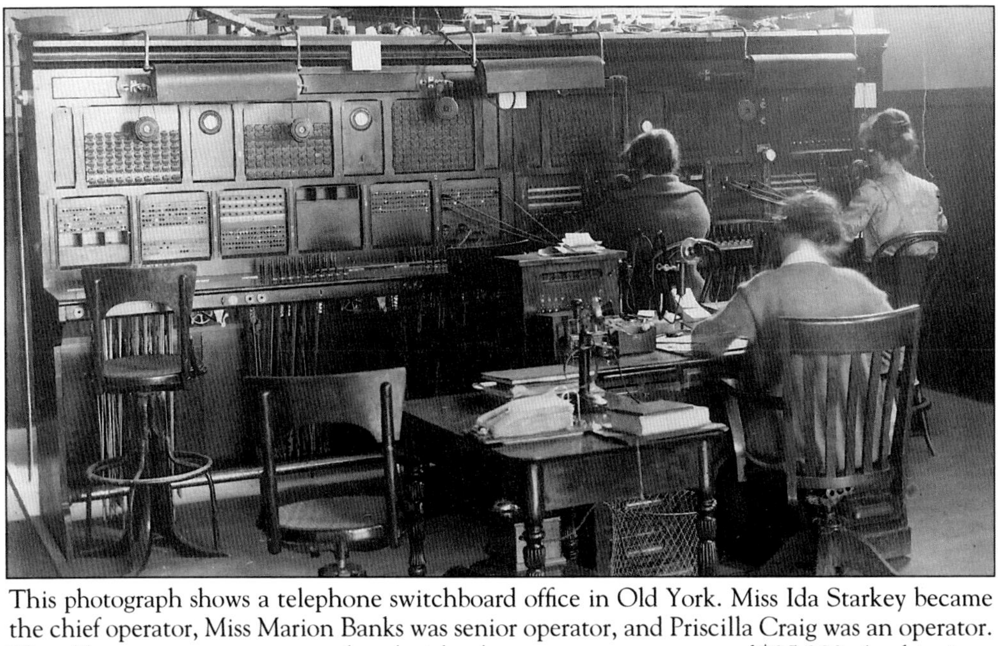

This photograph shows a telephone switchboard office in Old York. Miss Ida Starkey became the chief operator, Miss Marion Banks was senior operator, and Priscilla Craig was an operator. The old magneto system was replaced with a battery system at a cost of $25,000. At this time, the telephone exchange occupied one entire side of the Realty building.

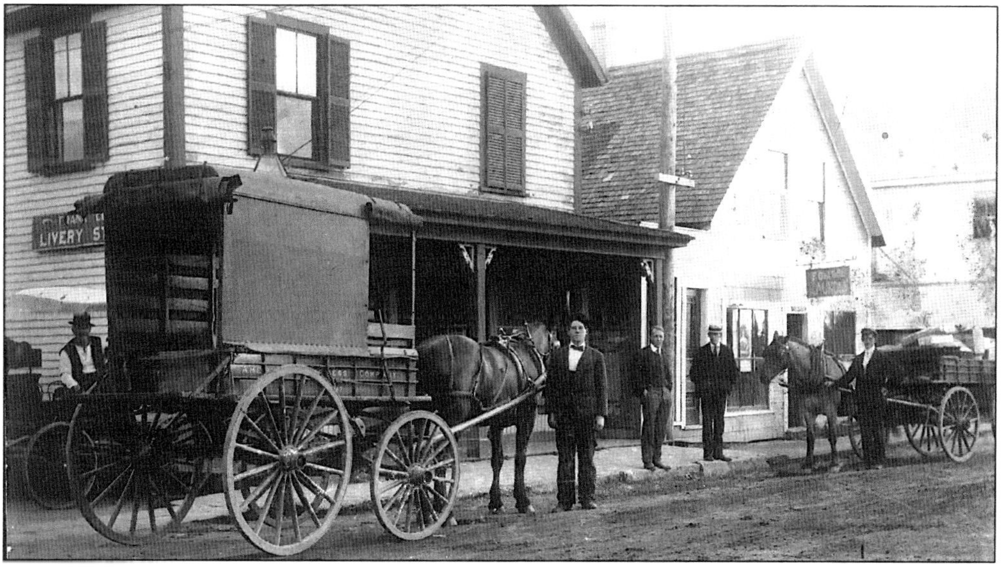

An American Express wagon in York Beach in 1905. These wagons carried much of the freight from the train and trolley stations. Cap Seavey is the man in the center of the picture. Cap worked for American Express for nearly 20 years, and at one time he worked as American Express agent for the York Harbor and Beach Railroad.

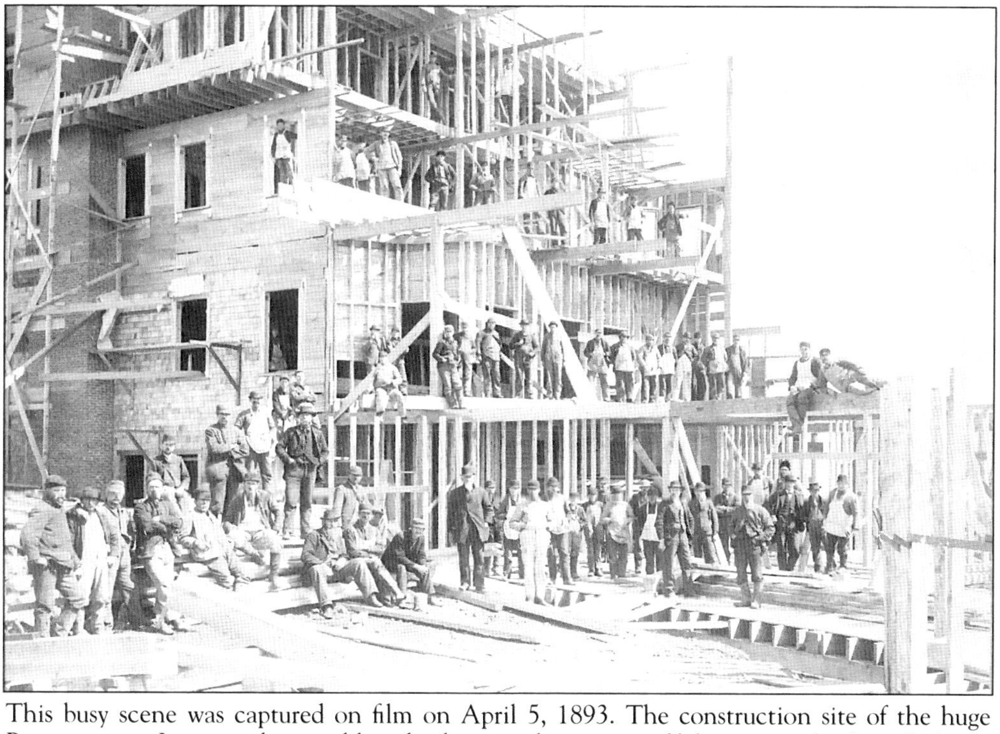

This busy scene was captured on film on April 5, 1893. The construction site of the huge Passaconaway Inn complex was like a beehive, with a swarm of laborers involved in all phases of the project.

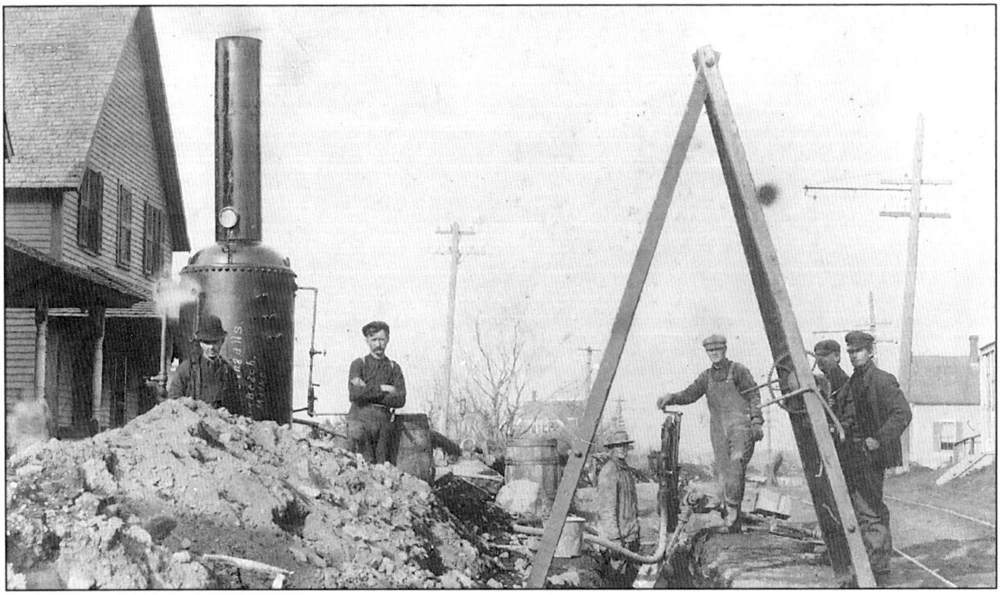

Digging trenches for water pipes on top of Hildreth's Hill in York Beach. Note the steam-driven drill and the trolley car tracks. The York Shore Water Company was organized in 1895 to supply the towns of York and Wells with pure water and to protect the waters of Chase's Pond.

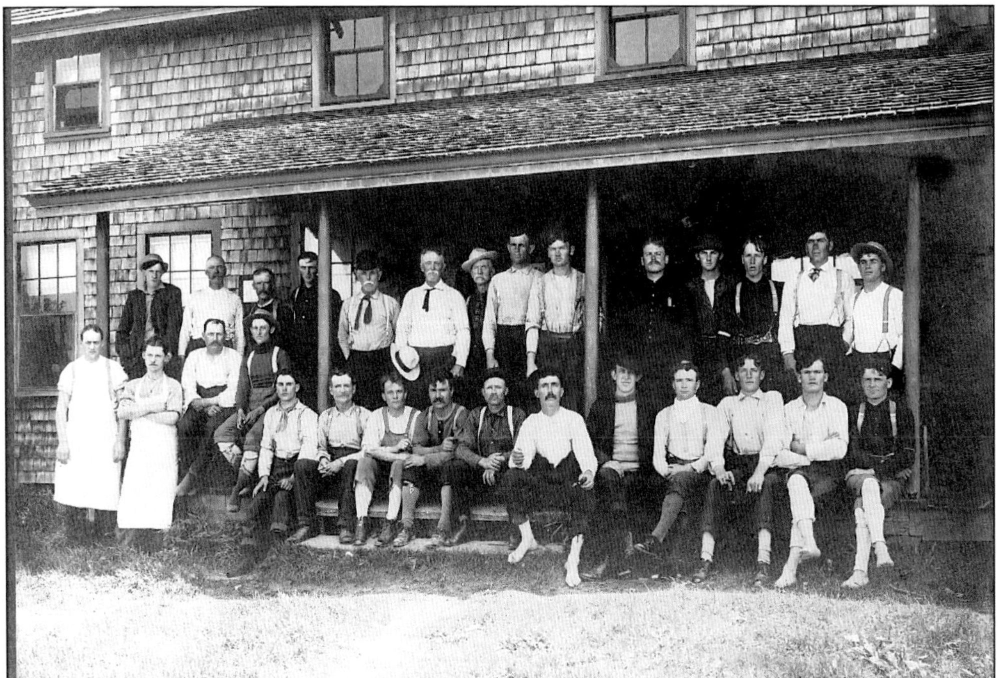

The Boom House on College Avenue in the early 1900s. Here, workers for the Hollingsworth and Whitney Paper Mill in Winslow (across the Kennebec River from Waterville) ate and slept. Most of those workers were Franco-Americans.

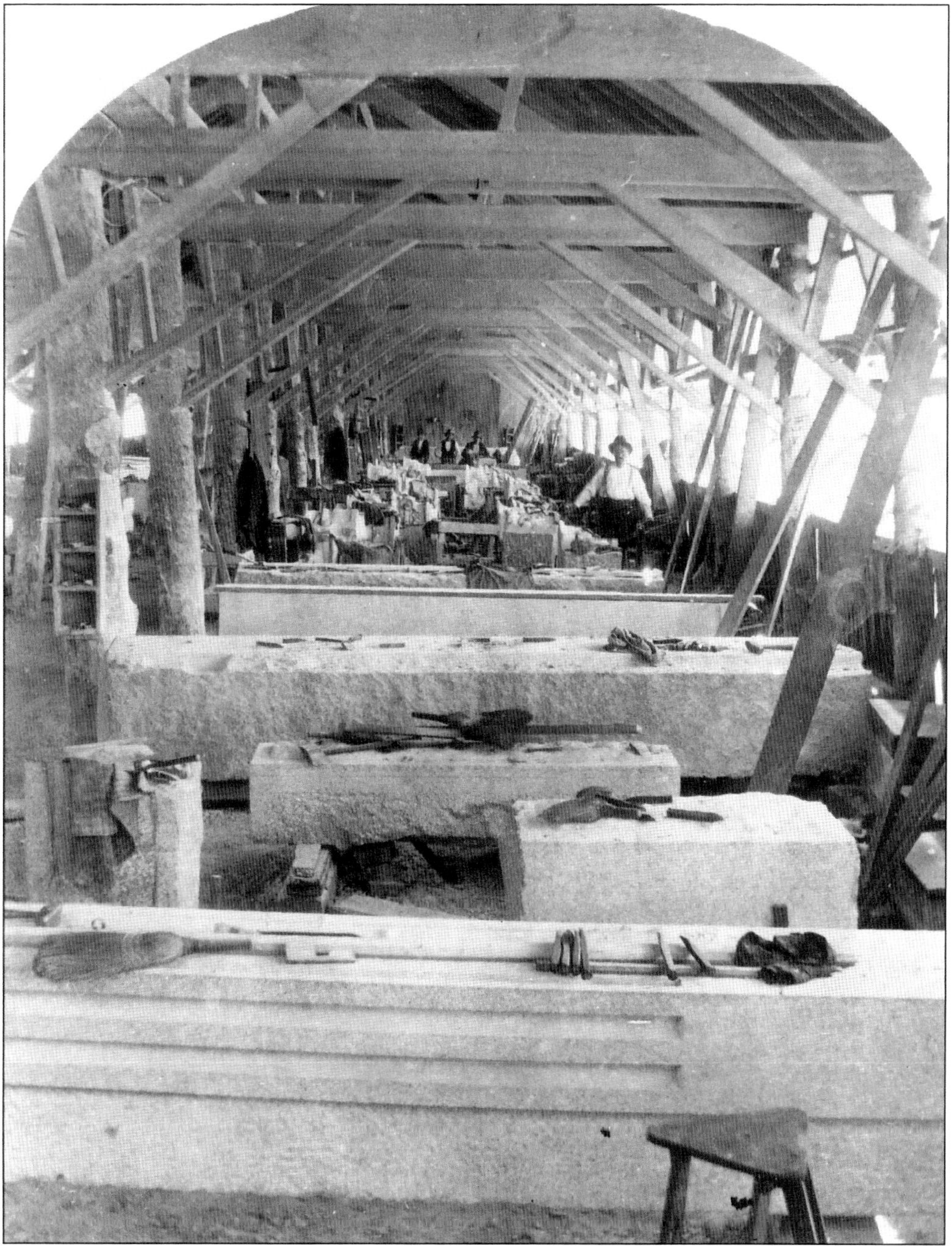

Granite carvers in the late 1870s worked inside several long sheds at Sands Stoneyard. Here, the stone for various jobs is shown with the carver's chisels, hammers, and other tools at their work stations.

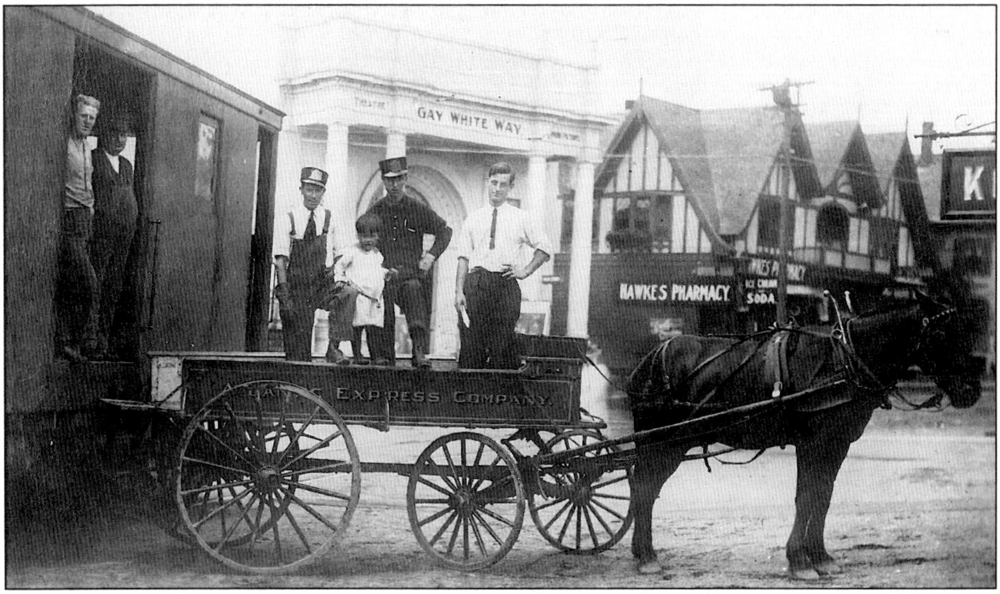

The Atlantic Express Company maintained express service over the Atlantic Shore Railway system for a number of years after 1912. Here merchandise is being transferred at York Beach Square to an express company delivery wagon. In the background is the Gay White Way, opened about 1910 by one Frank Ellis and featuring a dance hall and other attractions. A York Beach landmark for many years, it was torched by an arsonist on March 21, 1951.

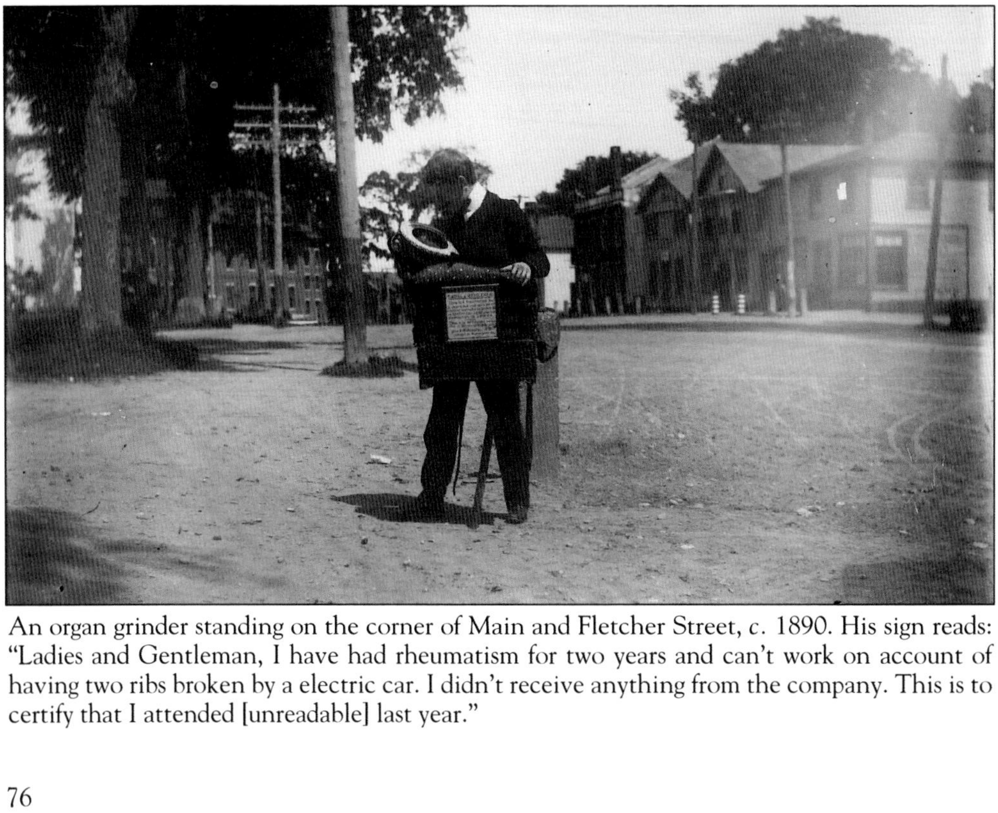

An organ grinder standing on the corner of Main and Fletcher Street, *c.* 1890. His sign reads: "Ladies and Gentleman, I have had rheumatism for two years and can't work on account of having two ribs broken by a electric car. I didn't receive anything from the company. This is to certify that I attended [unreadable] last year."

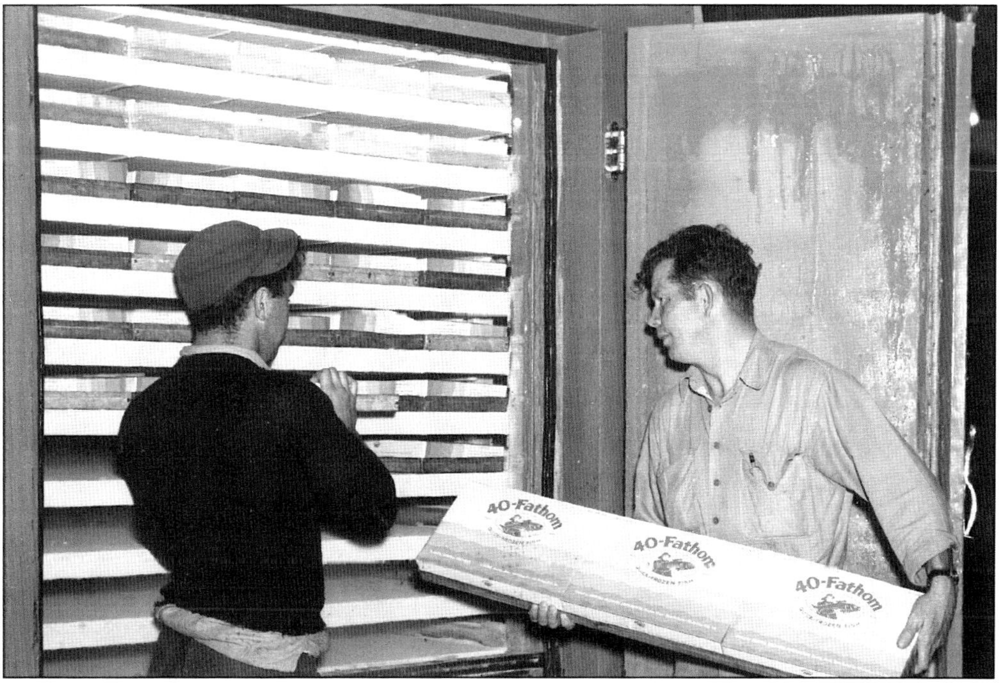

A 1940s photograph of a freezer full of Forty Fathoms frozen fish fillets packed by General Seafoods at their plant on Tillson Avenue.

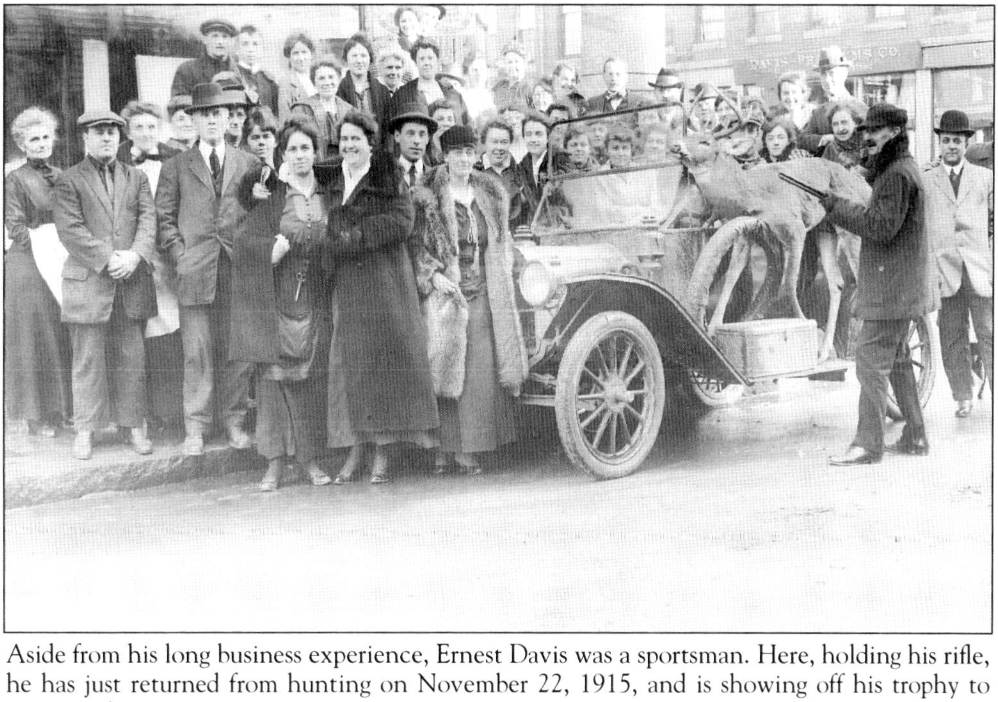

Aside from his long business experience, Ernest Davis was a sportsman. Here, holding his rifle, he has just returned from hunting on November 22, 1915, and is showing off his trophy to store employees.

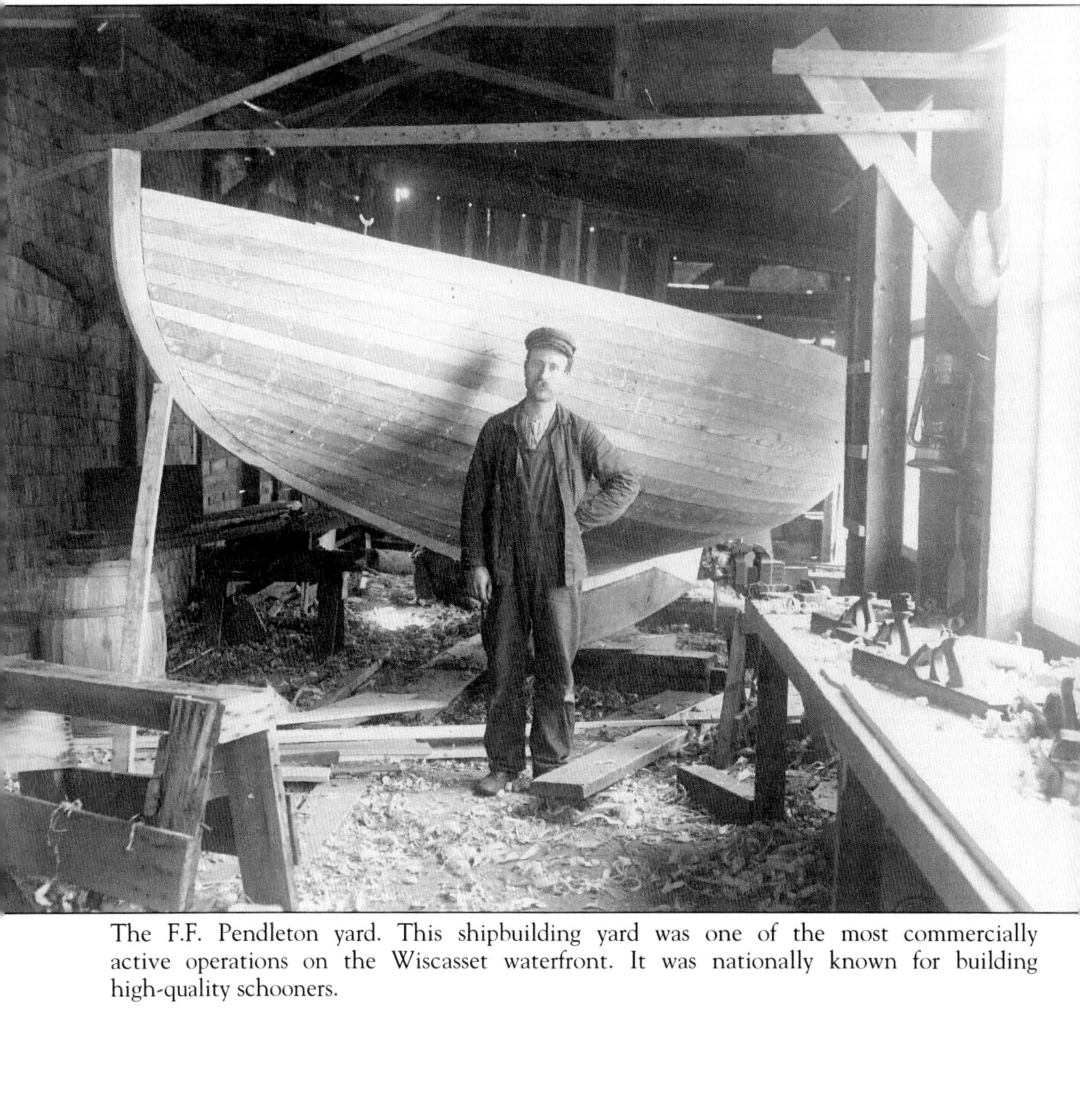

The F.F. Pendleton yard. This shipbuilding yard was one of the most commercially active operations on the Wiscasset waterfront. It was nationally known for building high-quality schooners.

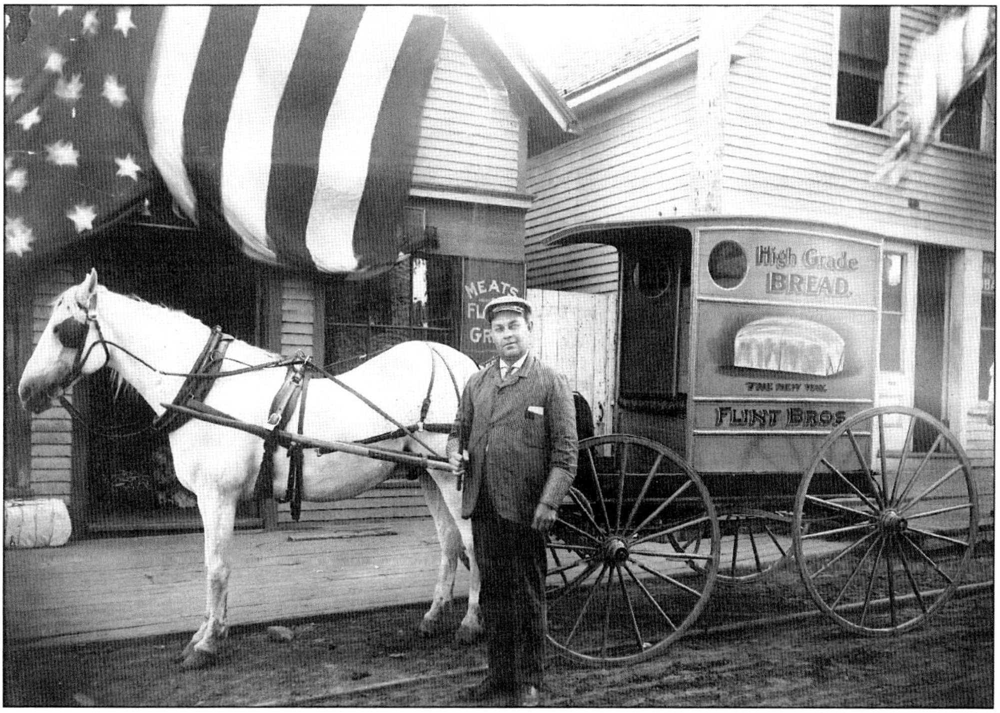

A Flint Brothers' Bakery delivery wagon with its advertising slogan.

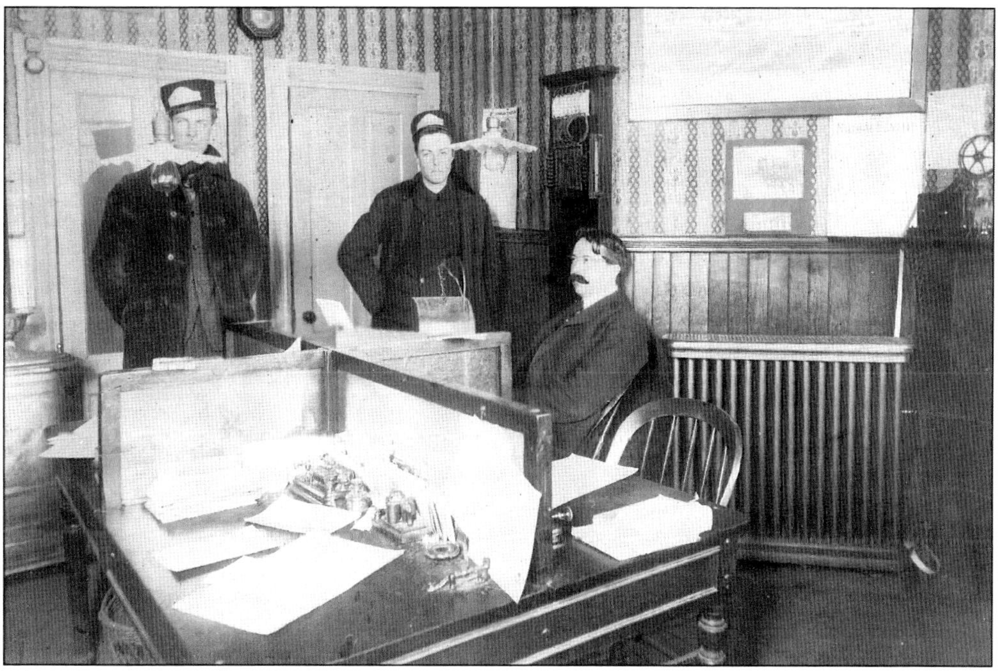

The telegraph preceded telephones and continued well into the 1900s. This interior photograph shows both operators and messengers at the Rockland office.

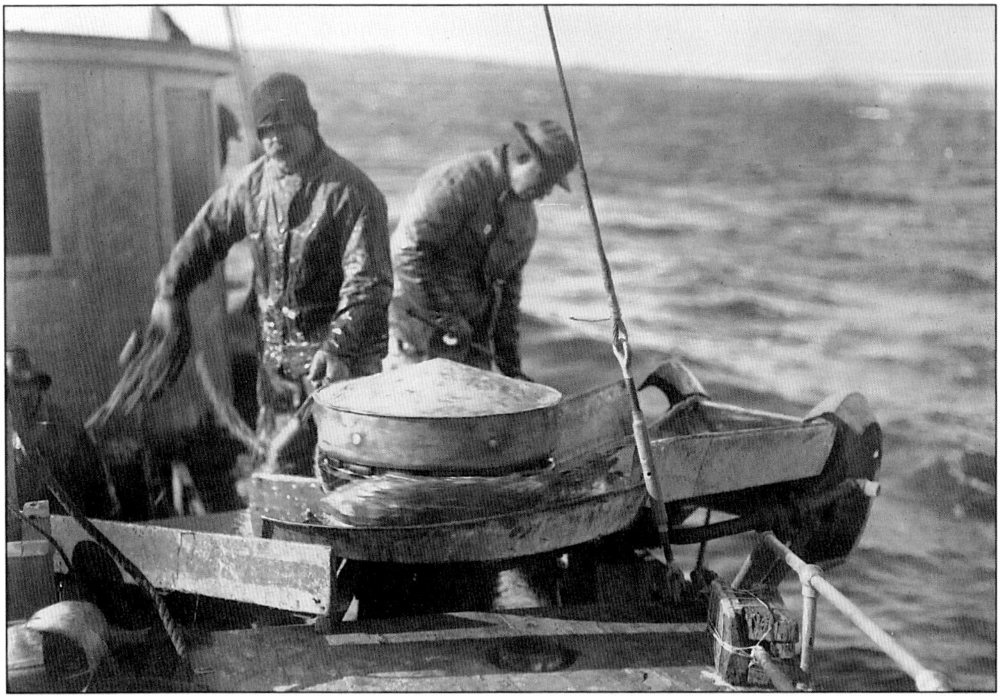

A new way of fishing, known as gill netting, was introduced in the early 1900s, with Hartley Huff in the forefront. Here Ed Perkins (left) and Charles McKay are aboard Hartley's boat, the *Ethel S*, c. 1920. (Huff Family).

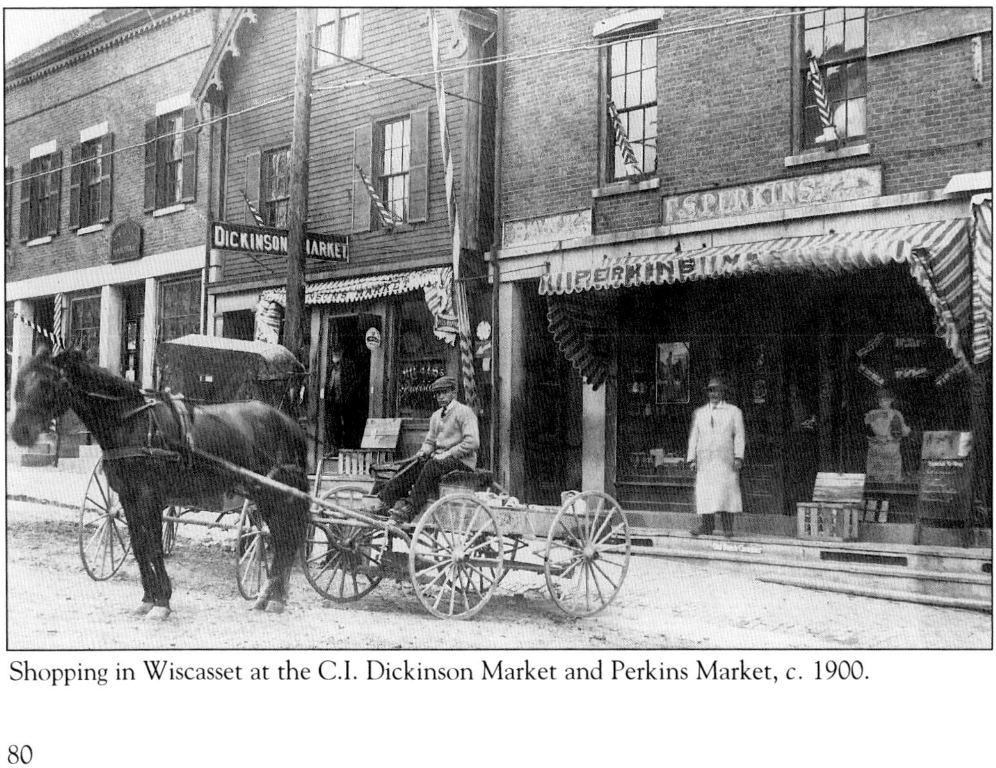

Shopping in Wiscasset at the C.I. Dickinson Market and Perkins Market, c. 1900.

Four

GETTING WET

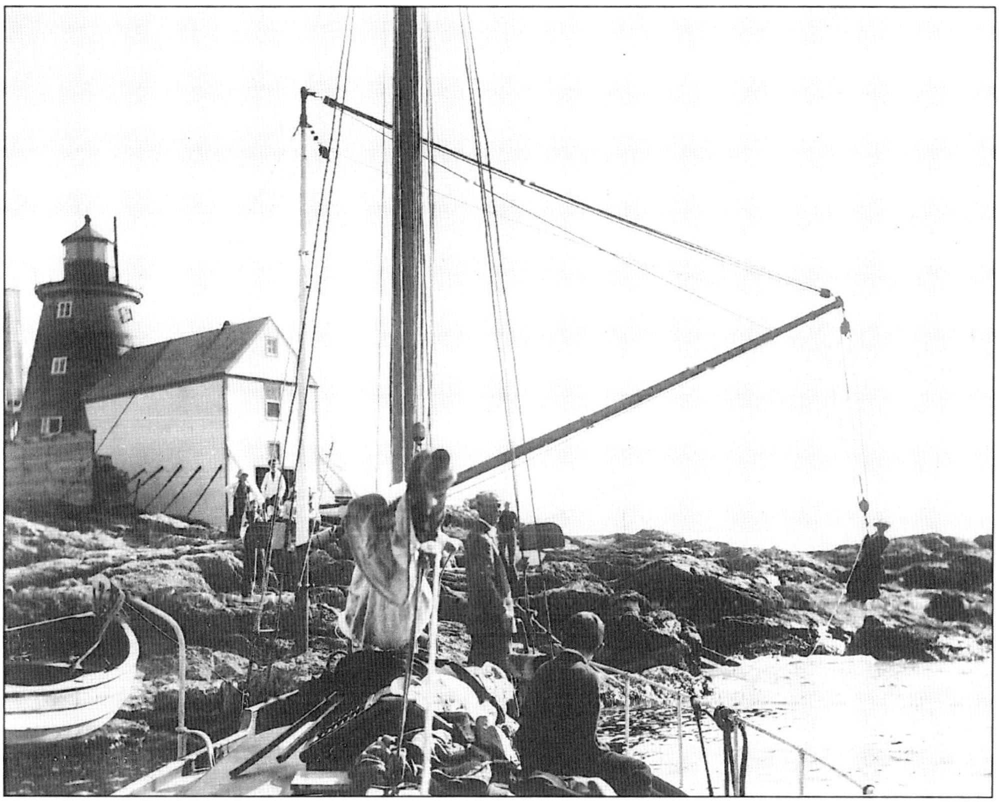

The Saddleback Ledge Lighthouse, built in 1839, was maintained by a keeper until it was automated in 1954. To go ashore on the ledge, it was necessary to be carried from your vessel in a bos'n's chair, swinging from a large boom, as the woman is doing in this photograph.

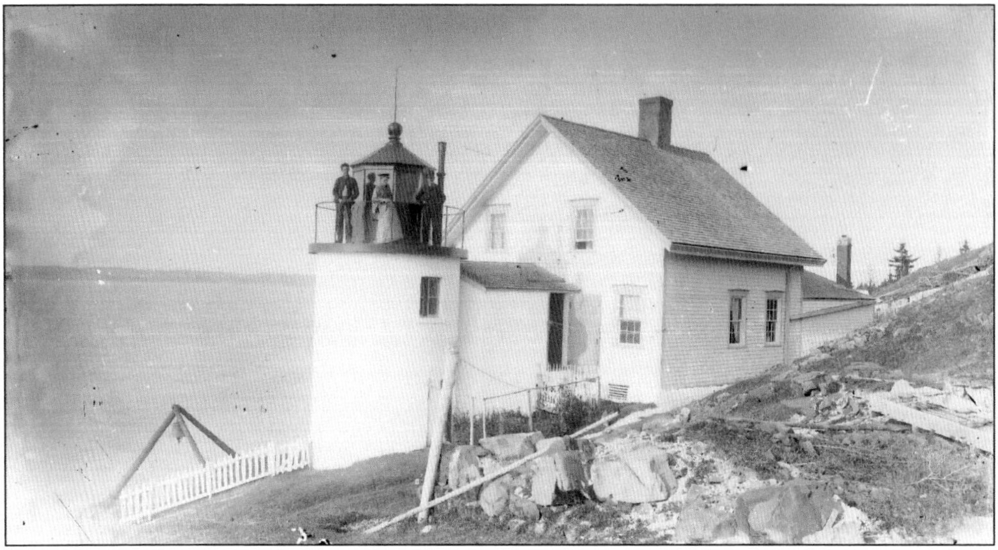

Ships in the vicinity of the island are protected by a number of lighthouses. This one, Brown's Head Light, stands on Vinalhaven's northwest shore. The lighthouse was first built in 1832 and was automated in 1987. Some of the keepers of the lighthouse were David Wooster, Howland Dyer, Benjamin E. Burgess, Charles T. Burgess, Alonzo Morong, Ernest Talbot, and Merrill Poor (U.S. Coast Guard 1945–55).

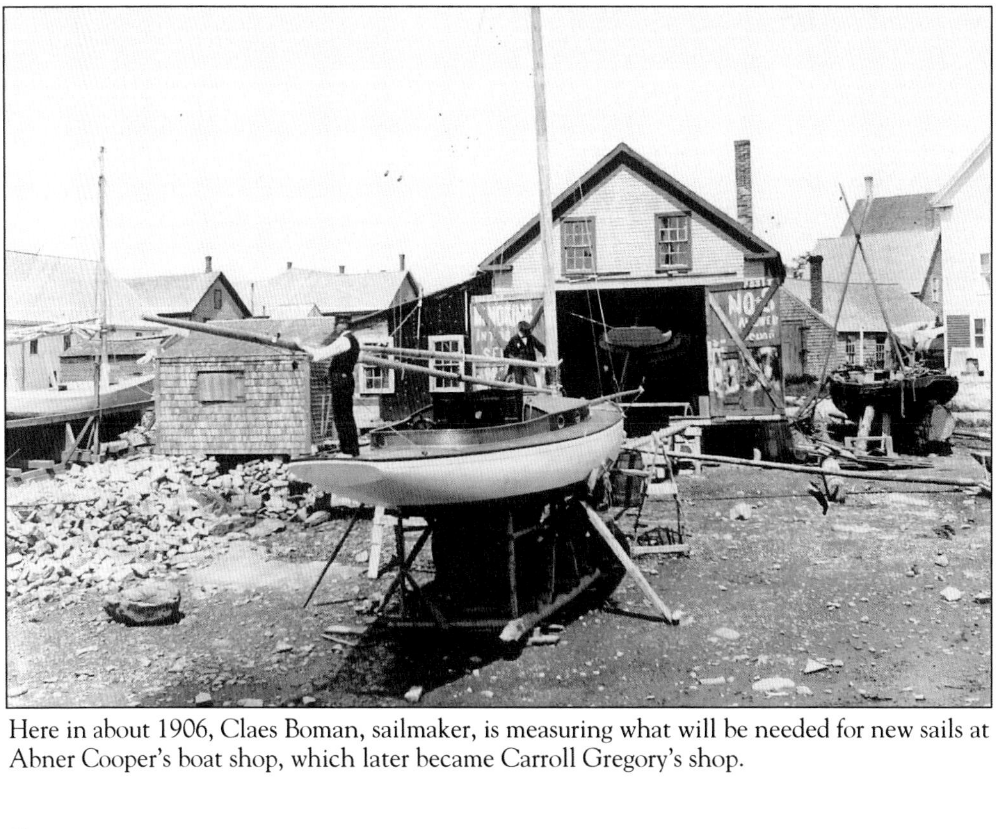

Here in about 1906, Claes Boman, sailmaker, is measuring what will be needed for new sails at Abner Cooper's boat shop, which later became Carroll Gregory's shop.

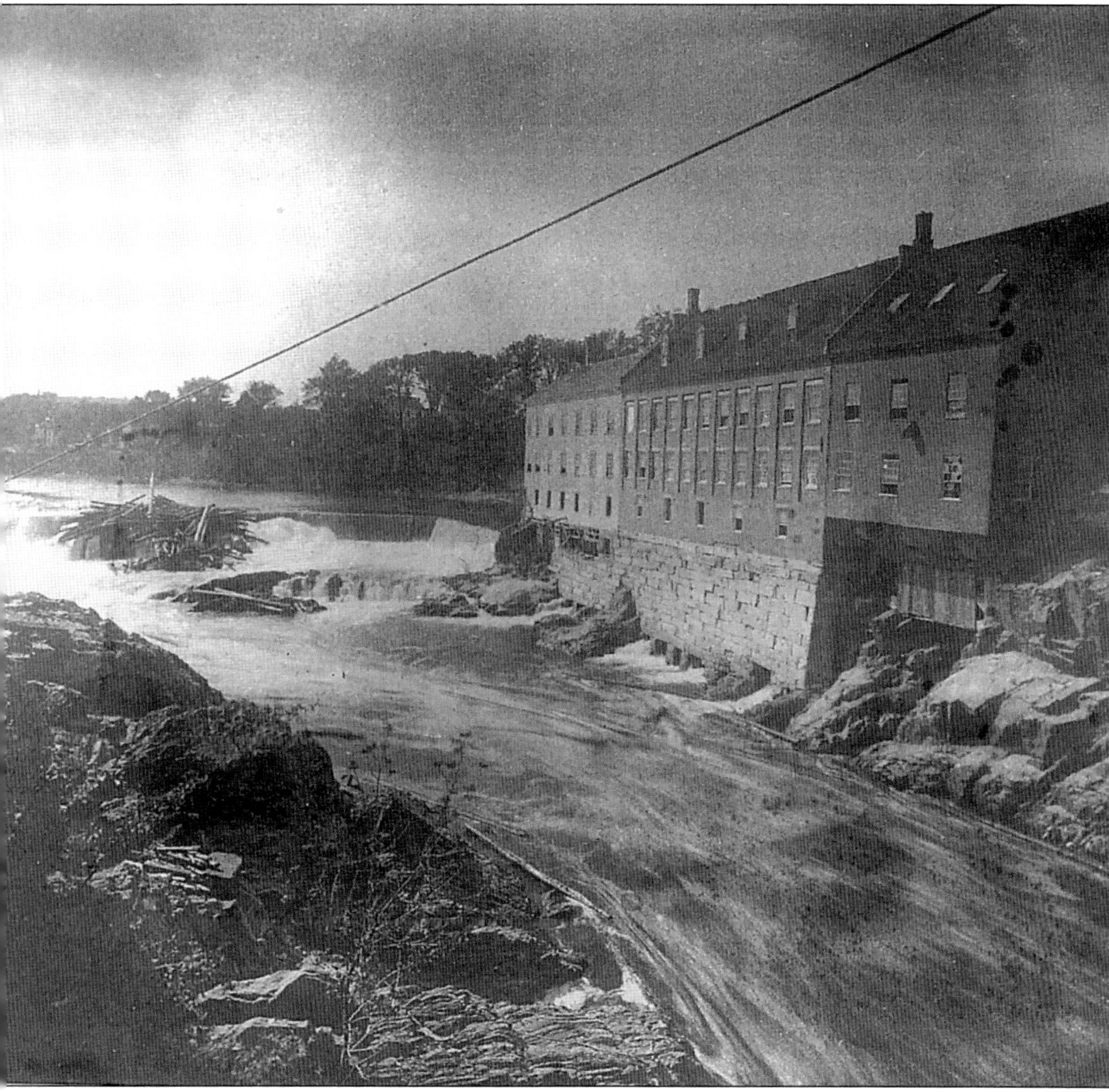

The railing of the North Channel Bridge is visible in the foreground. Wooden cribbing was being repaired in an effort to control the falls. The buildings to the left were part of the Weston and Brainerd Gristmill. During the 1800s Skowhegan Island was the site of many sawmills, woodworking businesses, carding mills, woolen mills, and corn and flour mills. (Wyman Collection).

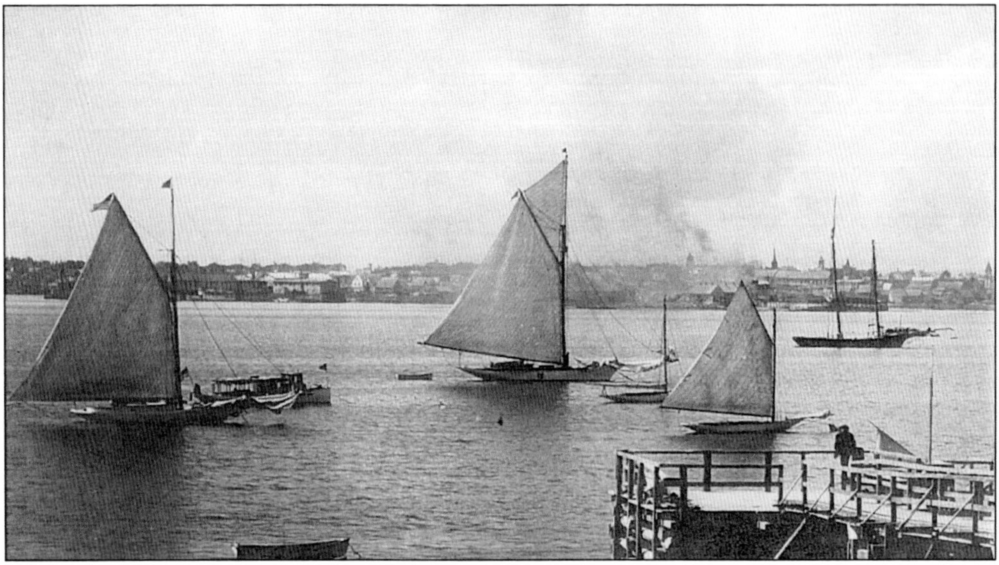

This description was taken from an 1892 publication: "This harbor, with its shore-built city, canopied by day with the 'Terebinthene' smoke, and illuminated at night with the brilliant fires of innumerable lime-kilns, presents a pleasing appearance from the water . . . and is considered by seamen to be one of the safest anchorages on the coast."

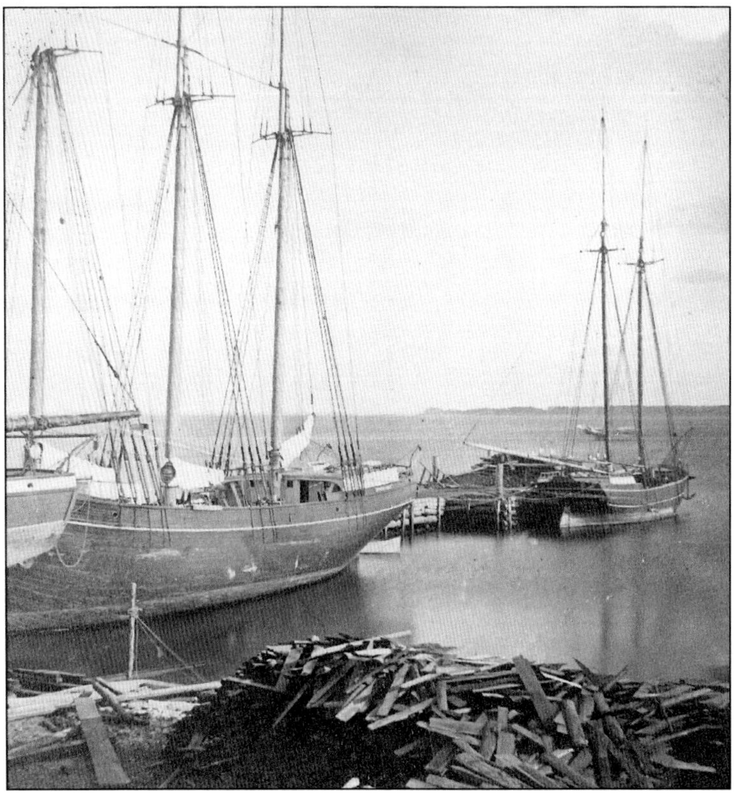

An 1870s view of Rockland's harbor from the railway wharf in the South End.

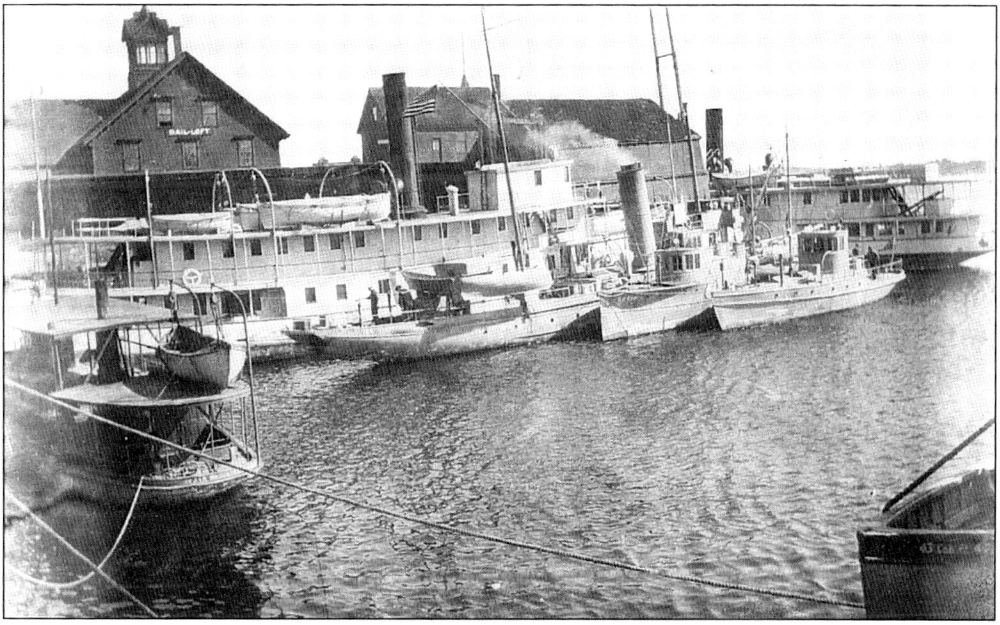

Tillson's Wharf, seen here with numerous steamboats and other craft. Located at the end of Sea Street, now Tillson Avenue, it was the center of steamboat activity in Rockland from its opening in 1881 until it was purchased and taken over by the U.S. Coast Guard following World War II. It cost an incredible $100,000 to construct and was considered a risky business venture at the time.

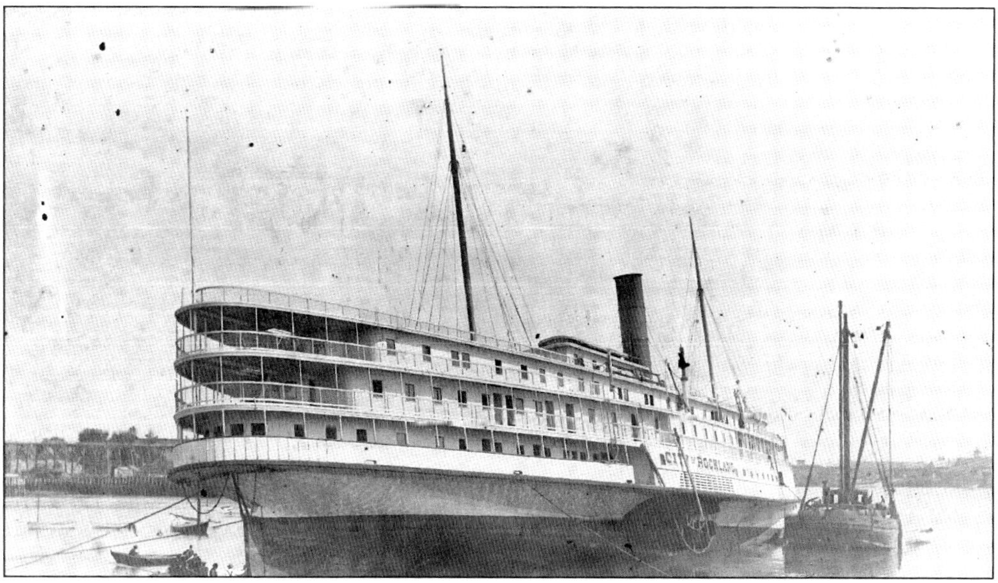

The proud *City of Rockland* was only four years old when she struck a ledge near Ash Island, south of Rockland. Her 400 passengers were rescued, and she was raised by salvage ships and towed into Rockland, where she was purposely beached (as seen here) so her hull could be patched temporarily. She was then taken to Boston for repairs and served until 1923.

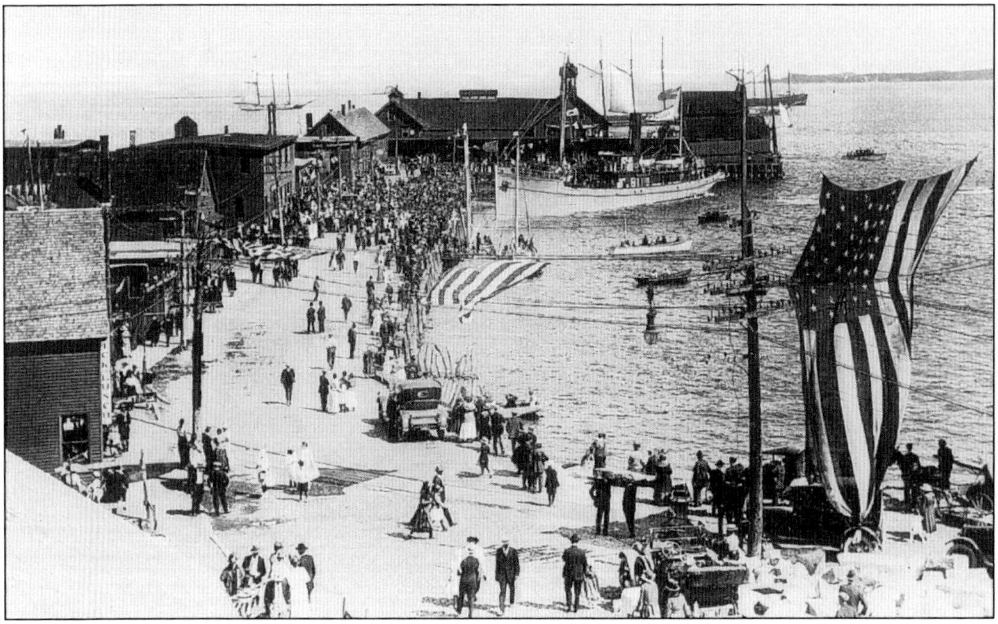

Pelican Day, 1919. This view is of the first of several steam fishing trawlers arriving at Tillson's Wharf. Its arrival was celebrated by hundreds of spectators.

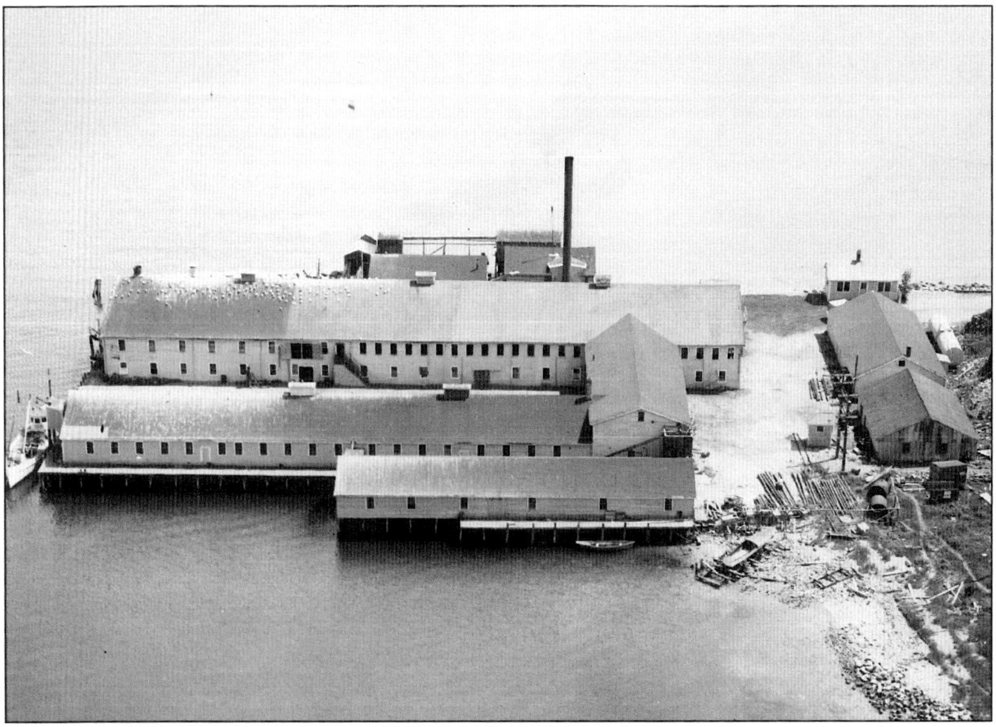

The Holmes Packing Company, a sardine plant near the public landing, burned in January 1985.

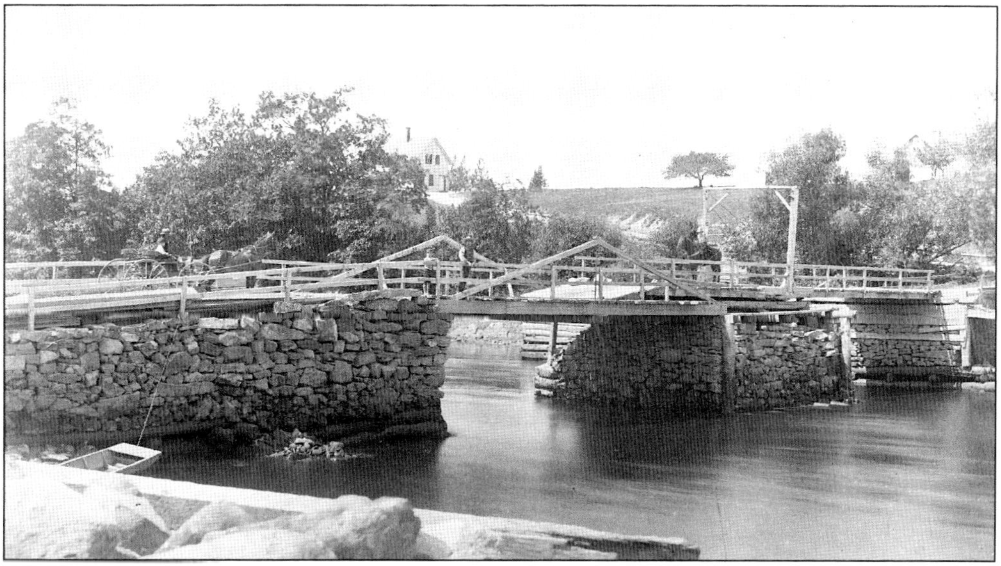

The Middle Bridge spanning the Eastern River, Dresden, 1880s.

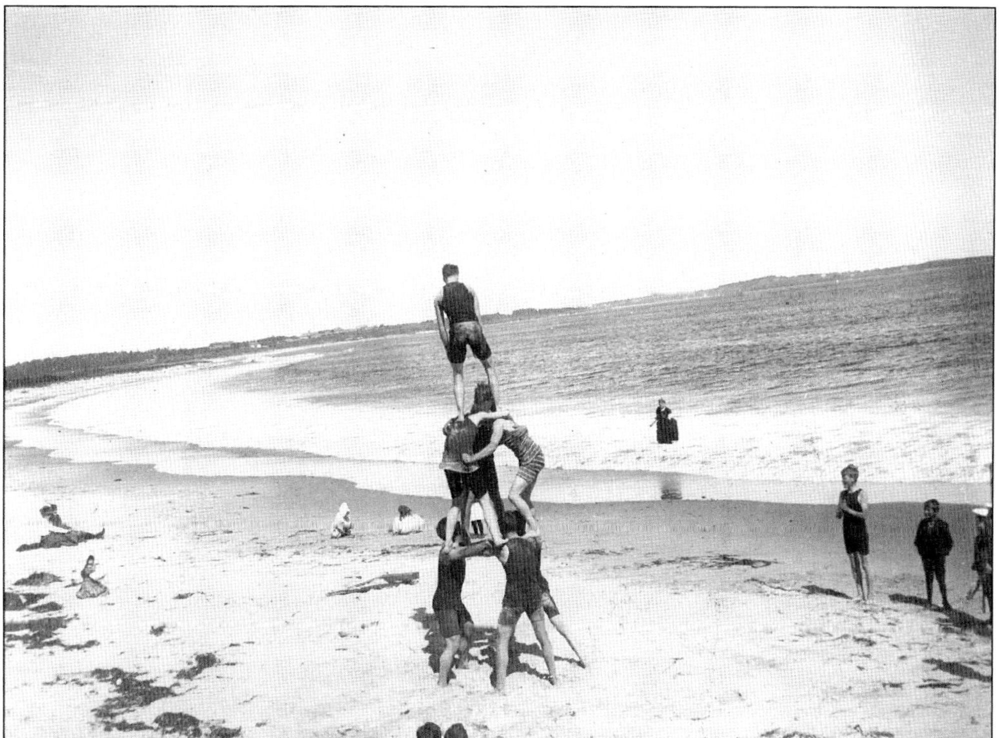

This photograph demonstrates that young people enjoyed themselves as much at the beach ninety years ago as they do today.

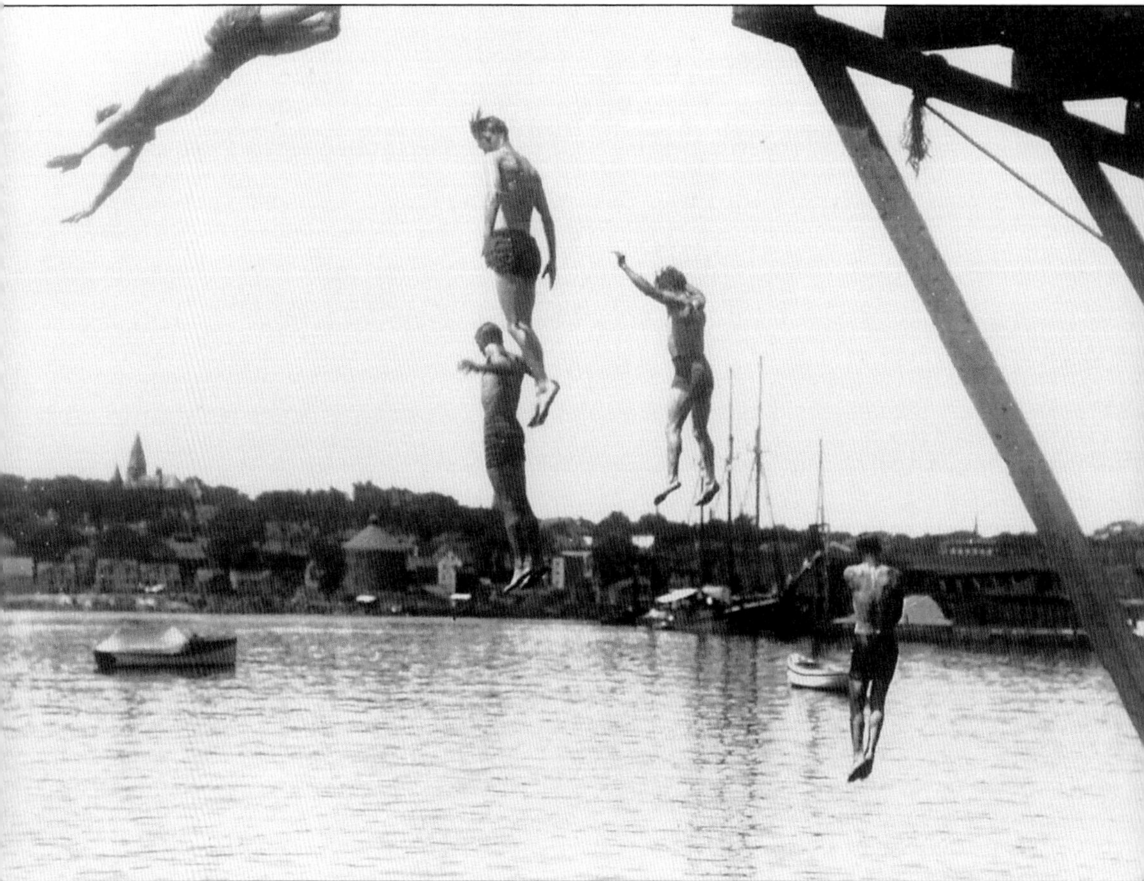

"If all your friends jumped off a bridge . . . " On hot summer days in 1914, Saco Wharf near the Saco Yacht Club provided a platform for diving into the cool waters of the Saco River. (McArthur Library).

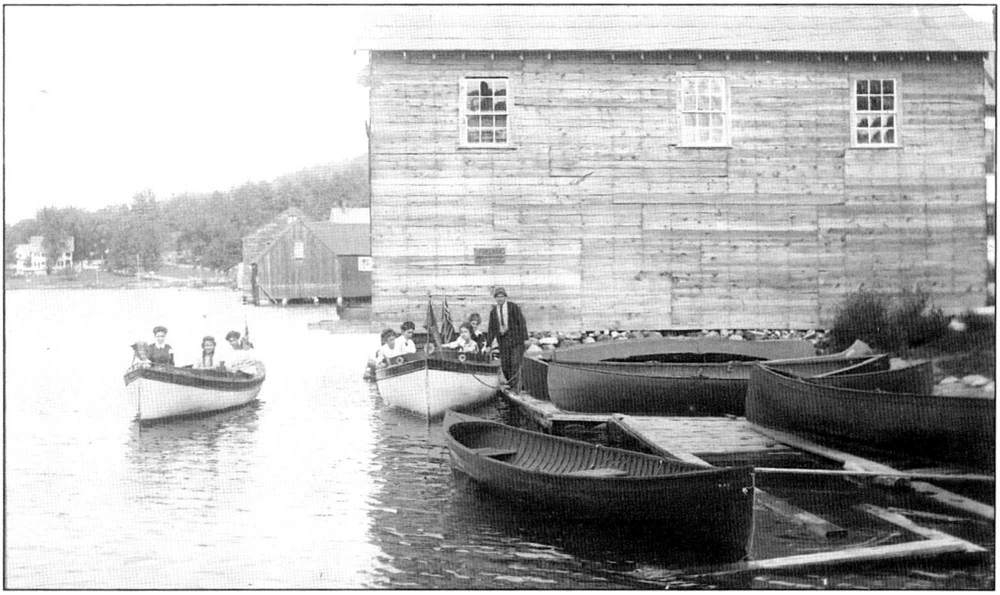

Harrison, as well as the other towns in the Lake Region, attracted droves of fishermen, canoeists, and excursionists. Boat rentals, such as this one owned by Percy L. Smith & Co. on Long Lake, did a thriving business as soon as the ice was out until after Labor Day. Excursionists in the launches *Alice* and *Osceola* are about to head down Long Lake, perhaps to Naples.

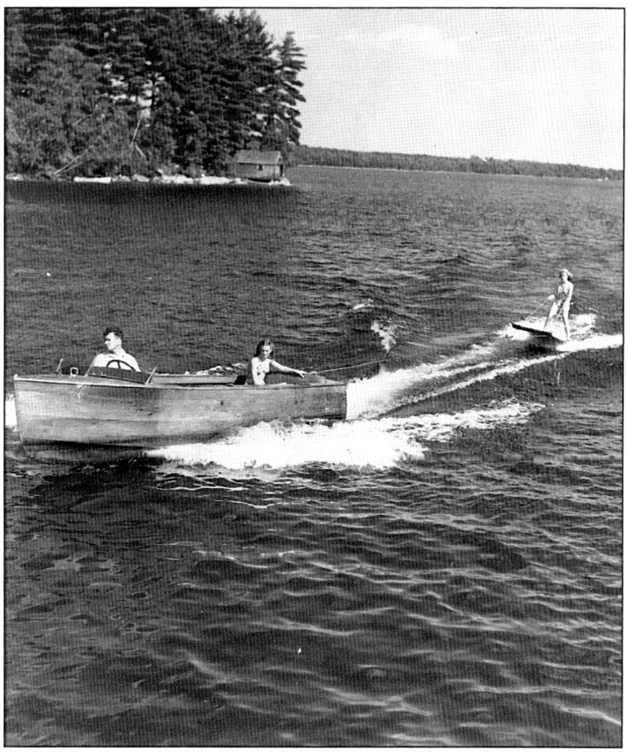

Before water skis were invented, aquaplaning behind a speedboat such as the Chris Craft was a popular sport on Maine lakes and ponds. Shown here on the west shore of Thompson Lake (known as The Cape), Frank Bean; his daughter, Janet Bean Swinchatt; and his niece, Patricia Bean Bourque, are taking full advantage of an opulent summer's day at the lake.

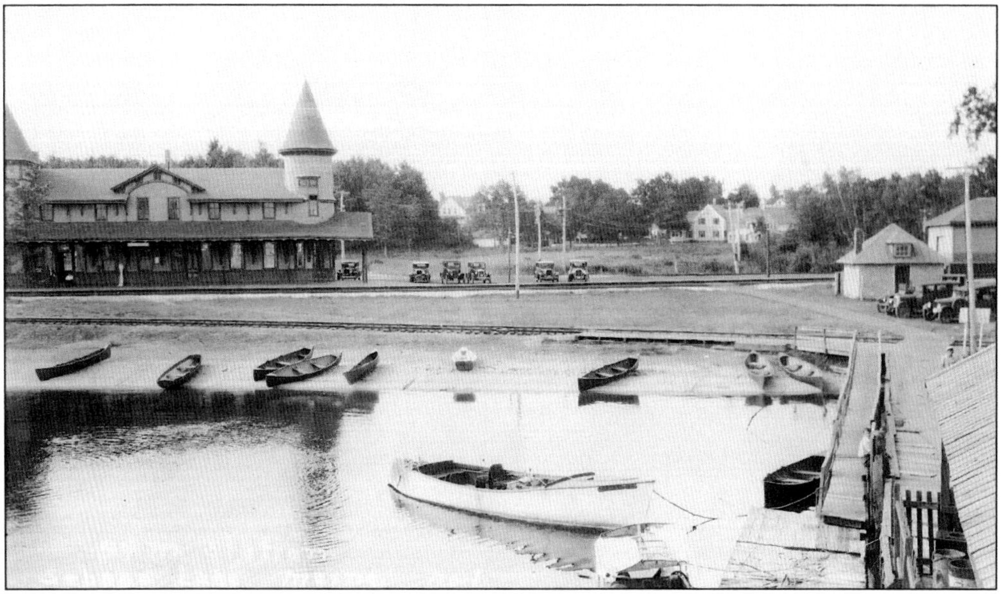

This is a view of the steamboat pier and waterfront at Sebago Lake Station. Sebago Lake Village is visible in the background. The spur in the foreground enabled groups of excursionists to step off served passenger cars onto the steamboat pier. The inboard motorboat was very likely privately owned, but most or all of the canoes and rowboats pulled up on the beach were probably rentals.

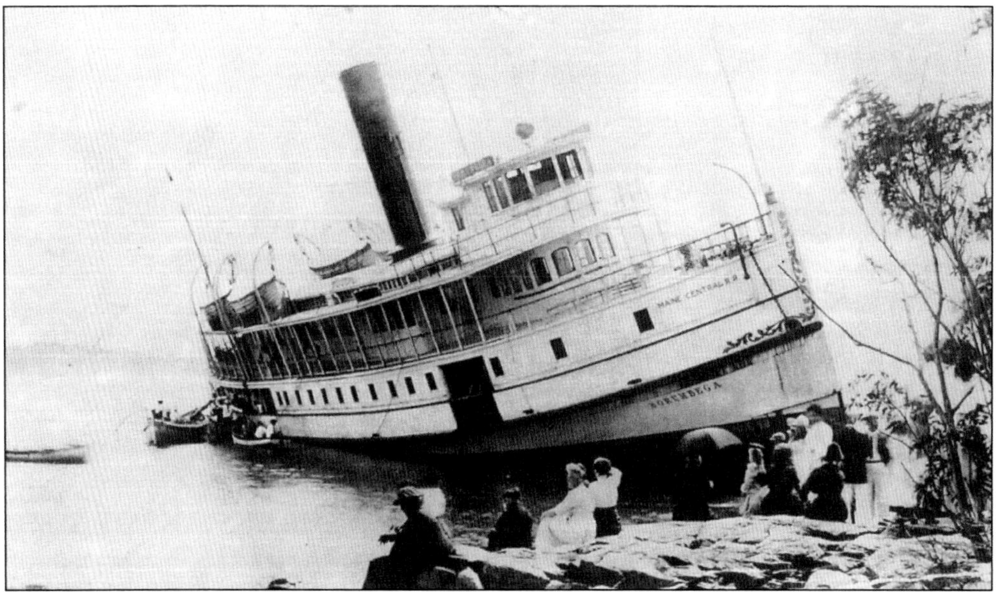

The *Norumbega* goes aground Bar Harbor.

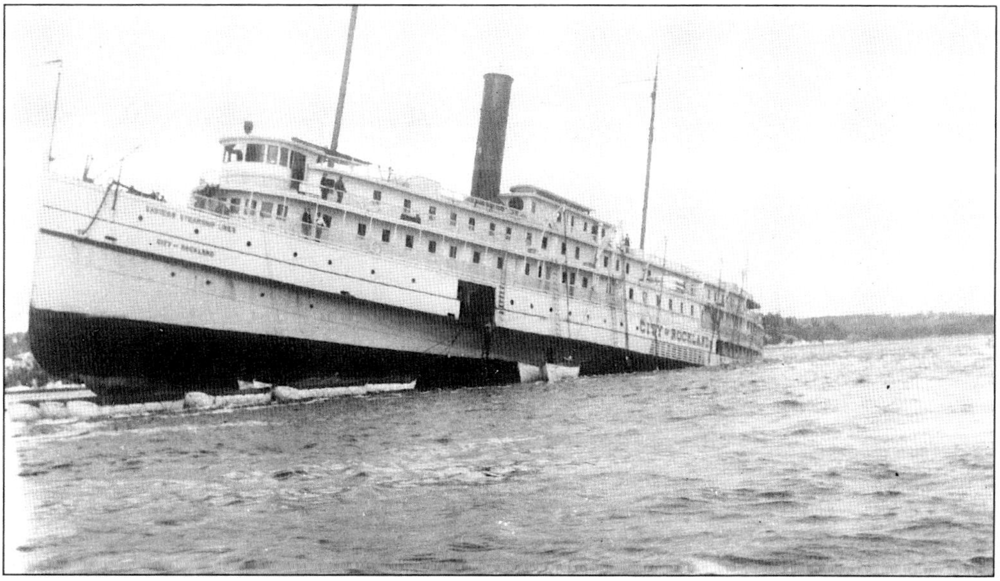

The *City of Rockland* of the Eastern Steamship Lines ran aground on Dix's Island off Cox's Head in the fog on September 2, 1923. She was hauled to Boston for repairs, but never returned to service; instead, she was condemned and burned off Salem, MA.

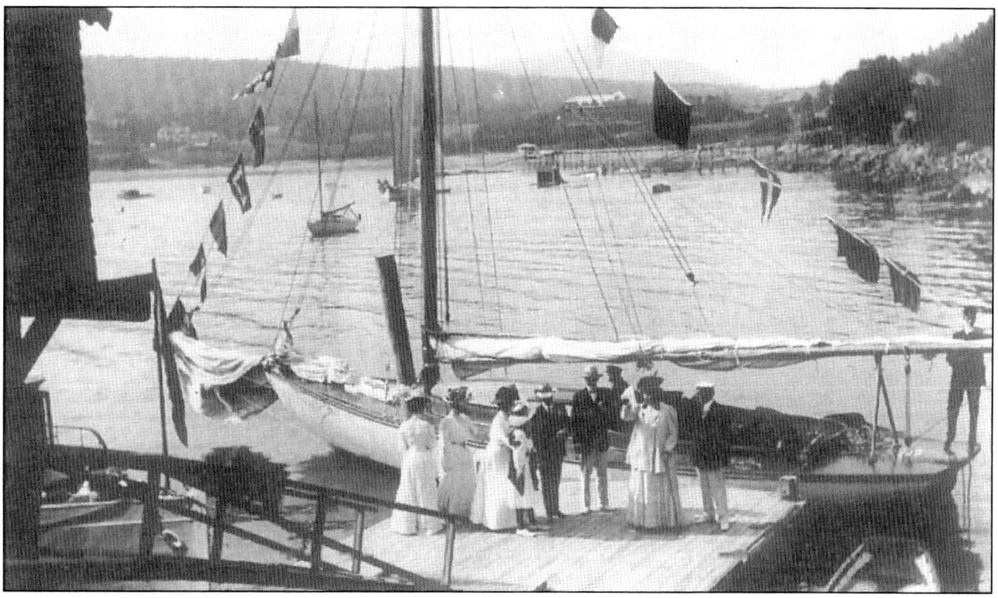

Before the Seal Harbor was built in 1912, yachtsmen used the steamship wharf as a landing. In this 1908 photograph, Mrs. Marcus Hanna (second from the right) is joined by fellow sailors to christen her sloop, Marcana, named after her late husband, before taking the vessel out. An enthusiastic sailor, Mrs. Hanna became one of the founders of the yacht club shortly after this photograph was taken. (Dunham Family Collection).

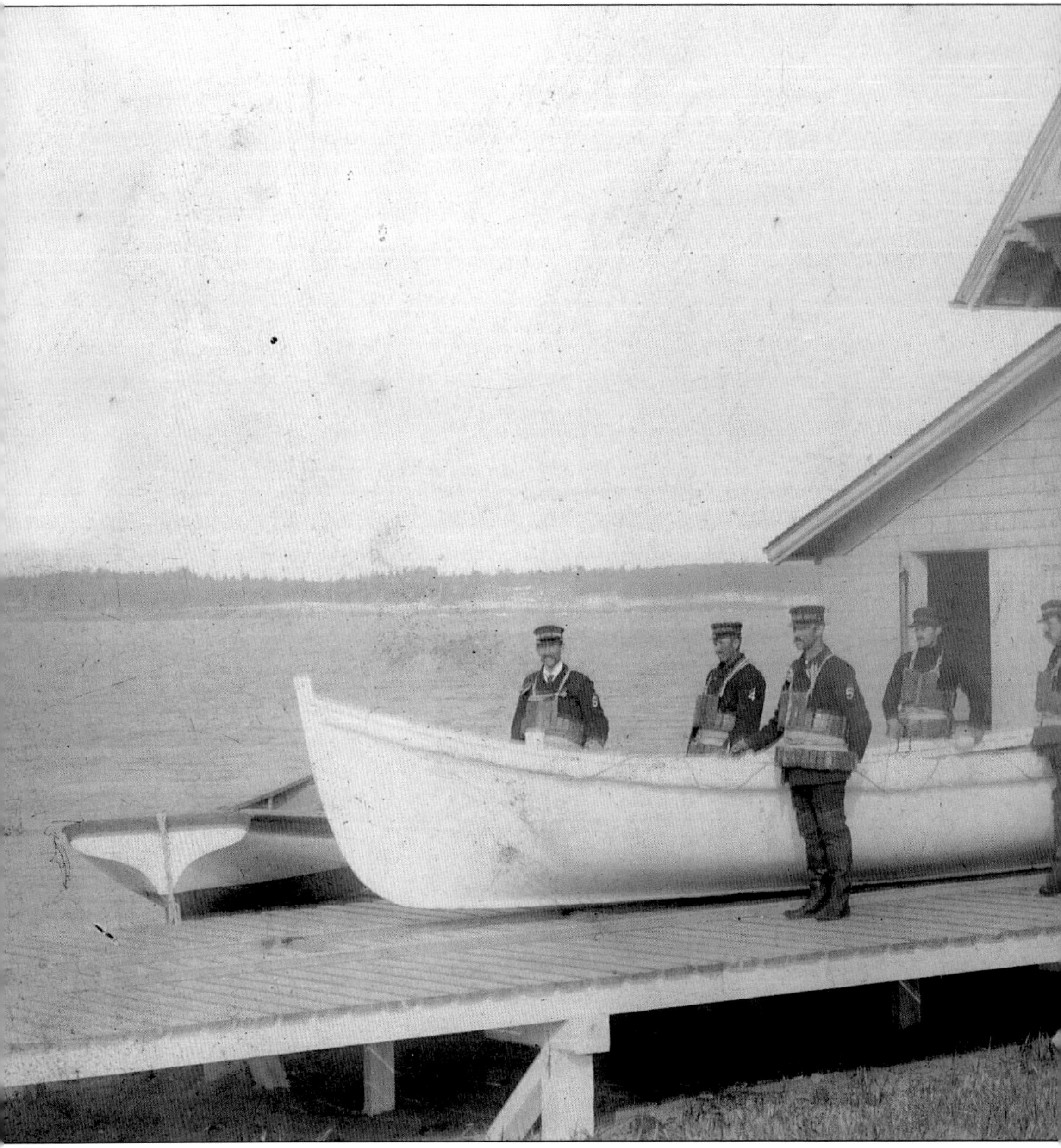

The Crumples Island Life-Saving station, or "The Crumples," was located on a group of islands off Jonesport. It served until 1904, when it was replaced by the Great Wass Island station. The station was typical, with a large boat-room on the first level and a smaller mess-room behind, where the crews assembled and ate their meals. The second floor housed the crew's sleeping quarters and extra cots for survivors. On October 23, 1880, patrolmen on duty here discovered the English brig *Kate Upham* with 11 men on board. She was disabled 3 miles from Red Head, on the easterly point of the island, during a fearful storm. Keeper Hall, seeing no answer to his warning signal hoisted to the masthead, assembled his crew and ran their new surfboat

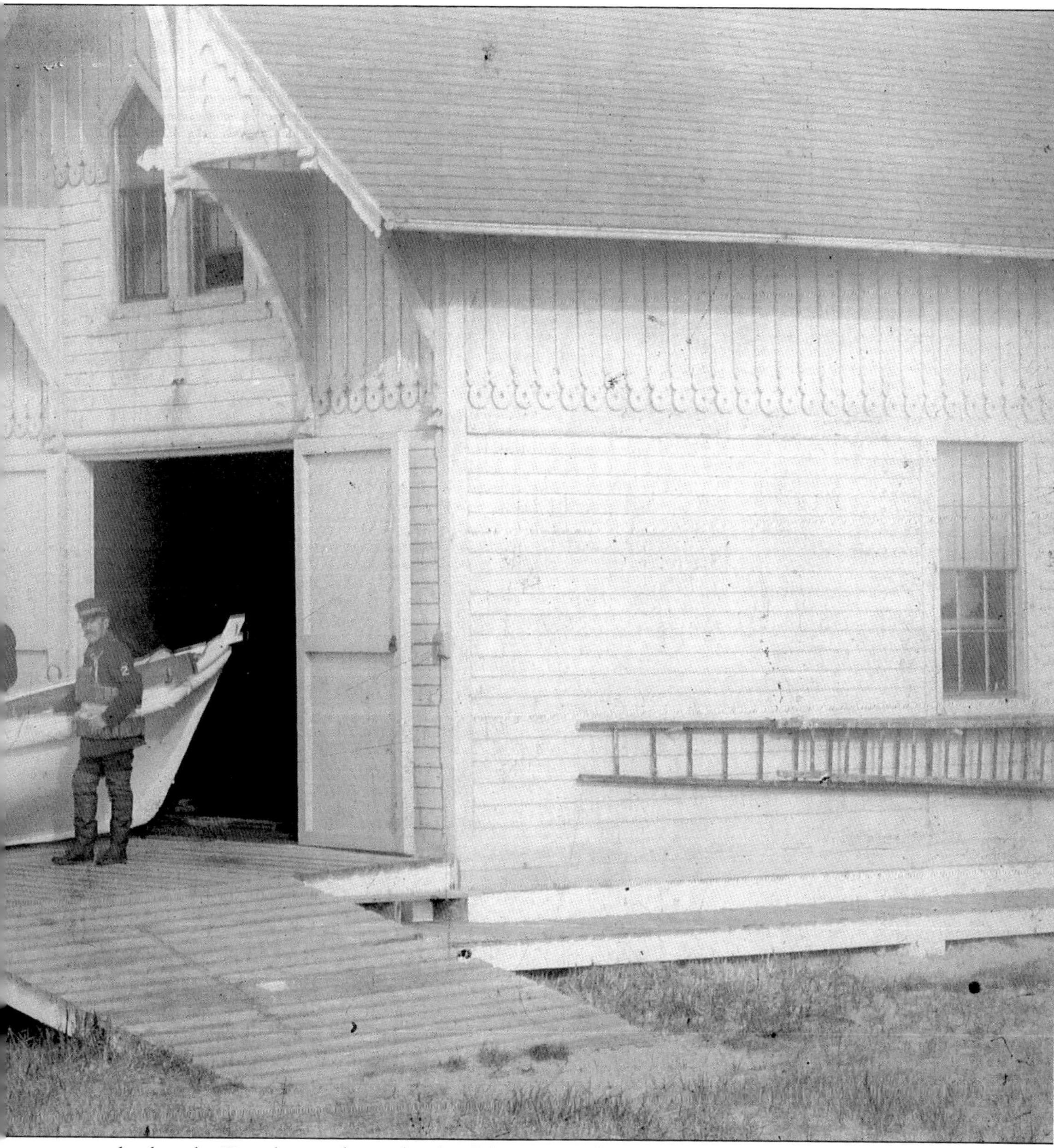

out to the beach. Grimly watching the fearful storm and angry sea, and attired in their cork life-belts, the crew launched, determined "to save the brig's crew or go with them." The crew soon entered the breakers, and with a 10-foot-high wall of water smashing at the boat, the crew pulled in a superhuman effort to get to the vessel's assistance. By watching the seas, the keeper was finally able to pull alongside and assist the crew into the boat. Afterward, the captain of the brig related thinking, "Good God, what can that little boat do?" He found out the answer after an hour-long pull by the surfmen, when he and his men were landed safely on the island.

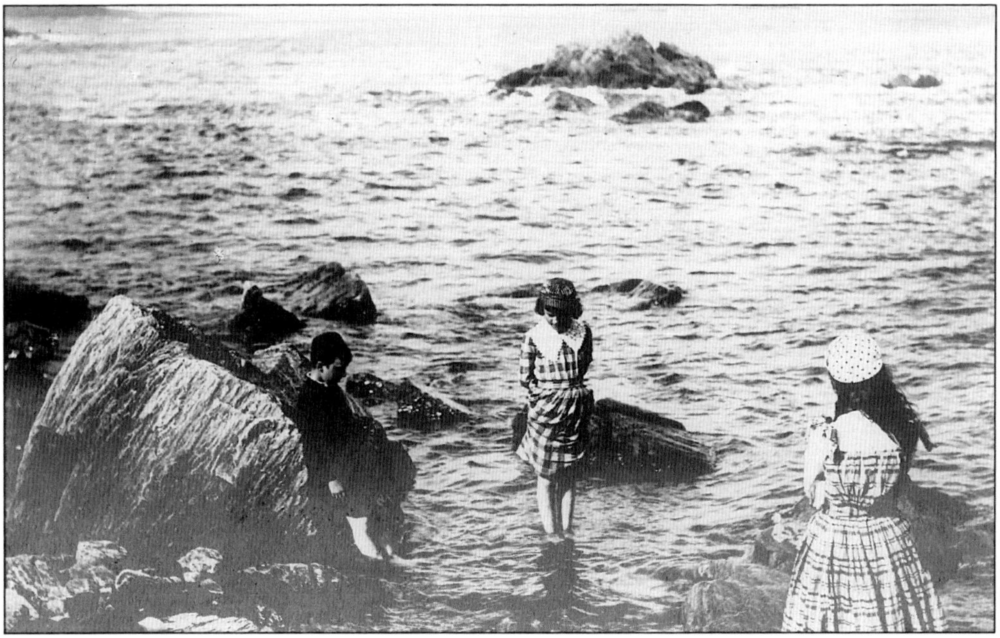

Living near the ocean provided its own entertainment for the children in Cape Elizabeth and South Portland. George G., Jane, and Emma Morse play in Delano Park around the turn of the century. (Robert Shuman family).

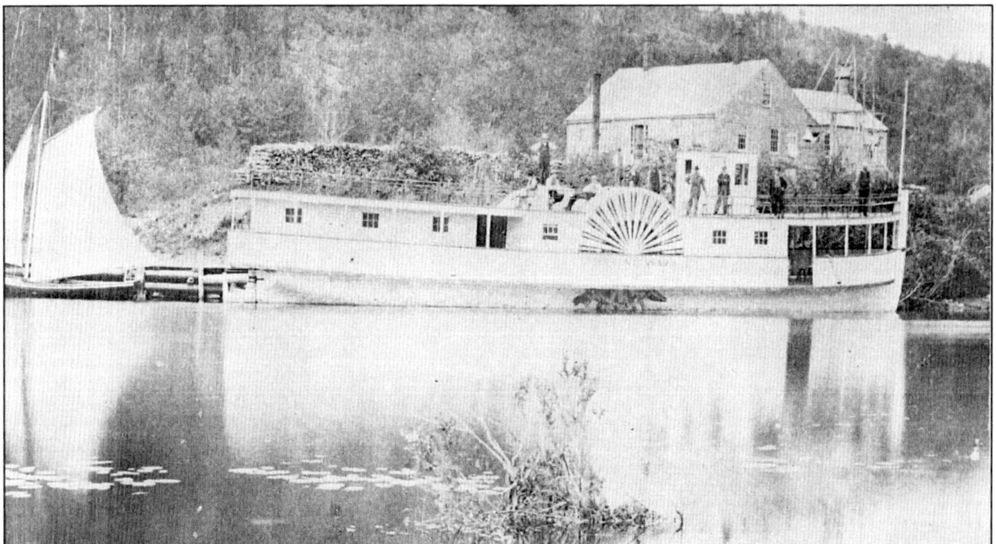

In 1868, Captain Crockett built the *Rippling Wave*. Made of lumber cut in Bowerbank, she was a 90-foot sidewheeler with spacious cabins, a full hurricane deck, and the capacity to carry five hundred passengers. The *Rippling Wave* was constructed by Major Bigney, who also built the Moosehead Lake steamboats, *Fairy of the Lake* and *Governor Coburn*. Note the large pile of wood on the shore, which was needed to fire the boiler of the *Rippling Wave*. (Beth Cawley).

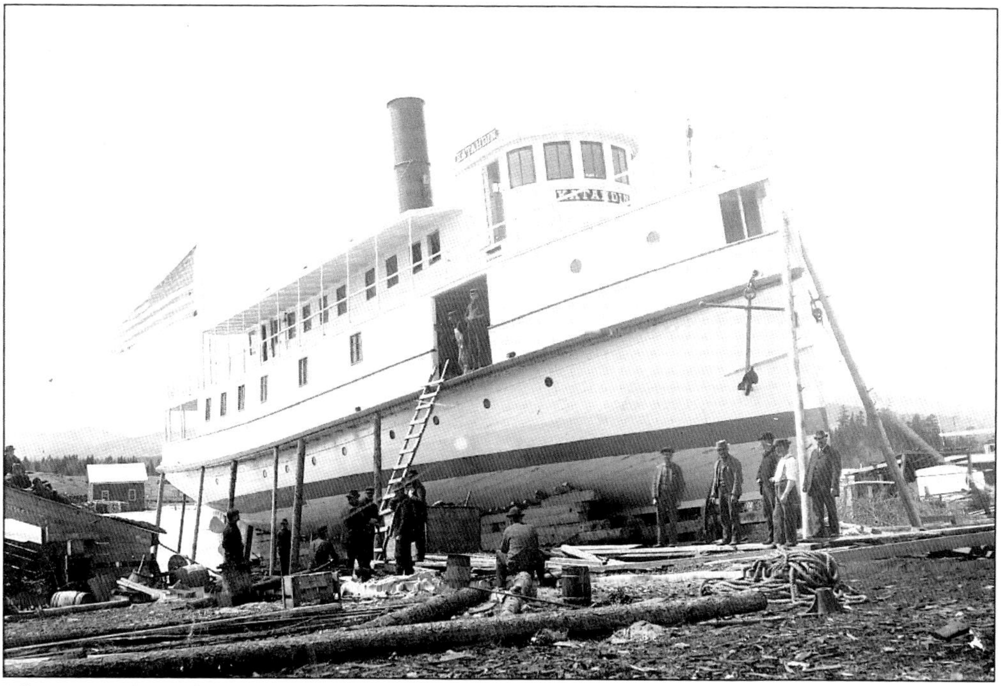

The original *Katahdin* steamboat in the lake with ice, 1900s. Both of these photographs were taken by Paul Johnson of Brownville. (H.A. Sangers Jr.).

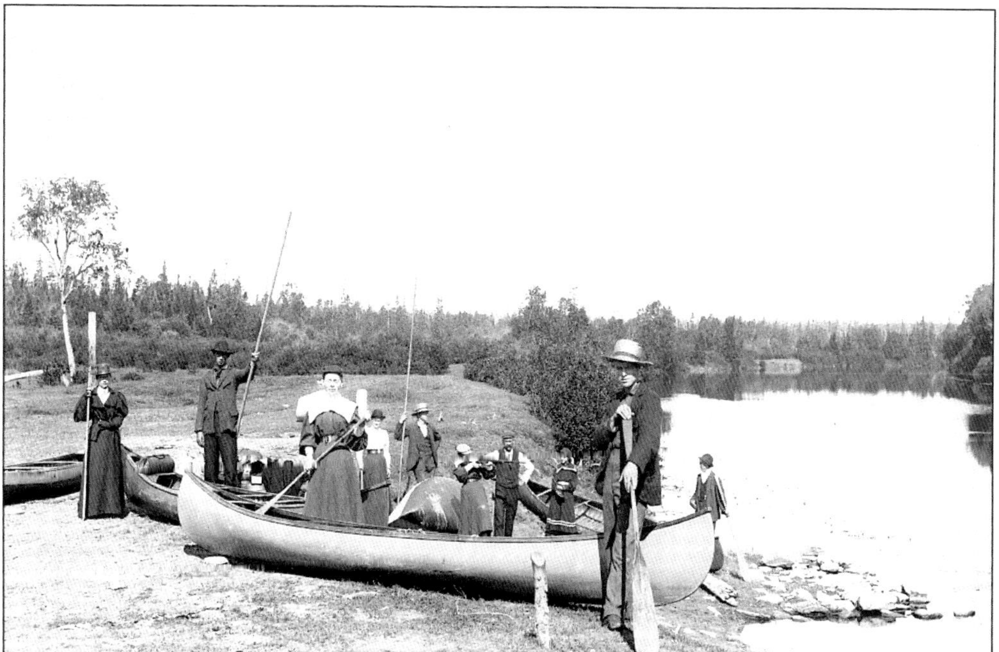

A portage for five parties in canoes on the Upper West Branch of the Penobscot, Northeast Carry to West Branch site, 1890s. (G.D. Hamilton).

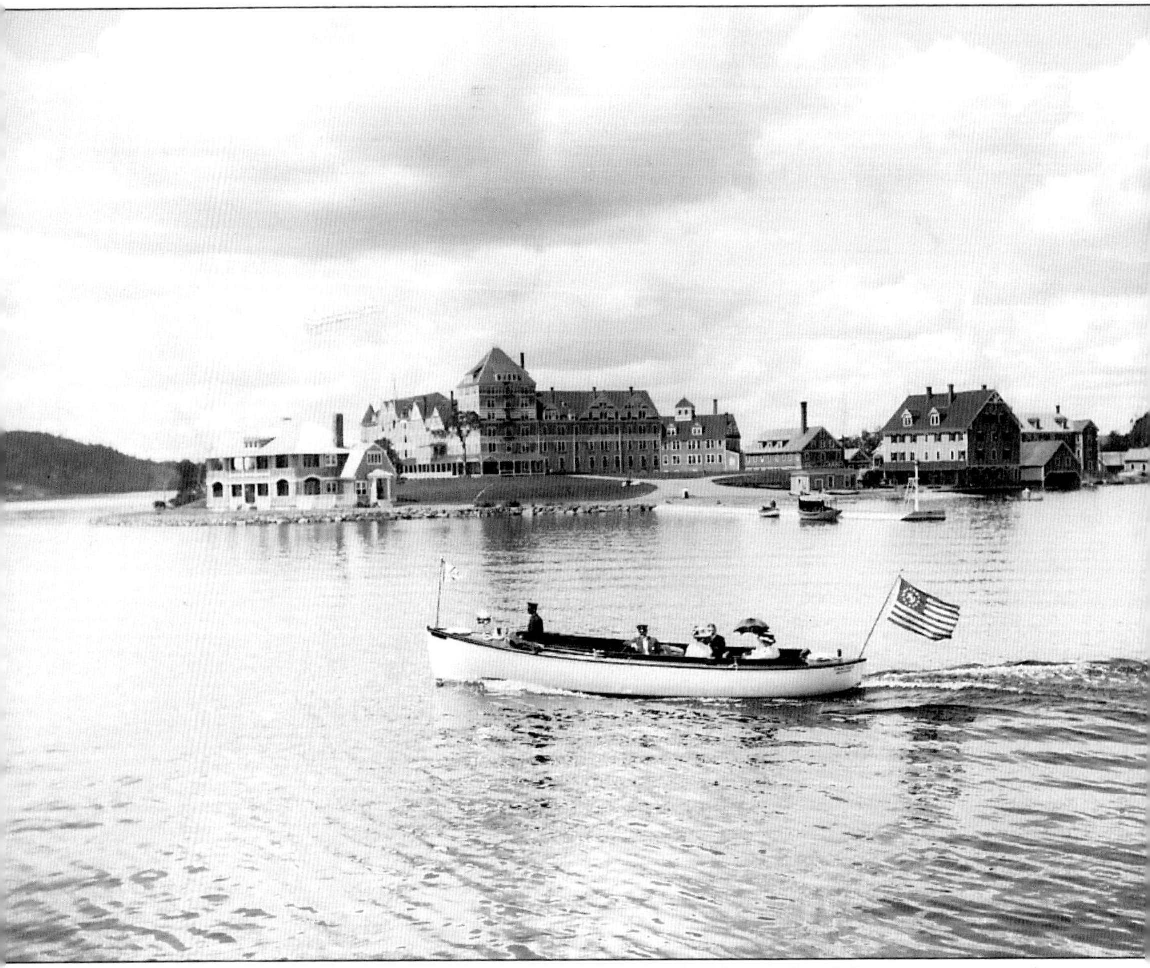

Water motoring at the new Mount Kineo House, 1910. The yacht club was constructed just a few years before the photograph. The boat is a Moosehead Lake Yacht Club launch frequently used between Kineo and Rockwood.

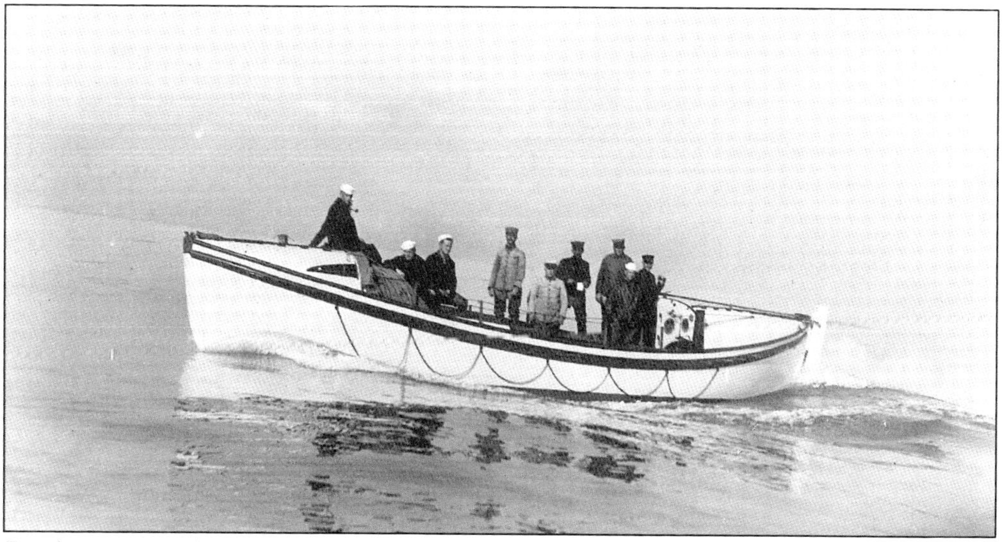

By about 1910, the Life-Saving Service began converting from pulling (oar) boats to the new motorized lifeboats. Though engines were still in their early stages of development, they afforded the life savers the ability to extend their range and to be less exhausted upon arrival. Thus, they would be better able to perform their rescue duties. Shown is a Coast Guard boat, probably a 34-foot motorized lifeboat, c. 1935.

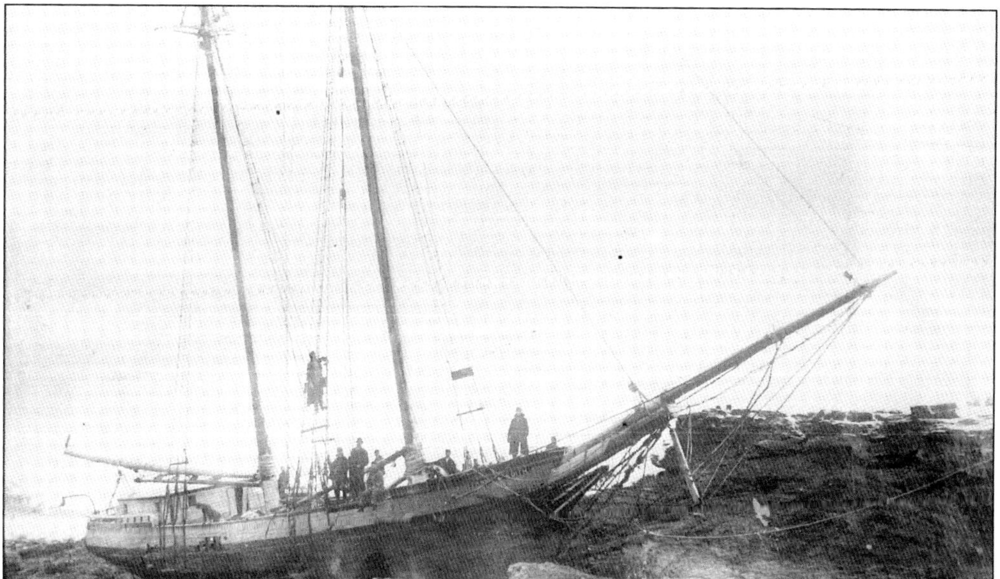

On December 4, 1900, the two-masted schooner *Fannie & Edith* anchored behind Richmond Island to ride out a storm that was intensifying in force. The small vessel put out two anchors, but when the winds picked up to a gale force, the chains parted and the *Fannie & Edith* was at the mercy of the storm. The vessel was swept across Saco Bay, and the crew could only watch as they neared the area known as Hubbard Rocks between Higgins and Scarborough Beach. (Prouts Neck Historical Society).

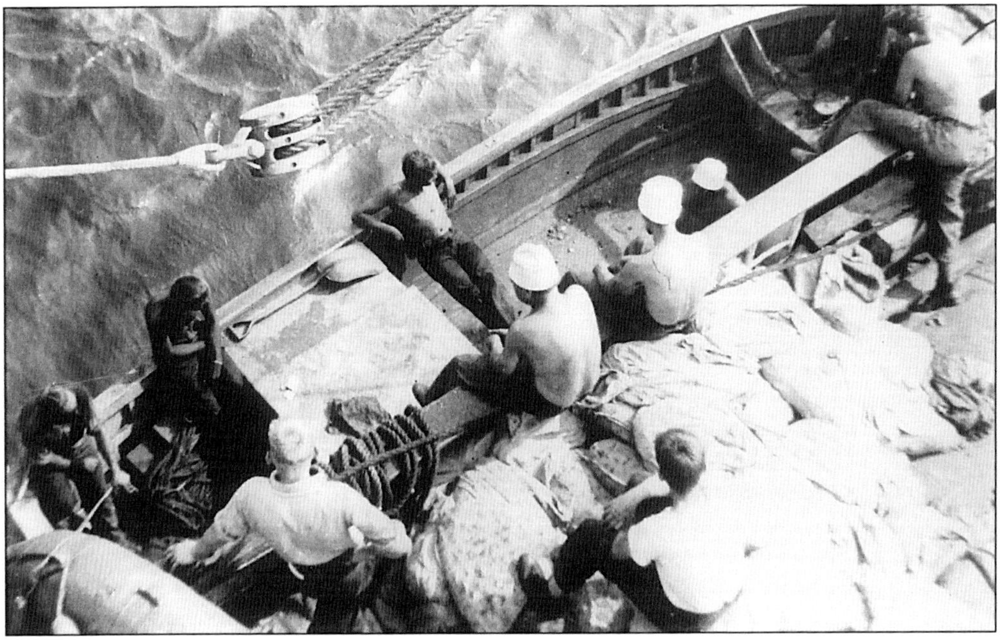

Once the USCG *Cowslip* reached its destination, the bags of coal were off-loaded into work boats that held approximately two tons. At the light station they were piled on the dock, tossed onto the shore, or winched up to the boat house.

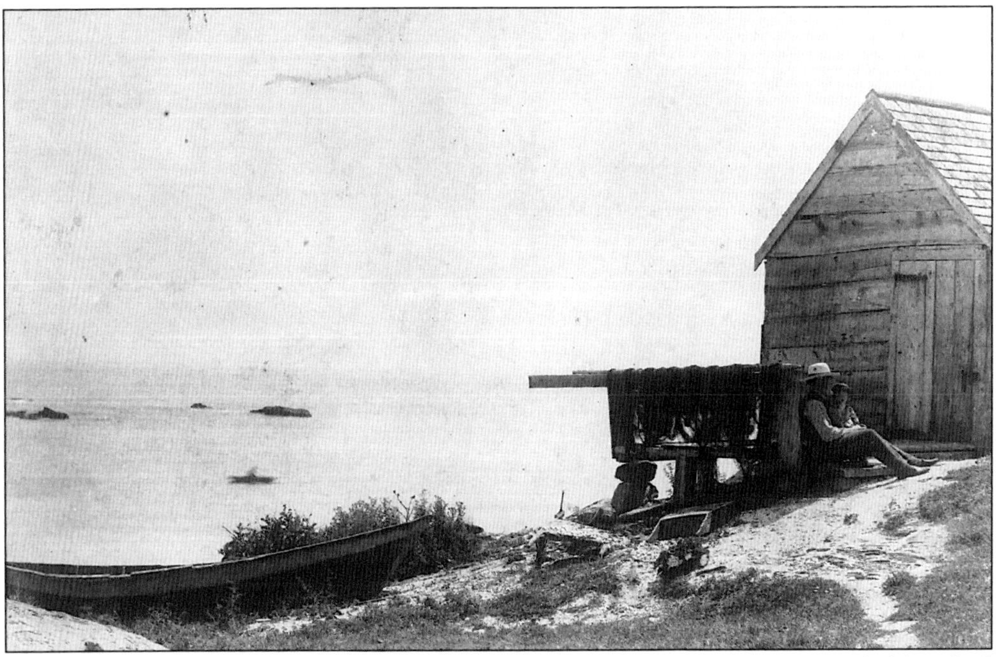

An idealized view of the life of a fisherman in the late 1800s. The area was probably tidied up before the picture was taken because it shows none of the litter that typically surrounds a fish house.

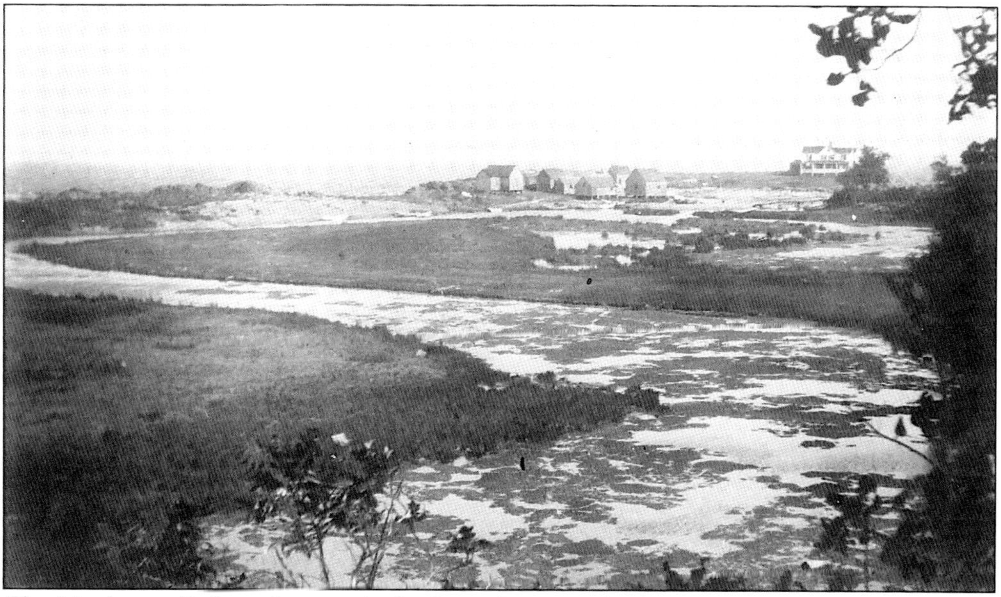

The Marshes at Perkins Cove with the Josias River in the foreground, c. 1900. Half a dozen fishhouses are located between the river and the ocean. The rebuilt Island House can be seen on the upper right and the footbridge is just in front of it.

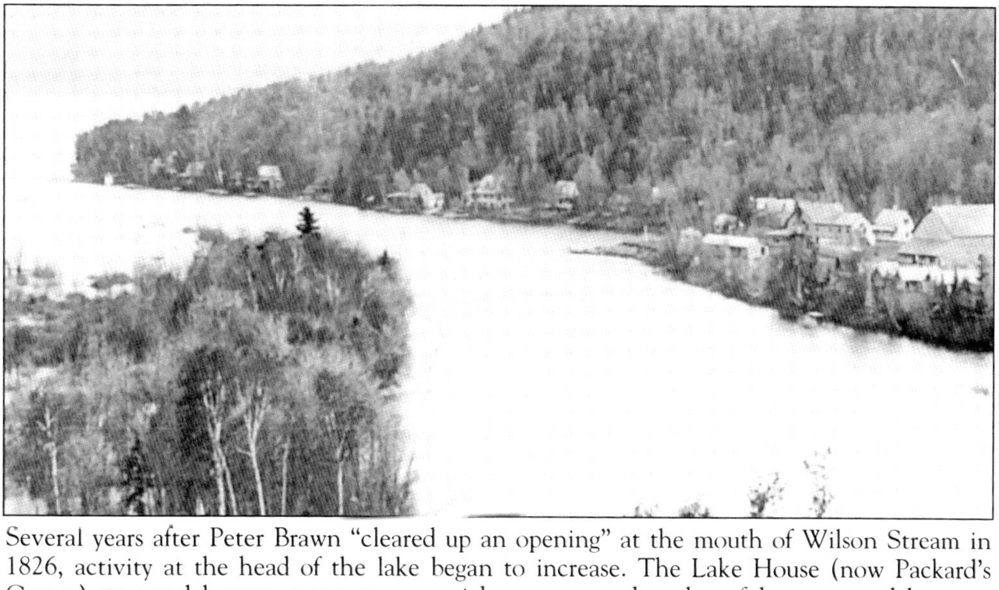

Several years after Peter Brawn "cleared up an opening" at the mouth of Wilson Stream in 1826, activity at the head of the lake began to increase. The Lake House (now Packard's Camps) attracted loggers, trappers, gum pickers, summer boarders, fishermen, and hunters. Steamboats traveled the channel, and lumbermen drove logs down the stream. In 1900, the area in the photograph above was the site of the first trip by a gasoline-powered motorboat. According to Marlborough Packard, the boat gave "a very discouraging performance." It belonged to Angus and Dave Campbell and ran from Packard's Landing to the mouth of Wilson Stream during its only run. Wet batteries abruptly halted its maiden voyage, and the boat had to be towed back. (John Parsons).

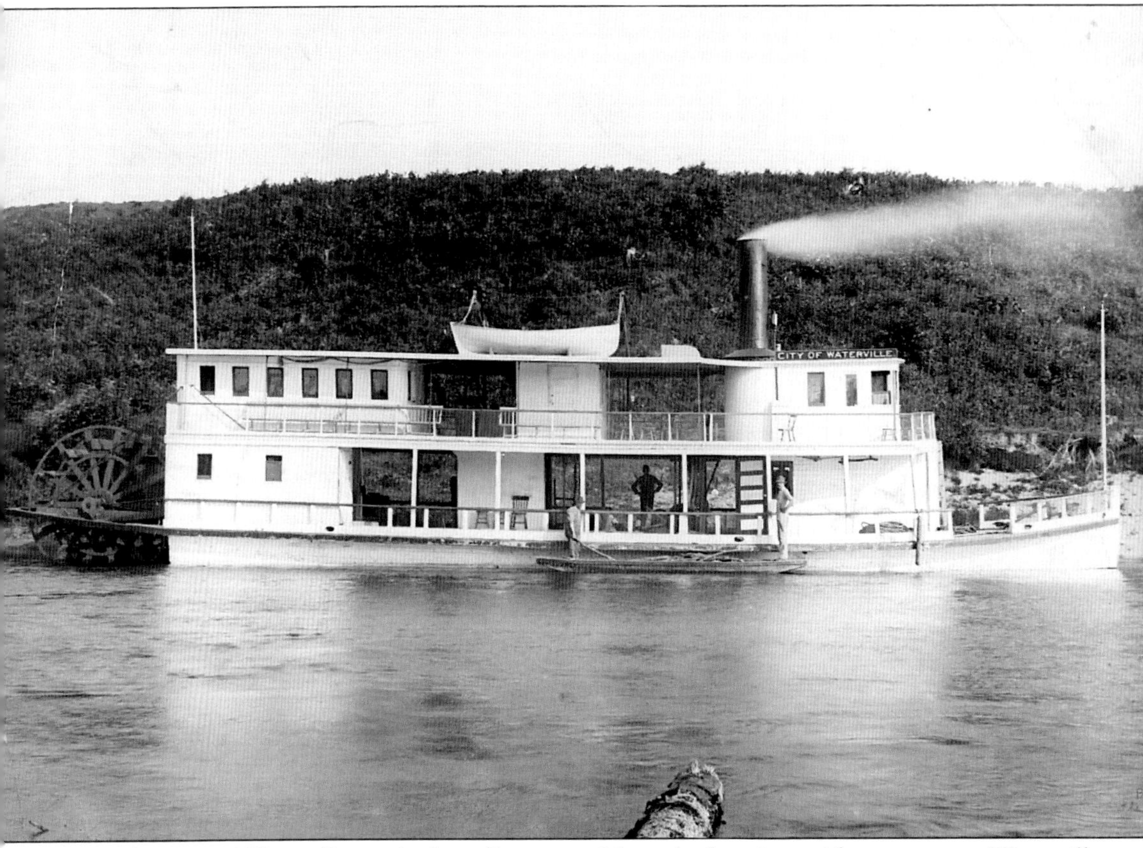

The *City of Waterville* was built in Bangor and launched on its maiden voyage to Waterville in 1890. It was an attempt to restore steam navigation to the Kennebec River. Unfortunately, the craft ran aground several times, failed in its mission, and was later sold to a Virginia firm. It does, however, look really elegant.

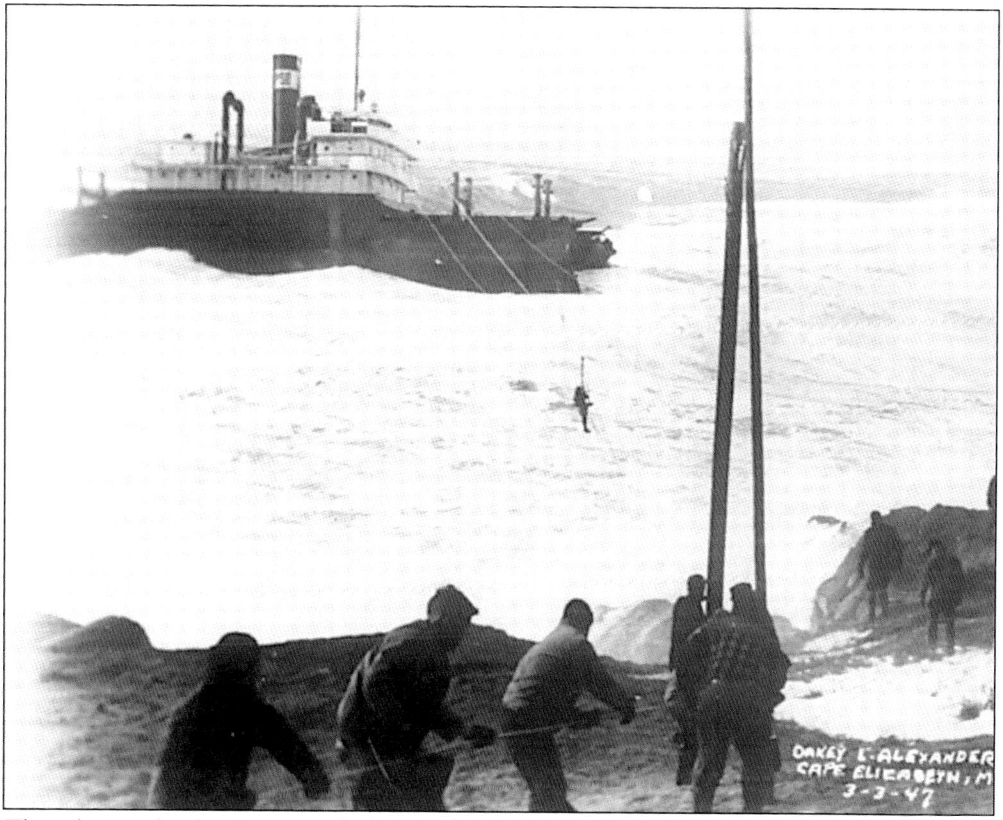

The advent of radio direction finding and other navigational aids improved safety all along the coast. However, even today there are times that nature still has her way over man's achievements. In March of 1947, the collier *Oakey L. Alexander* broke in two on the rocks off Cape Elizabeth. The U.S. Coast Guard crew was quick to respond and succeeded in rescuing the crew using the breeches buoy, one of the last times the Coast Guard would use this apparatus.

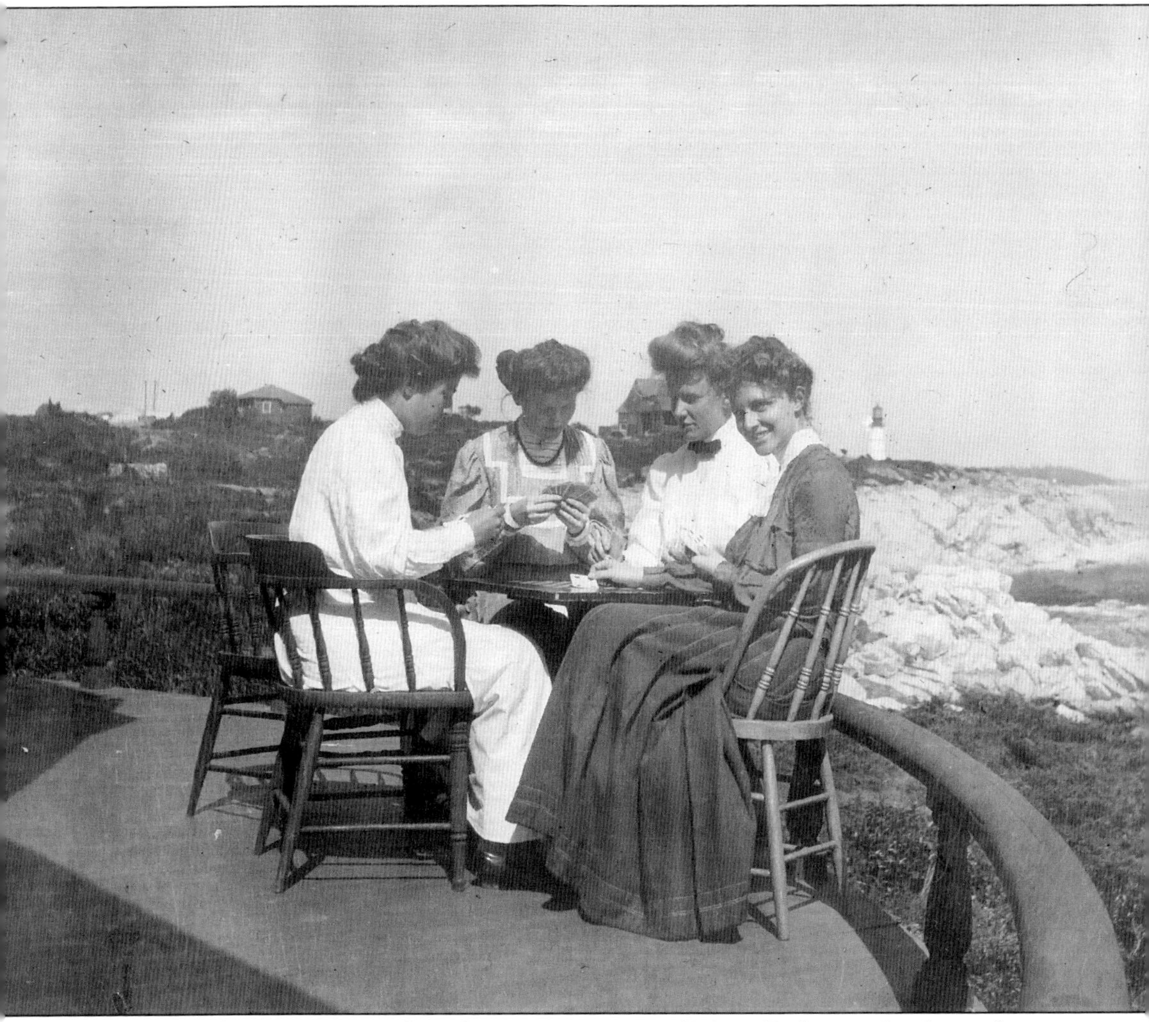

The circular piazza surrounding the Morse cottage at Delano Park provides the perfect ocean perch for an afternoon card game. Popular games at the time were Whist and Authors. (Robert Shuman family).

Five

Maine Life

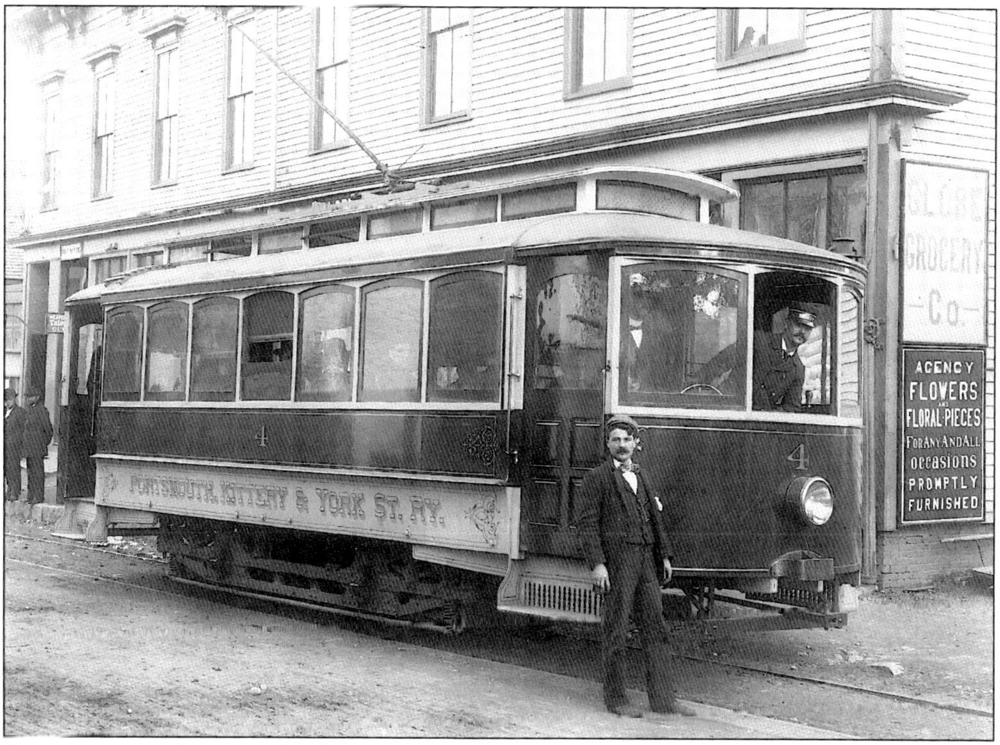

En route to the Badger's Island ferry landing, PK&Y No. 4 stops for the photographer in front of Wentworth Hall on Government Street, Kittery. Like three identical cars, Nos 2, 6, and 12, No. 4 had plush-upholstered seats of the walkover type and was nicely warmed in the winter by electric heaters. Wentworth Hall was destroyed by fire in 1925, two years after trolley service in the town ended.

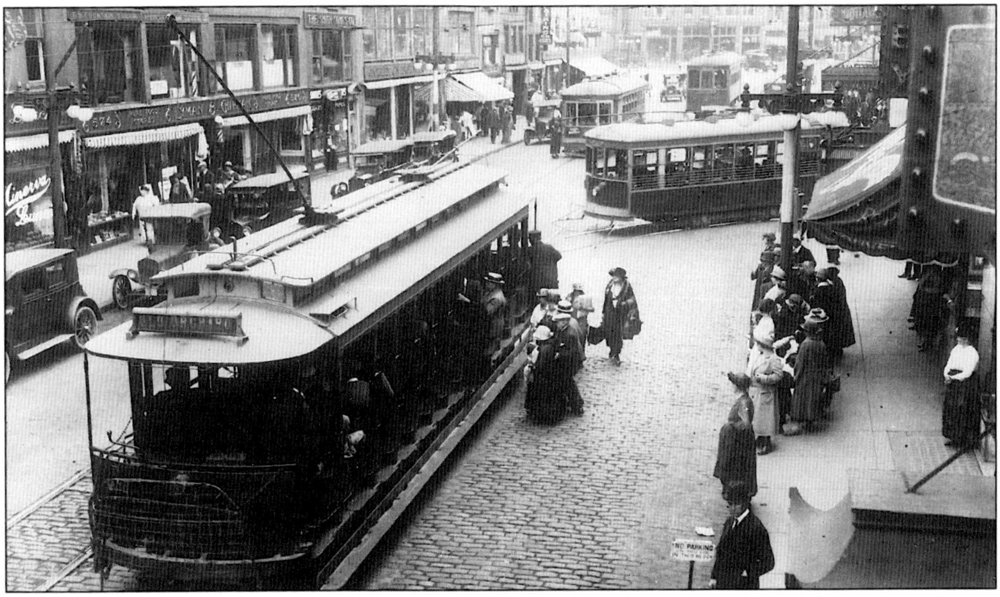

This Old Orchard-Bound open car boards passengers at the intersection of Congress Street and Forest Avenue in Portland about 1920. We're looking toward Congress Square—the intersection of Congress, High, and Free Streets. The car was to continue along Congress Street to Railroad Square and then run along St. John Street, past Union Station, to Danforth Street.

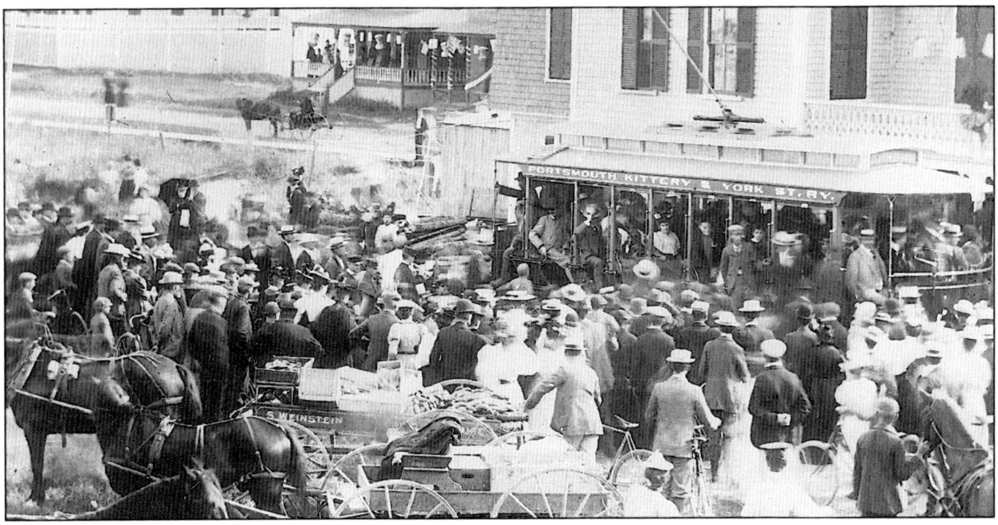

Portsmouth, Kittery & York Street Railway (PK&Y) operated its first through trip from Badger's Island, Kittery, to York Beach via Kittery Point, York Village, and York Harbor on Friday, August 27, 1897. The four-wheel open trolley was greeted by a sizable crowd when it arrived at the resort around 3:30 in the afternoon. The PK&Y was absorbed on November 1, 1903, by the Portsmouth, Dover & York Street Railway, which was consolidated with the Atlantic Shore Line Railway on February 1, 1906, and became the latter's Western Division. All trolley service between Badger's Island and the resort ended March 17, 1923.

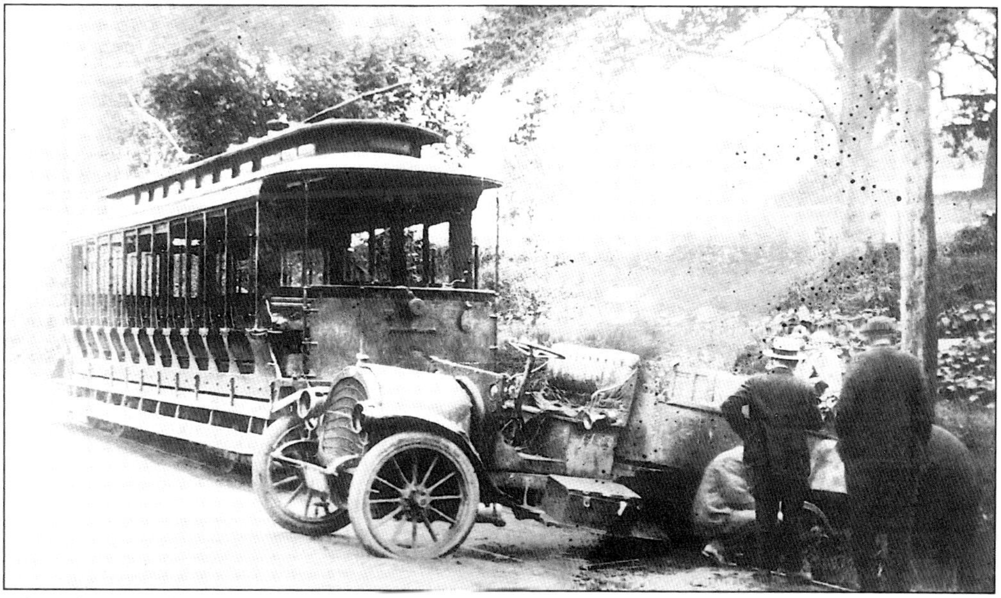

This photograph appears to show a trolley-truck collision at Rice's Hollow on Government Street, Kittery, in 1916. Actually, the motor vehicle skidded into the ditch before the electric car, headed for South Eliot, Eliot, and Dover, came along. There are no passengers on the trolley, and the crew is nowhere in evidence. How long the track was blocked is anybody's guess.

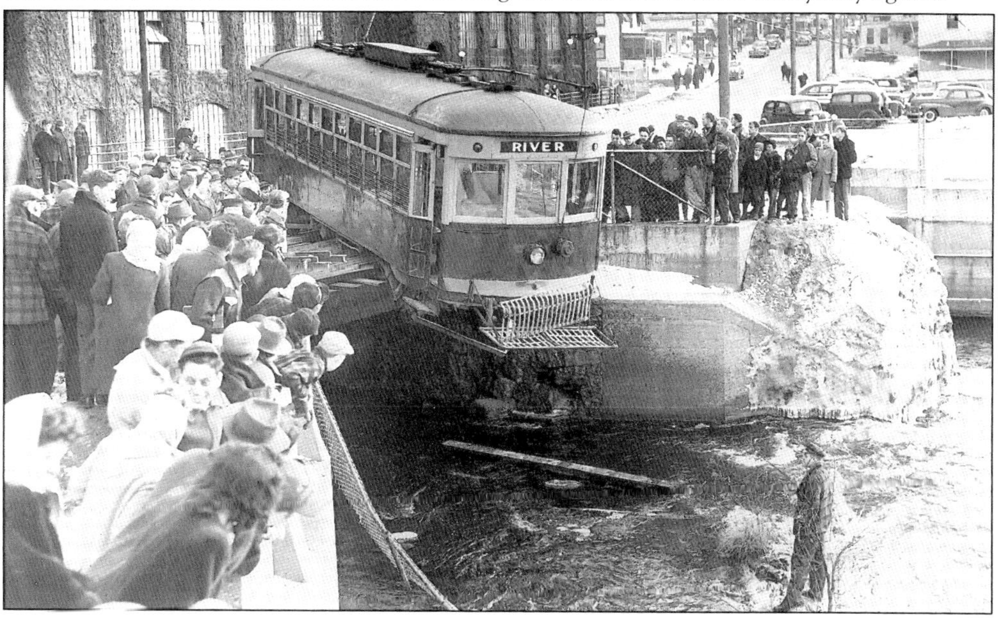

The destination sign was appropriate when Car 90 derailed on Mill Square bridge in Sanford village on February 6, 1947, and almost plunged into Mousam River. Operator Stanley Cram jumped to safety and 17 passengers escaped through a rear door. This accident left the York Utilities Company with only one passenger car, resulting in the start of bus service on the River Street line on April 2nd.

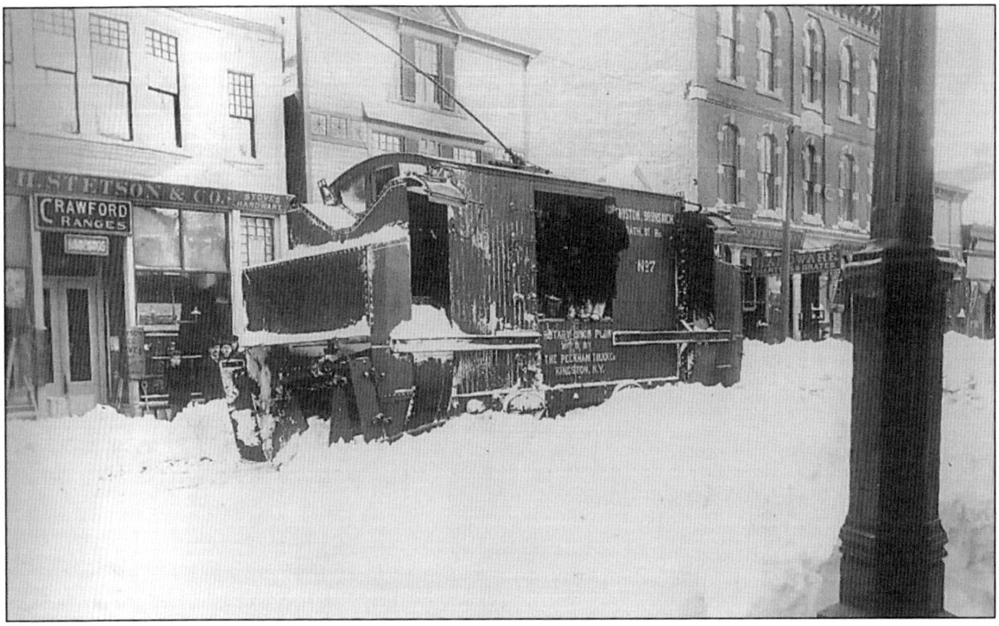

The Great Blizzard of 1888, Lisbon Street, Lewiston. The trolley tracks are being plowed by a #7 rotary plow manufactured by the Peckham Truck Company, Kingston, New York. Notice the store signs advertising the J.H. Stetson Co., Crawford Ranges, and the Knight Hardware Co.

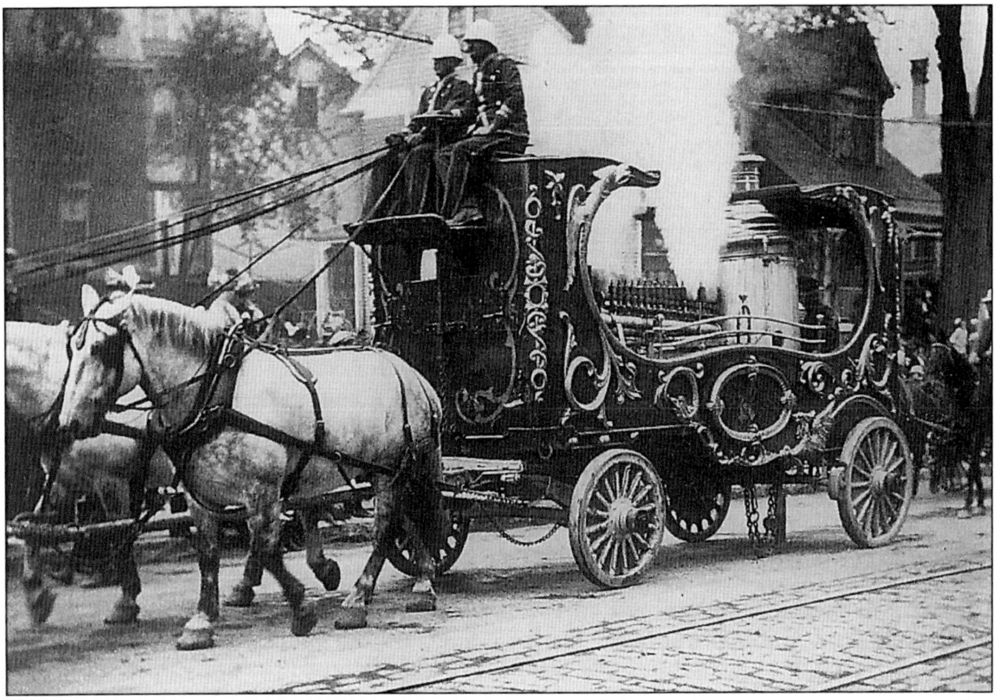

The Ringling Brothers Circus, June 10, 1911, Main and Sabattus Steets, Lewiston. Notice the signs advertising A.E. Harlow Candy Company, Caskets. (G. Herbert Whitney).

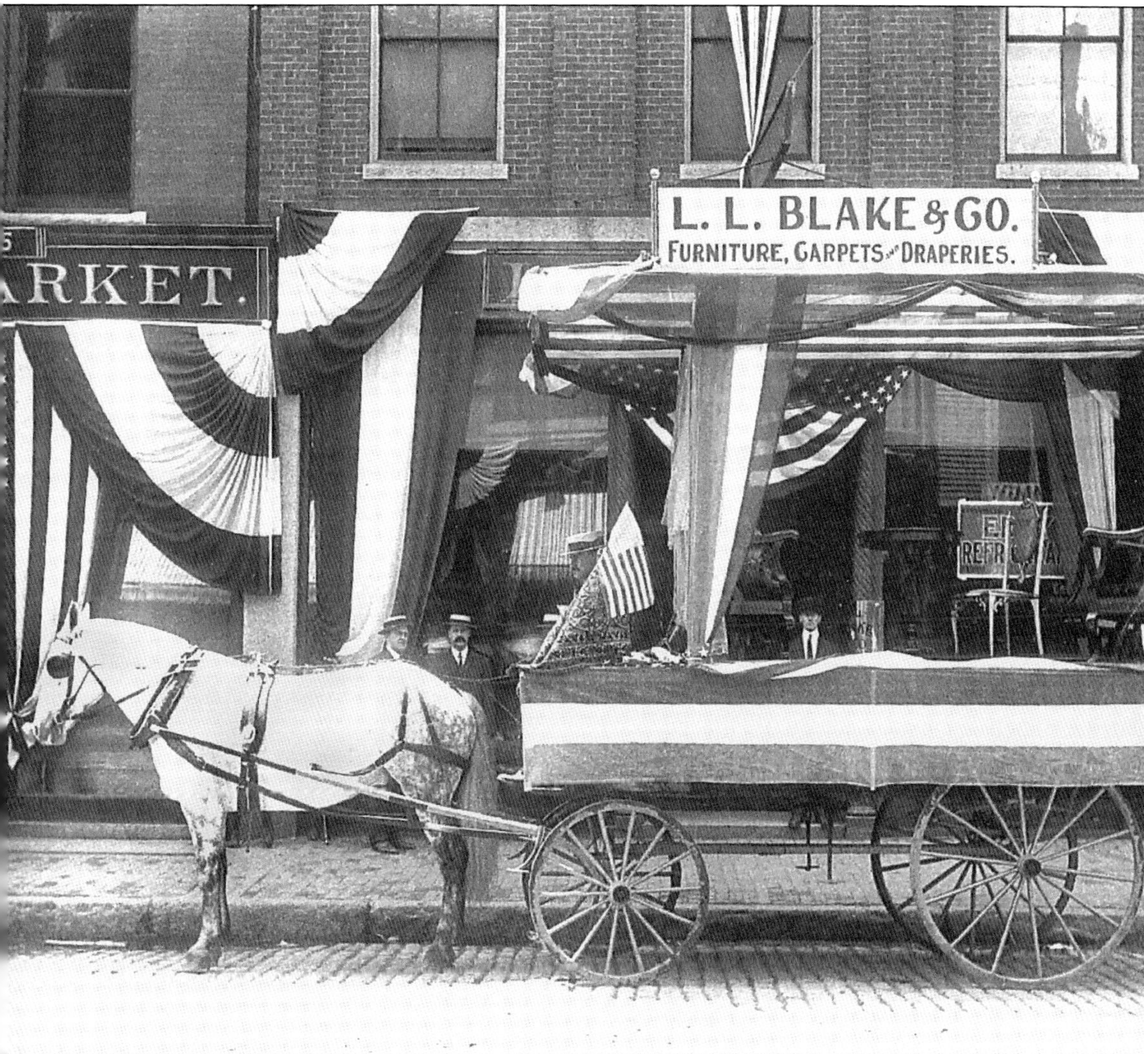

L.L. Blake and Company, 155 Lisbon Street, Lewiston. The company float was all ready to join the 1910 parade. Not the cobblestones that were used for paving the streets. L.L. Blake and Company sold furniture, carpets, and draperies. Notice the little American flag on the horse's ear. A gentleman is looking out the second-story window, probably giving some last minute suggestions for the float.

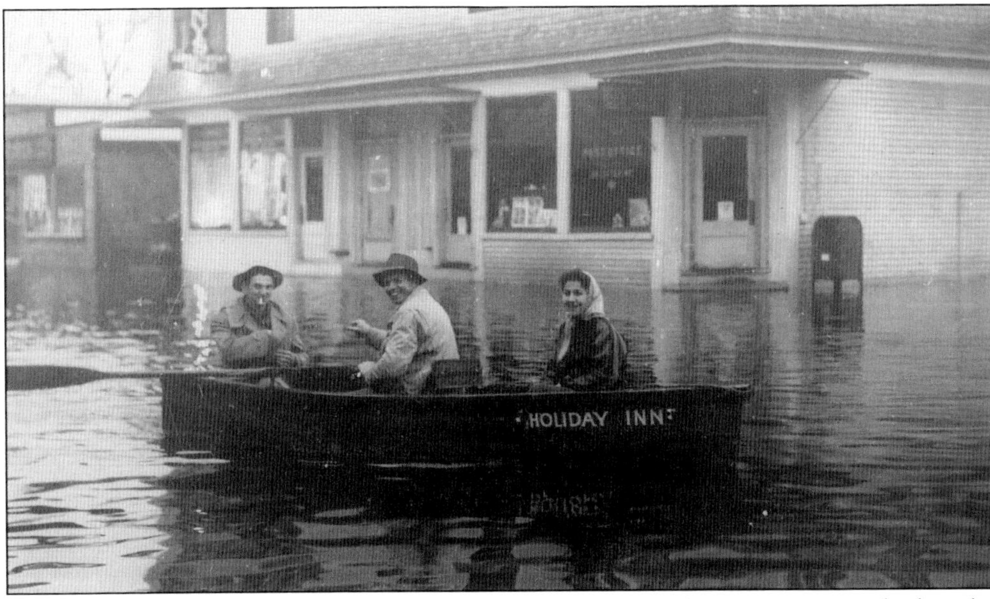

Heavy snowfall during the winter combined with excessive early spring rains resulted in the rapid melting of the snow, which, in turn, caused the water level of Highland Lake to rise. The upper part of Stevens Brook could not contain the deluge of water pouring in, and Post Office Square on Main Street and Depot Street were transformed into a miniature Venice. Although the merchants here in the Square suffered severe losses, these three people are obviously enjoying a rare boating experience.

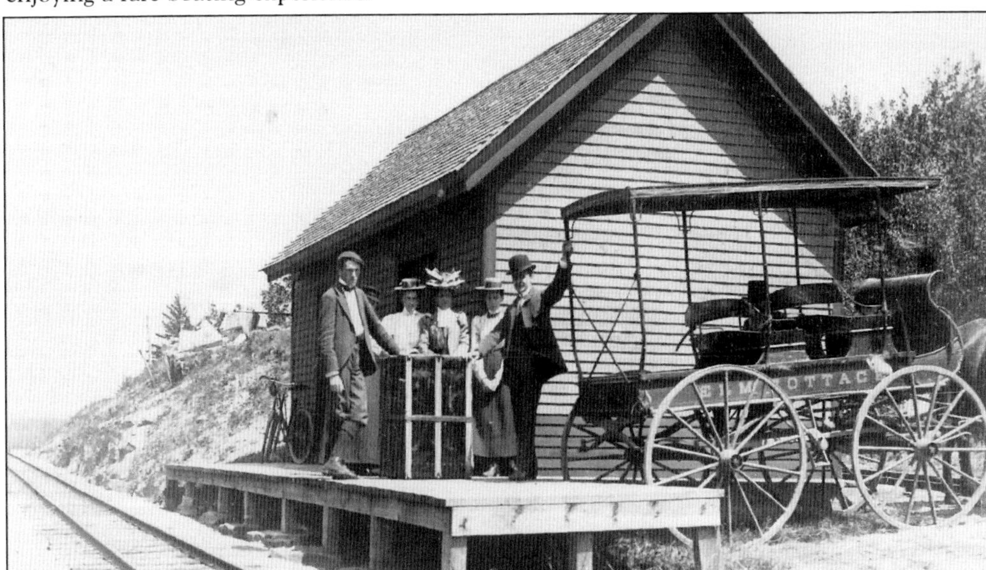

The lakes and ponds in the Lake Region were attracting summer visitors before the turn of the century. Guests of the Elm House at Hancock Pond, owned by the Babbs for many years, appear to be waiting for the arrival of the train. The Lakeside Station, near Joe Bennett's cottage, was constructed in 1894.

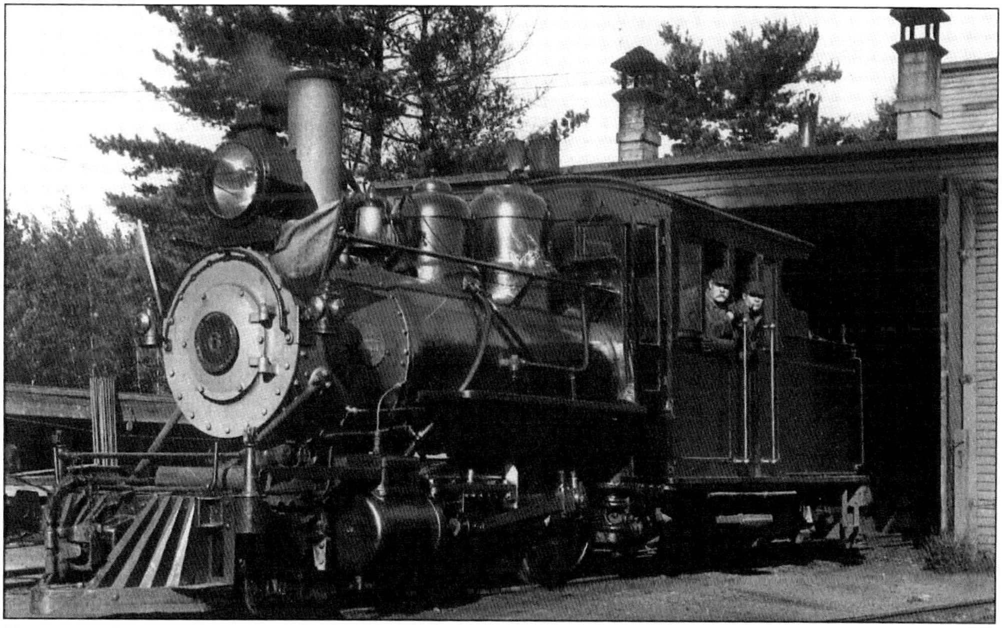

Engineer Oscar Ham and an unidentified fireman are visible as they peer from the windows of Engine No. 6 in front of the engine house. This shiny new locomotive built by the Baldwin Locomotive works in 1907 was the heaviest locomotive used on the line until No. 7 was added in 1913.

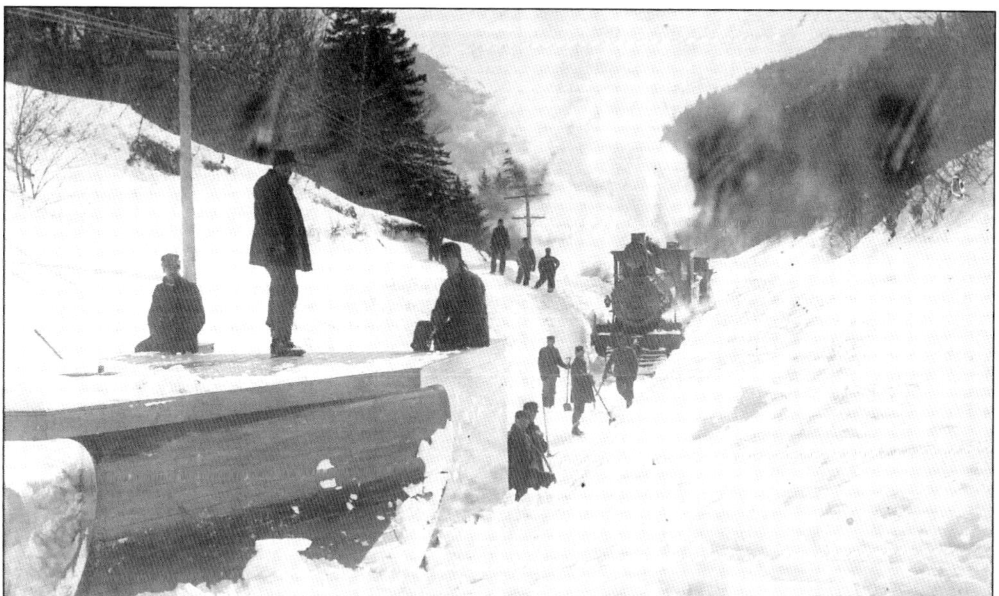

Snowstorms such as this February blizzard in 1927, which buried the Lake Region under 22 inches of wet snow, were extremely costly to the railroad, which by then was struggling. Here the plow and the flange digger were almost useless. Nearly the entire line had to be picked and shoveled by hand.

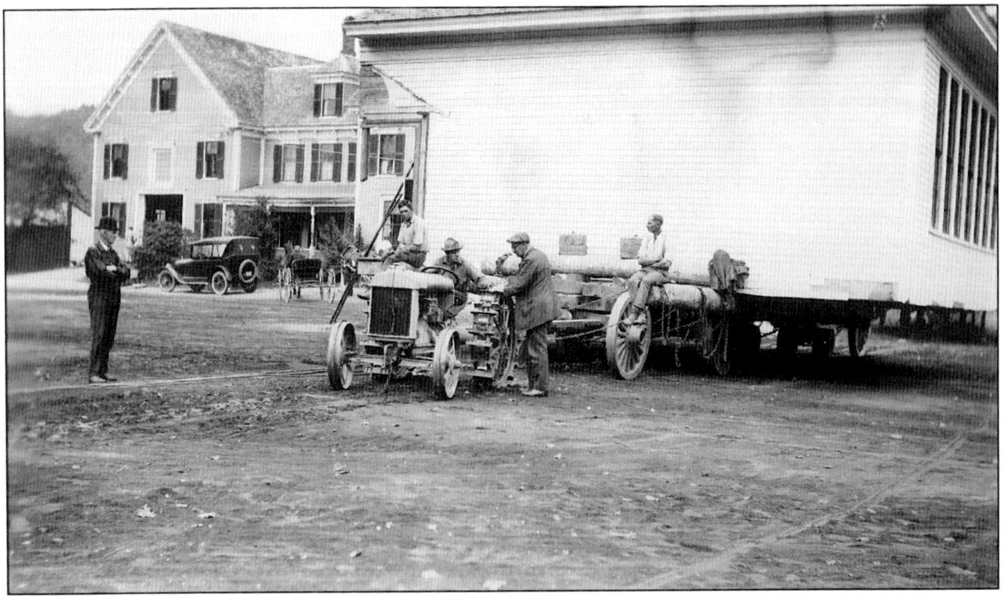

When the Portland Water Company purchased the industrial village of Smith's Mills—just a few miles up the lake from Sebago Lake Village—and all the buildings were destined to be razed, the town of Standish moved the Smith's Mills school to School Street in Sebago Lake Village square. The driver remains unidentified, but the others are, from left to right: Percy Manchester, Dr. Moulton, John Cole, and Fred Chapman.

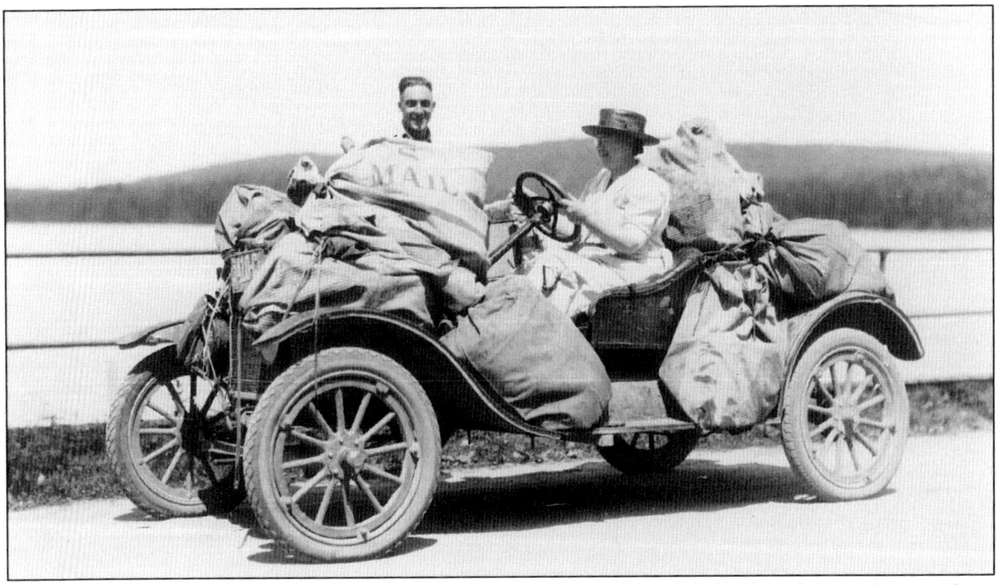

Flora Chute Jewett made daily trips in this modified *c.* 1920 model-T Ford over the winding road (Route 114) to East Sebago and then on to the Mattocks Station (East Baldwin) to pick up bags of mail and then return to the Naples Post Office, where the mail would be sorted and much of it delivered by mail boat on Long Lake, Brandy Pond, and down the Songo Rover to Sebago Lake. Long Lake is visible in the background.

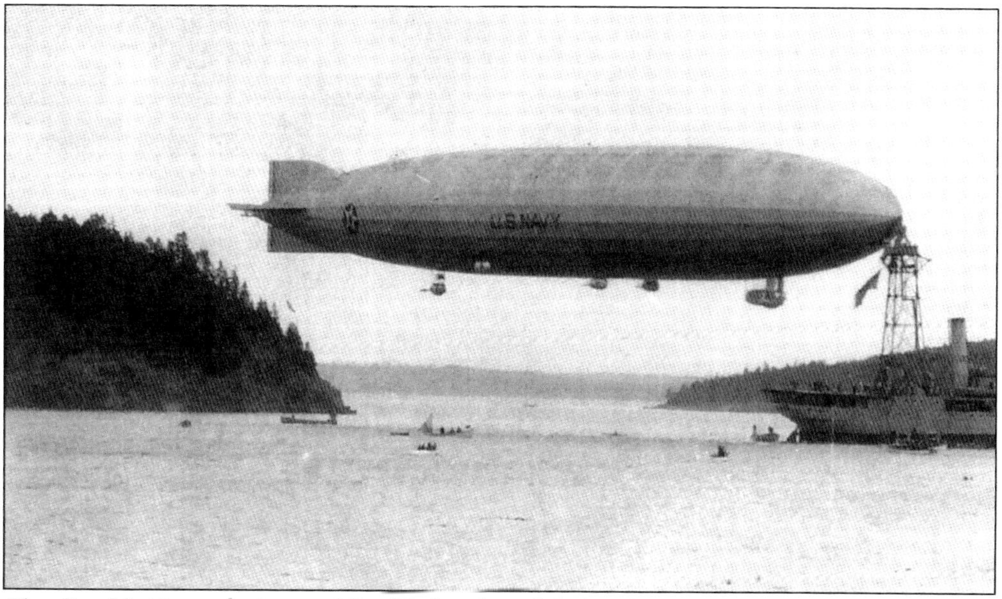

The dirigible *Shenandoah* visited Bar Harbor from July 3—5, 1925. Its incredible size can be determined by comparing it to the battleship and the smaller steamer. (Raymond Strout).

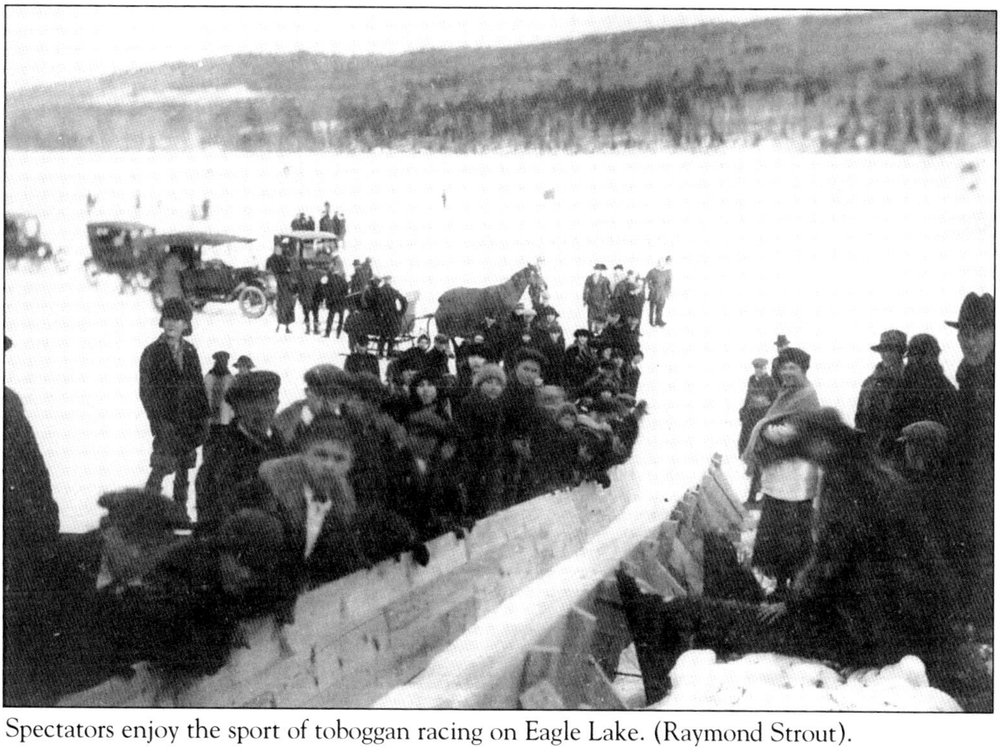

Spectators enjoy the sport of toboggan racing on Eagle Lake. (Raymond Strout).

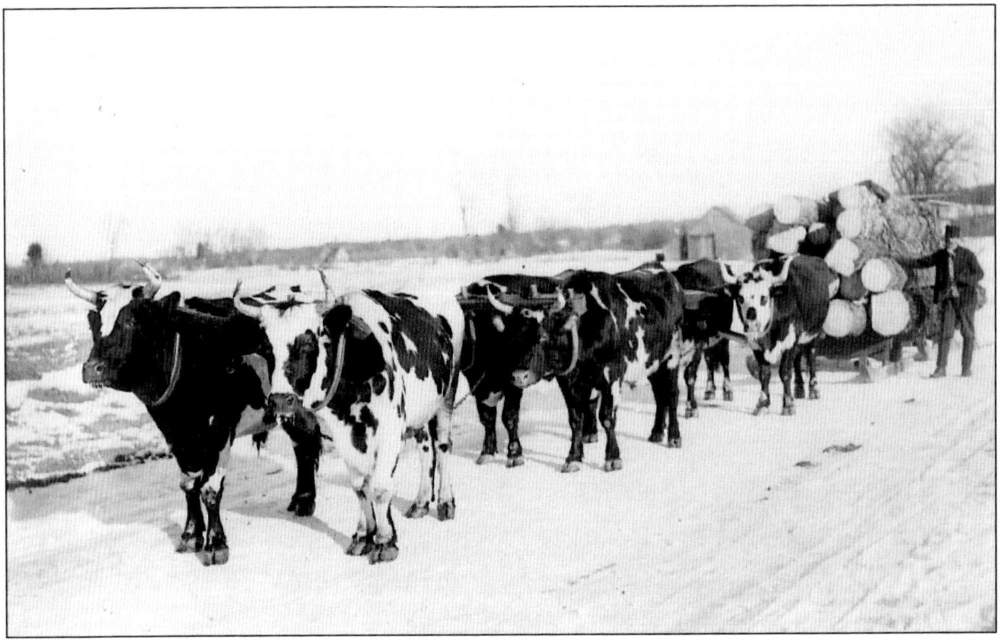

A team of oxen hauls logs on a winter snow sled. (G.D. Hamilton).

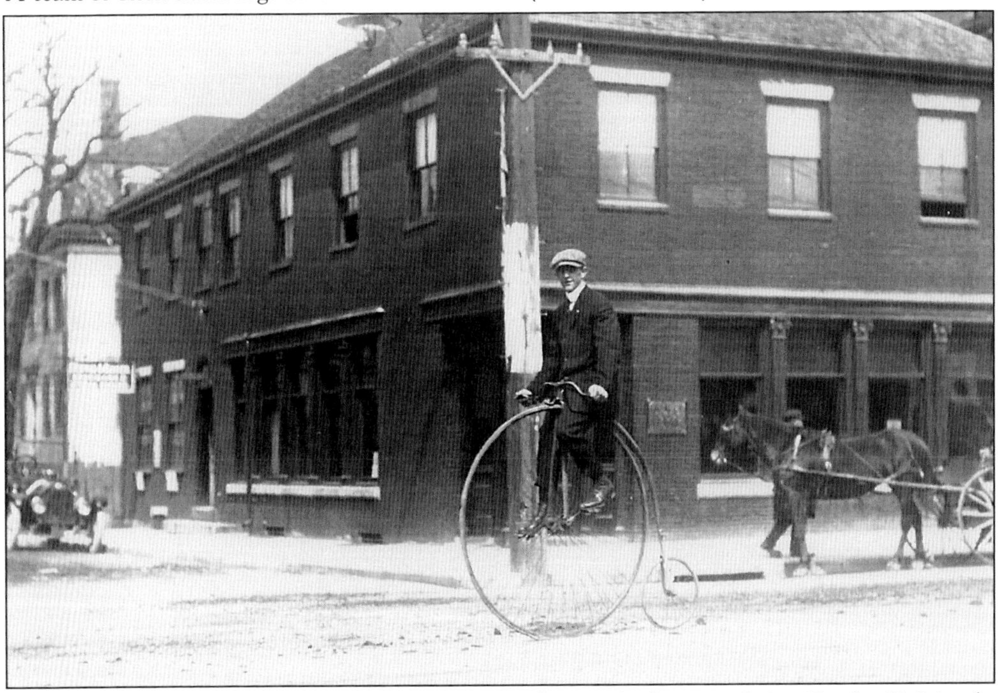

Taken at the corner of Storer and Main Streets, this 1912 photograph by Charles E. Moody captures the three favorite modes of transportation of the day. Archie R. King pedals the "Bone Breaker" or "Penny Farthing"-style bicycle, on the right is a horse and carriage and on the left is a "new fangled" automobile. (McArthur Library).

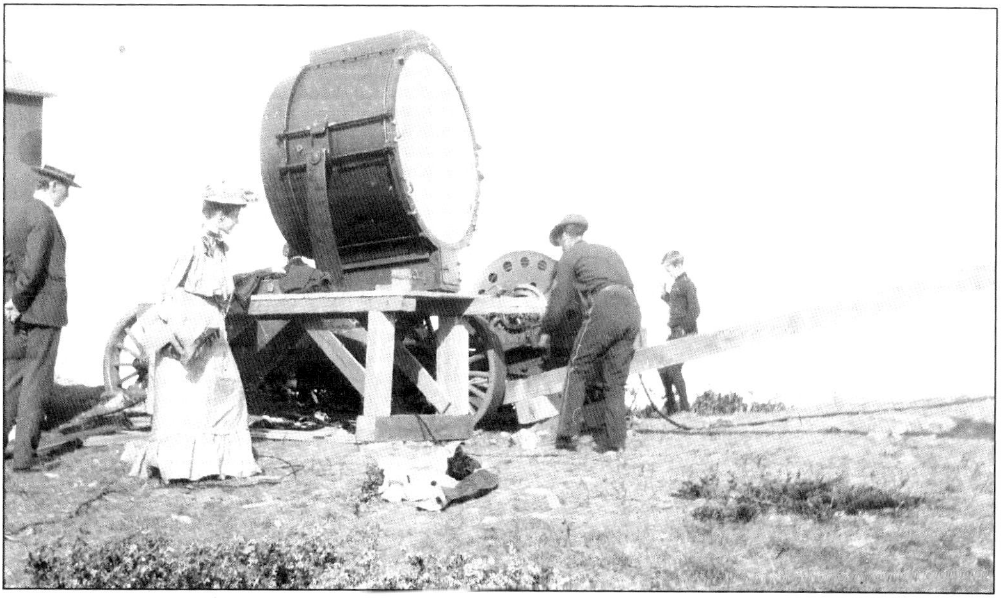

One of the three largest search lights in the world is positioned at Delano Park, Cape Elizabeth, to illuminate enemy vessels that might try sneaking into the harbor after dark, c. 1898. (Robert Shuman family).

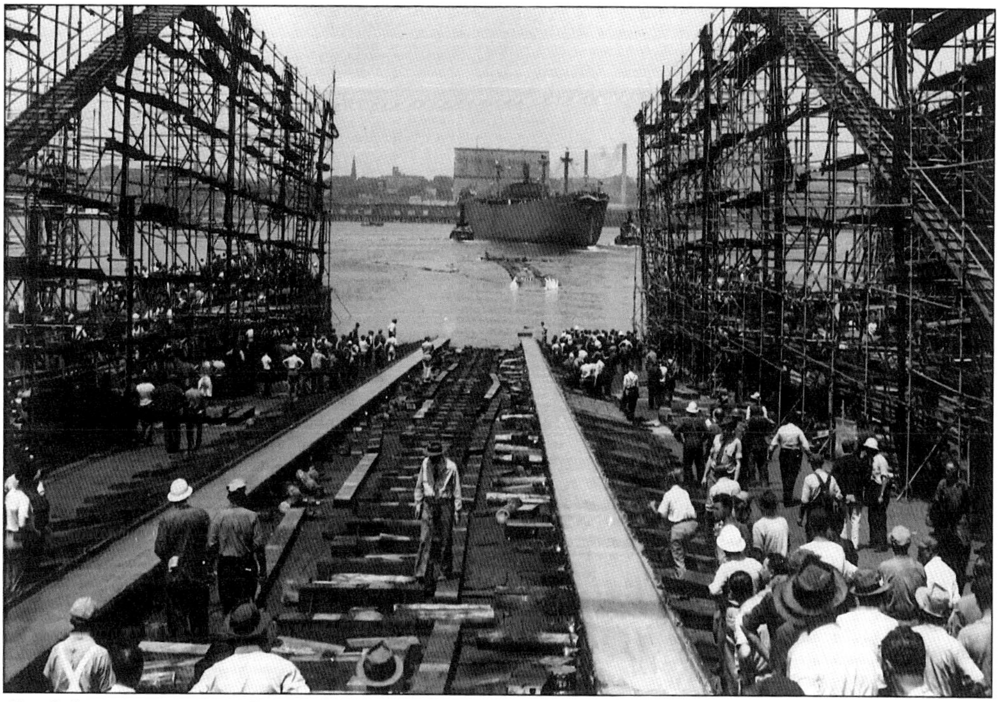

On July 13, 1942, Hull 203 heads out to sea from the West Yard, with Portland's Grain Elevator in the background. That year, six Liberty Ships were launched at one time, a notable feat. (Edward Langlois).

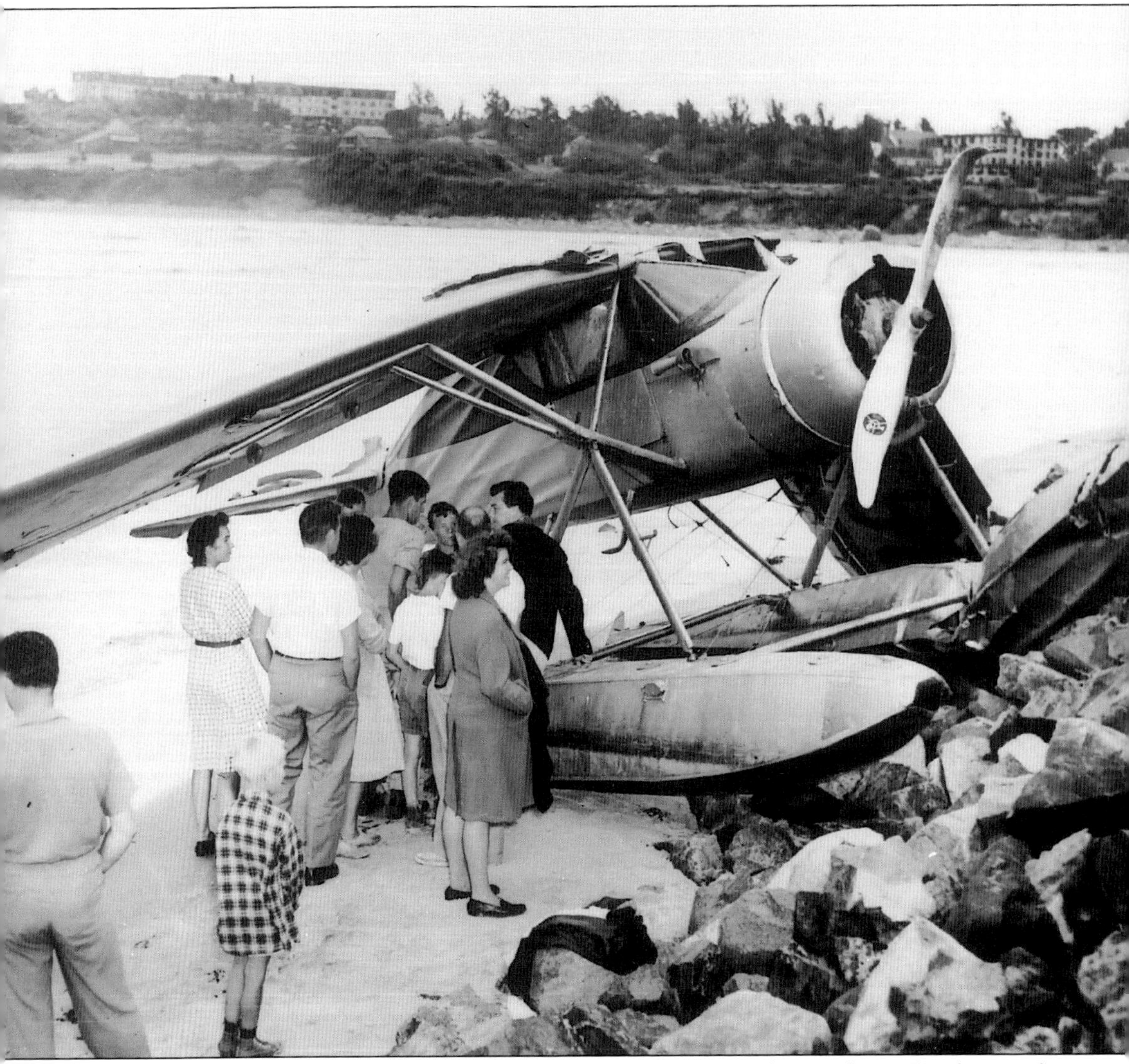

Visitors used many forms of transportation to reach Ogunquit, but in the 1950s this seaplane fell short of the mark and was badly damaged. However, it did provide an additional attraction for tourists. The aircraft crashed at the mouth of the river and Hutchin's wrecker pulled it up on the rocks ahead of the rising tide.

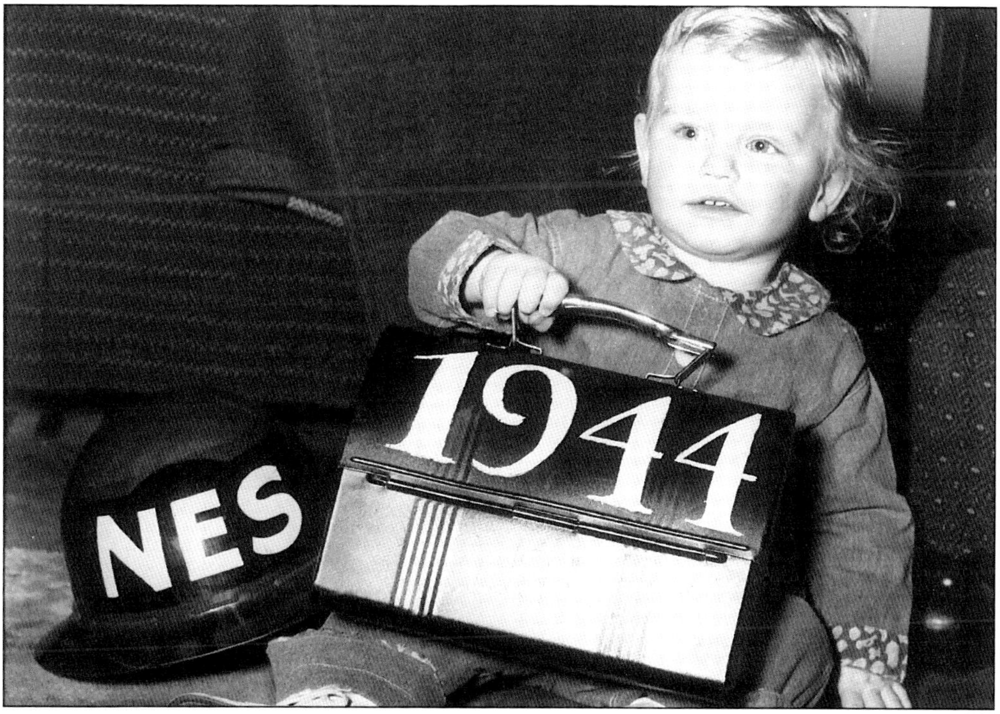

This youngster, in hightop leather "walking" shoes, holds Dad's (or is it Mom's?) lunchbox, proclaiming the year 1944. (Edward Langlois).

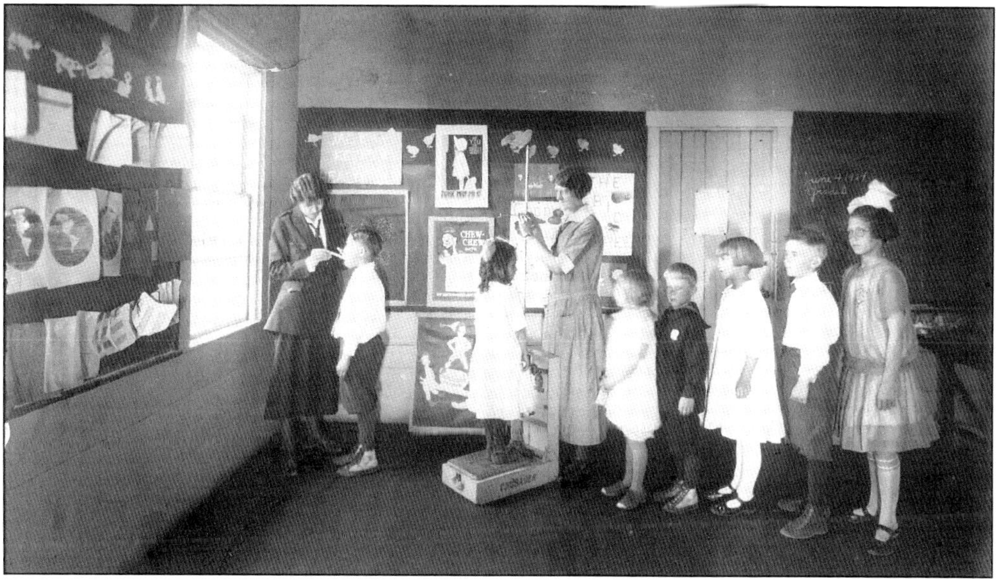

This photograph, taken on June 4, 1924, shows "healthy day" at the Highland School on Old County Road. It was the duty of the public health nurse to measure and weigh children and teach health pointers. This position was held by Eliza Steele from 1929 until her retirement in 1969.

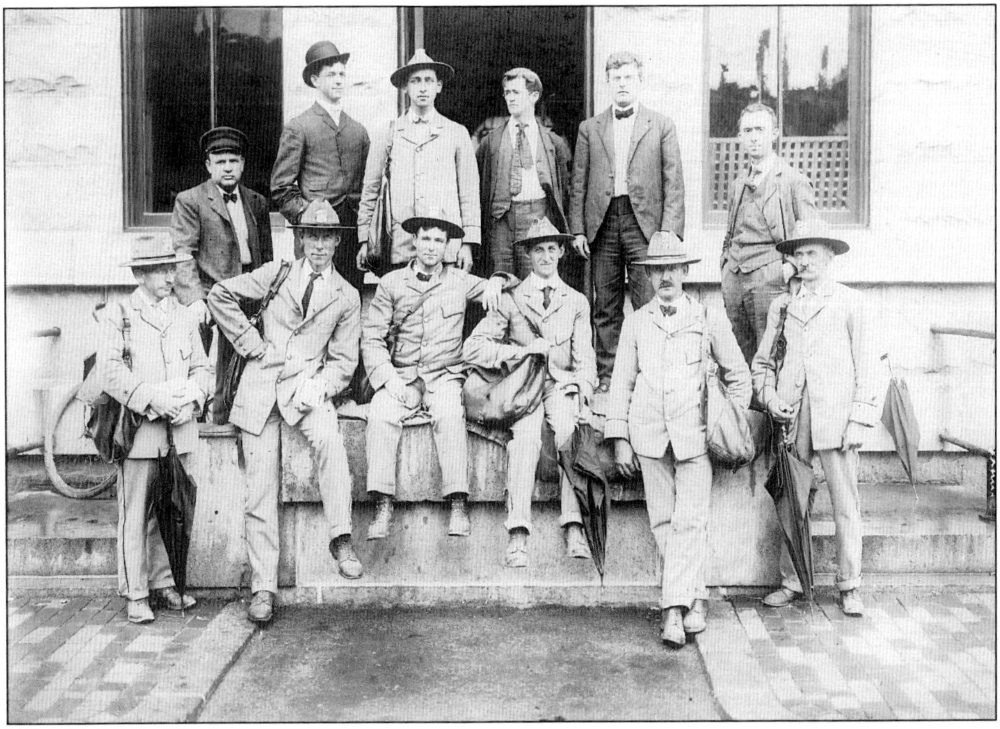

Early letter carriers, ready to deliver the afternoon mail, had umbrellas against the rain, hats for the heat, and bicycles for speed. At that time, mail was delivered twice a day.

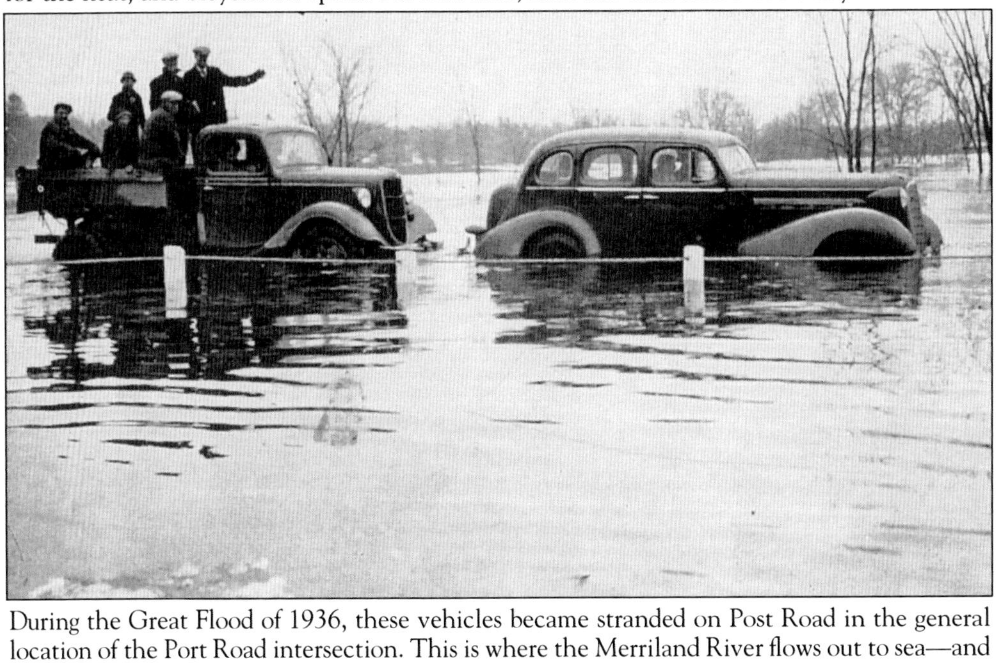

During the Great Flood of 1936, these vehicles became stranded on Post Road in the general location of the Port Road intersection. This is where the Merriland River flows out to sea—and occasionally over its banks, as can be seen here.

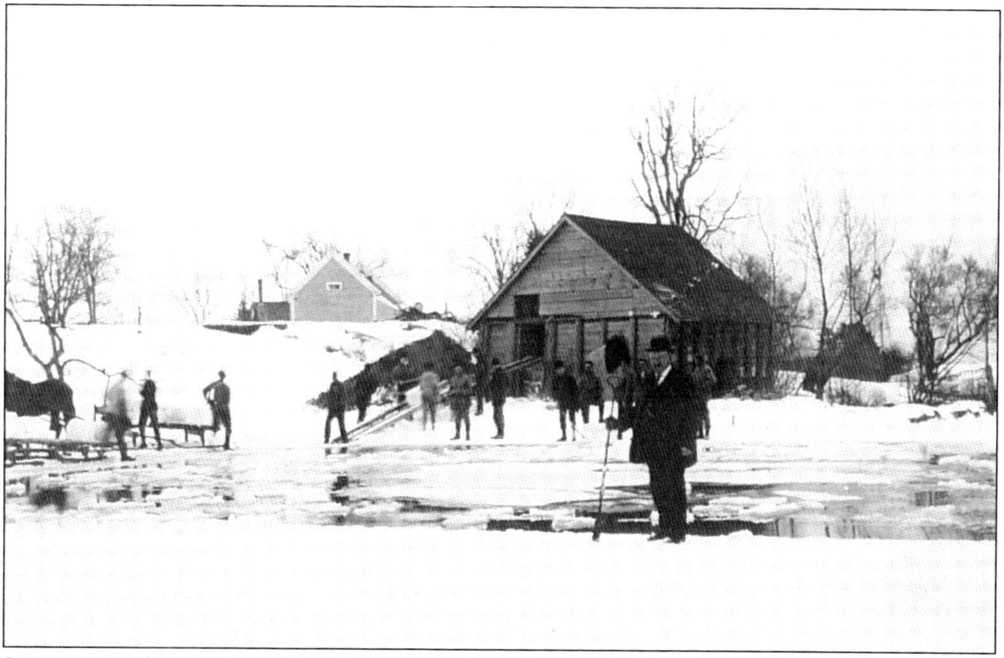

January was the usual month to harvest ice from the ponds. Mill Pond provided the ice which C.E. True used at the Elmwood Hotel. The ice house adjacent to the pond shows the slide on which the chunks were mounted. Packed in saw dust, the ice would last through the summer.

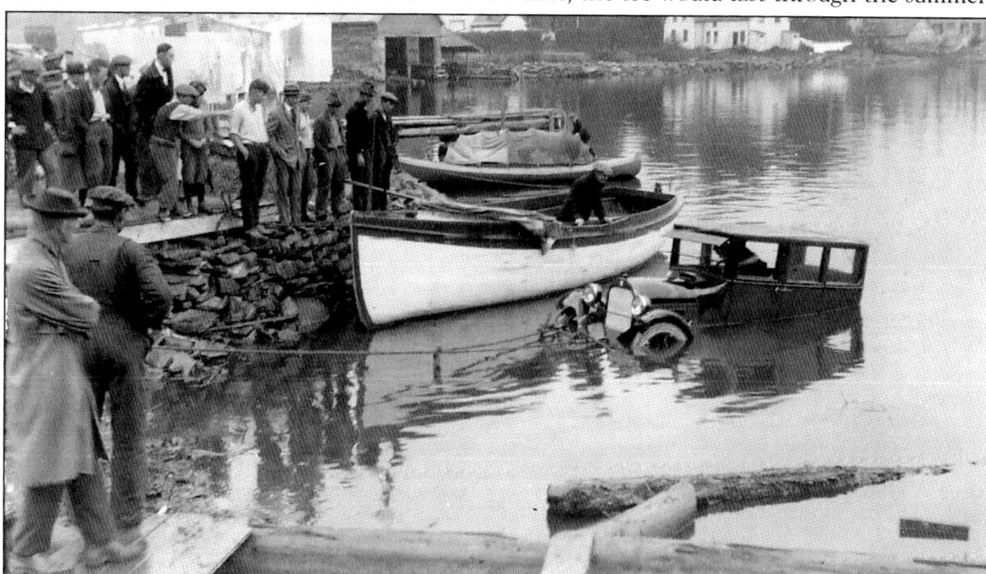

Several people who looked at this photograph said this was when Molly Mountain reversed the car into Moosehead Lake and Woody Bartley jumped in and saved her life. Woody, the father of Tony Bartley, reportedly received the Carnegie Medal for this act. The caption written by H.A. Sanders Jr. reads "Rescuing the Durant of John Brown after he backed off of the wharf." (H.A. Sanders Jr.).

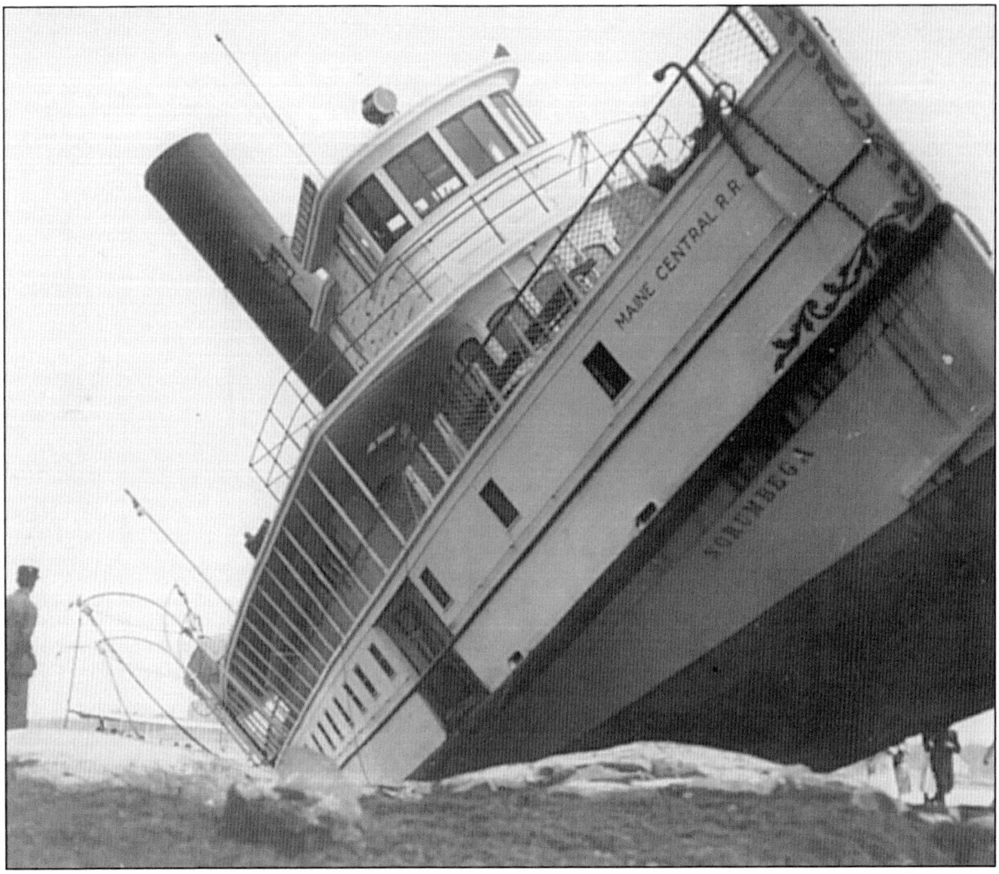

An example of the excellent service provided by the Life-Saving Service was exhibited by the crew of the Little Cranberry Station in 1883. On November 13–15 of that year, a heavy westerly gale had been blowing, causing vessels all along the coast to drag or part their moorings and be driven ashore. During this period, the Little Cranberry crew responded to no less than five vessels requiring assistance and was successful in bringing these crews to safety.

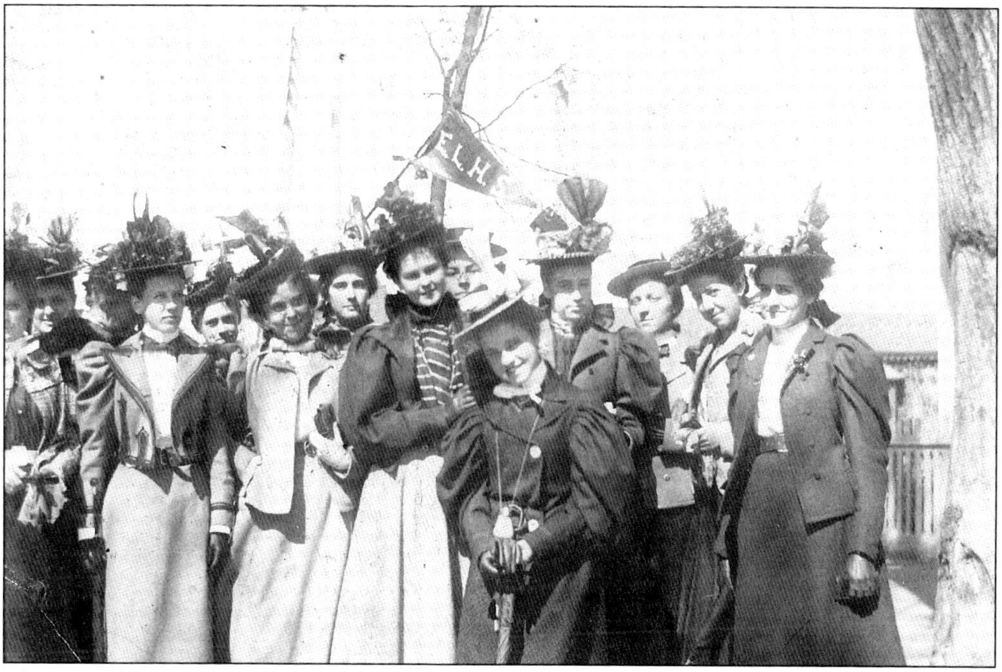

These well-wishers attended the football game between Portland and Edward Little High School in 1897.

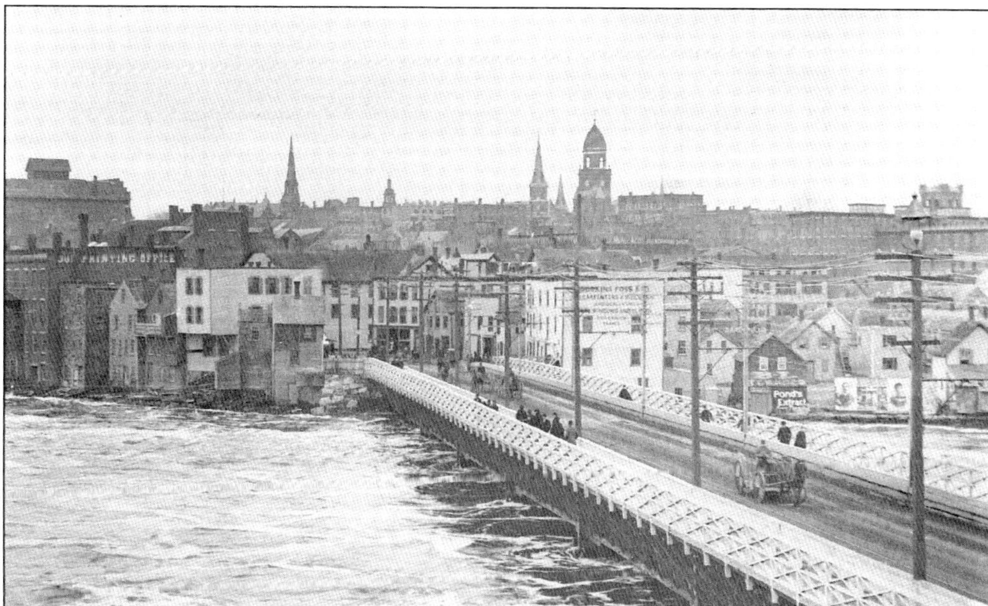

The Flood of 1896, which began after a heavy rainstorm at the end of February and beginning of March, washed away the two bridges connecting Auburn and Lewiston. This photograph below shows the Old North Bridge, prior to the flood.

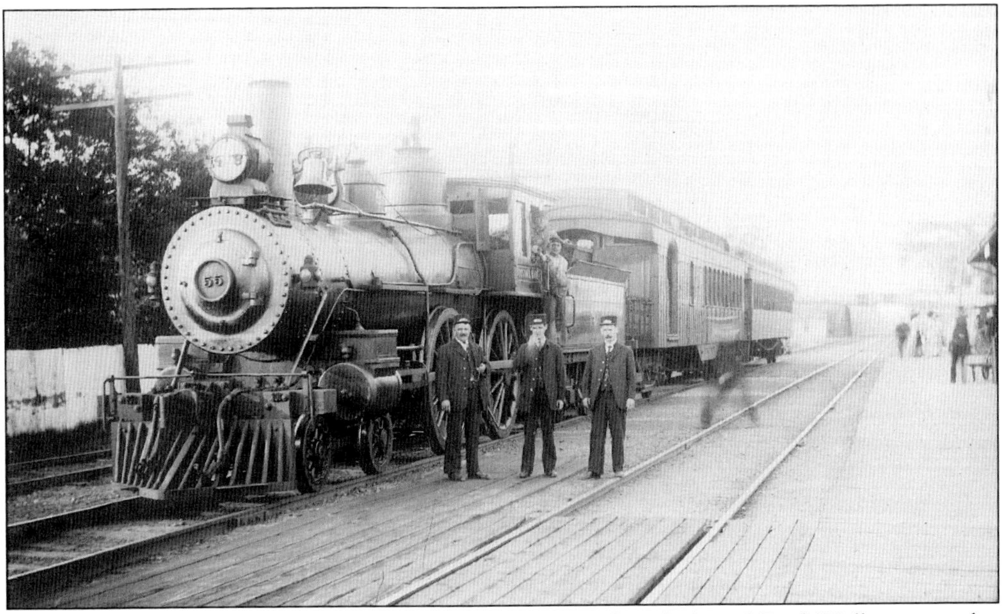

Charles Walker is on the on left, the center man is unidentified, and Fred Walker is on the right in this photograph of a locomotive and cars at the station. The overpass on Black Point Road can be seen in the distance.

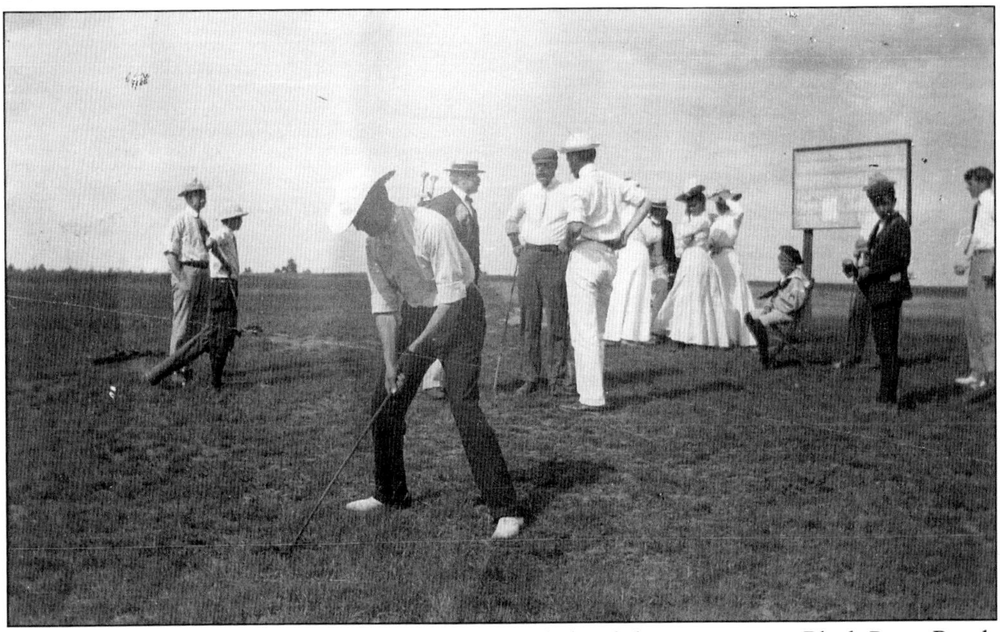

In 1900, a group from Prouts Neck rented property behind the cemetery on Black Point Road, and established the Owascoag Golf Club. A 9-hole course was laid out. It was primitive by today's standards, but has been described as picturesque. Formerly a sheep pasture, the rolling grounds were dotted with juniper and blueberry bushes. Even though it was very basic, the players found the course to be a challenge. (Dino and Barbara Giamatti.)

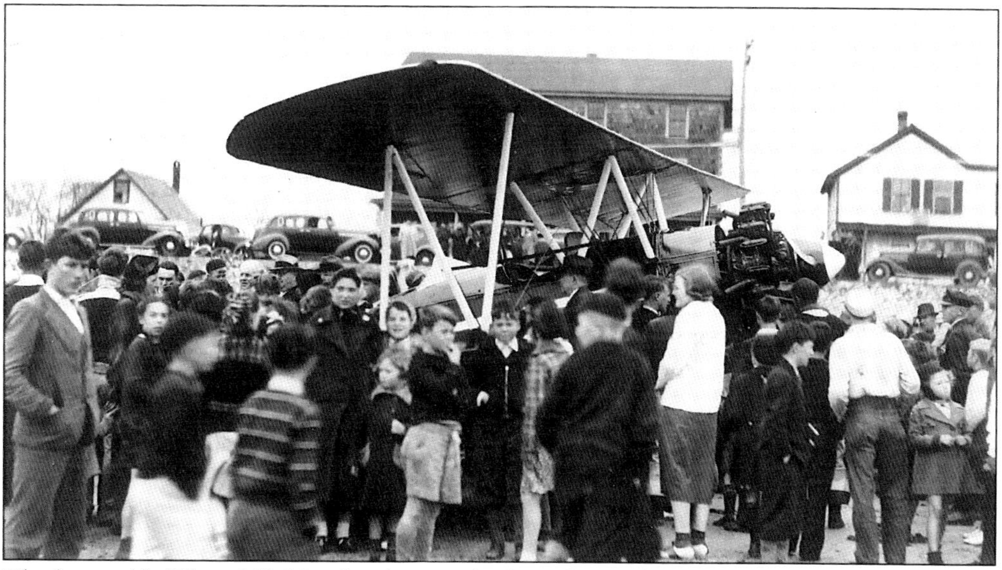

The honorable Edward C. Moody raking rocks from the road. He lived at the Moody Farm on Ridge Road. At that time the road was simply a lane leading to the farm. Moody's *Handbook History of the Town of York: 1623–1914*, was read by many generations of York residents who were interested in the history of the community.

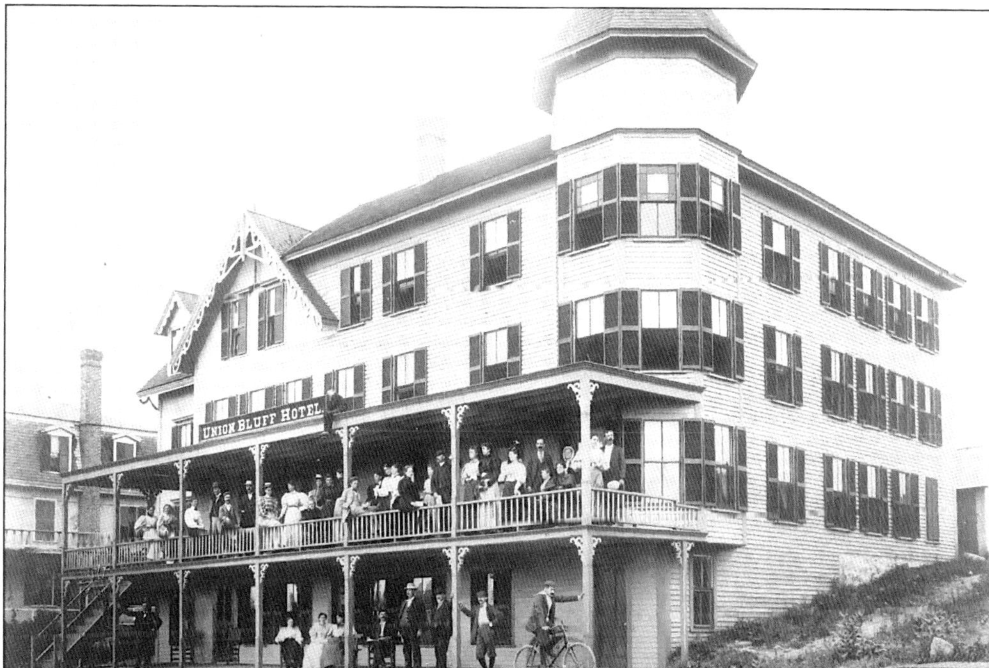

Guests fill the porches of the Union Bluff Hotel, originally the Driftwood Hotel. Here the top porch has been removed and rooms added to the rear and to the third floor. A tower has been added on the right.

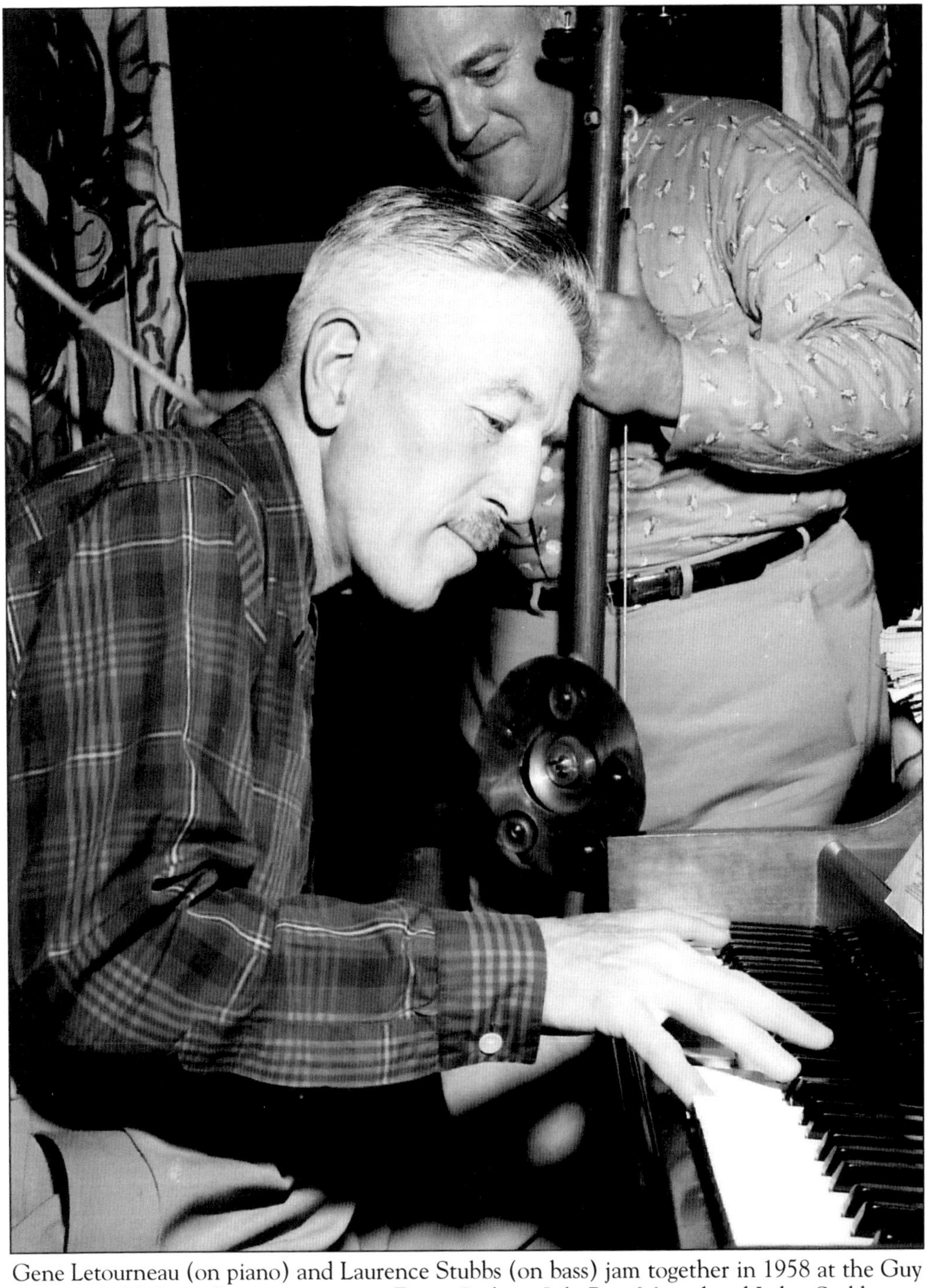

Gene Letourneau (on piano) and Laurence Stubbs (on bass) jam together in 1958 at the Guy Gannett Publishing Company camp at Forest Park on Lily Bay, Moosehead Lake. Stubbs was the general manager of the company in the 1940s and 1950s, while Letourneau is dean of Maine outdoor writers after more than sixty-five years with the *Central Maine Morning Sentinel*.

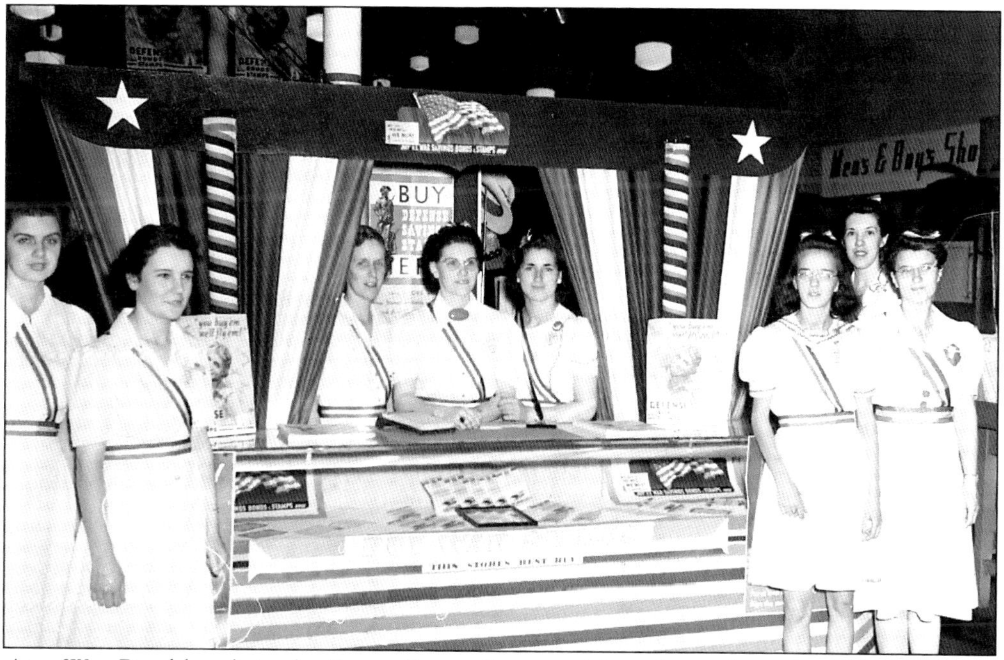

At a War Bond booth in the Emery Brown Store on Main Street during World War II are, left to right, Joan Nadeau Willette, Winifred McPhee, Bertha Sterling, Bernadine Tracy, and three unknowns.

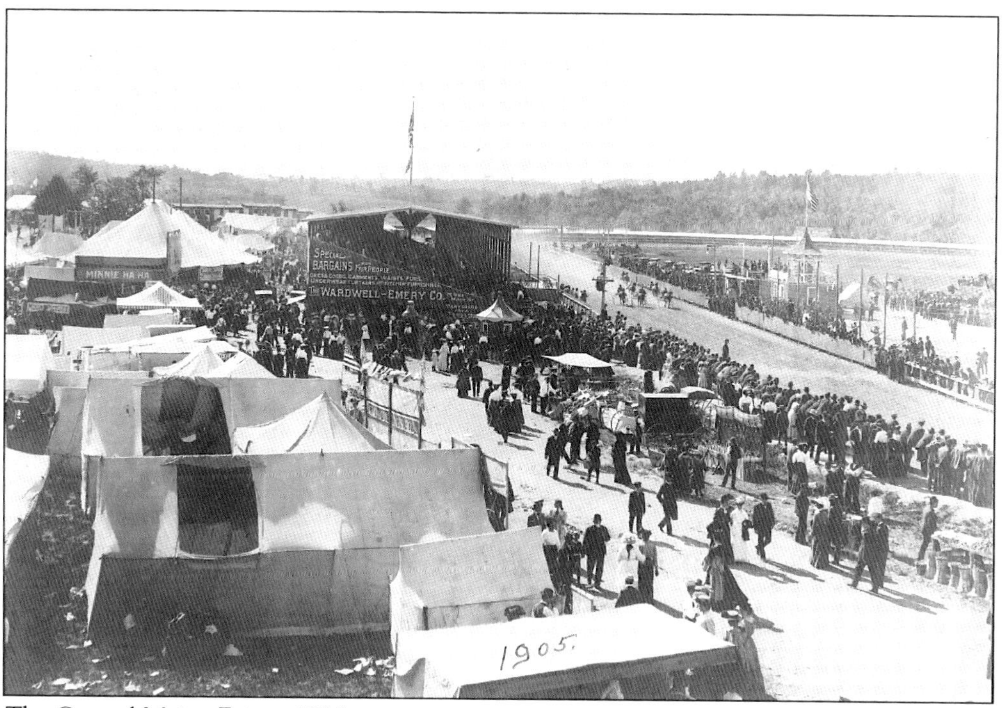

The Central Maine Fair in 1905.

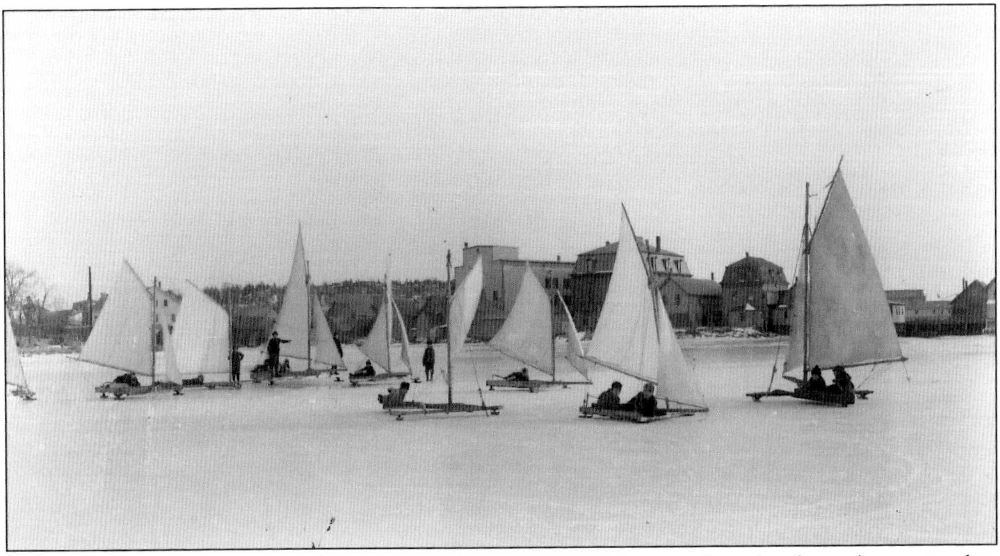

Ice boating on Carver's Pond was a popular winter pastime on the island, as shown in this photograph from 1897. Now, at the beginning of the twenty-first century, ice boats have returned to Carver's Pond.

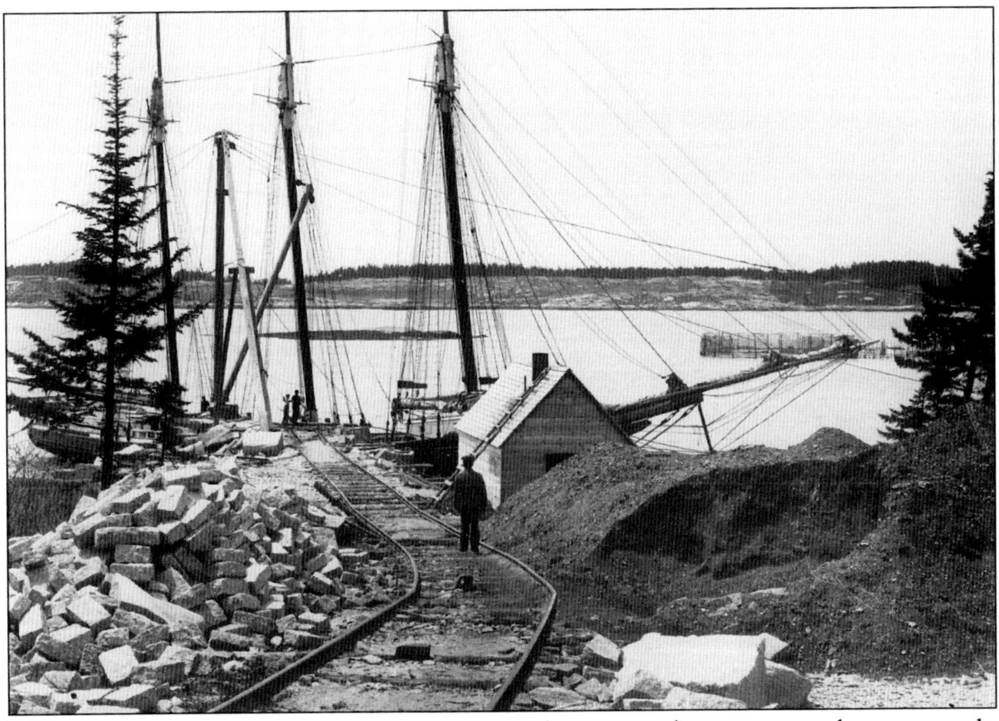

The proximity of Vinalhaven's granite quarries to the primary shipping route, the sea, is made clear in this picture of a small hillside quarry. The paving blocks cut here were carried by gravity to the shipping wharf in small rail cars that were hauled back up the hill by horses. To the right of the quarry is a large fish weir, an indication of the island's other major industry.

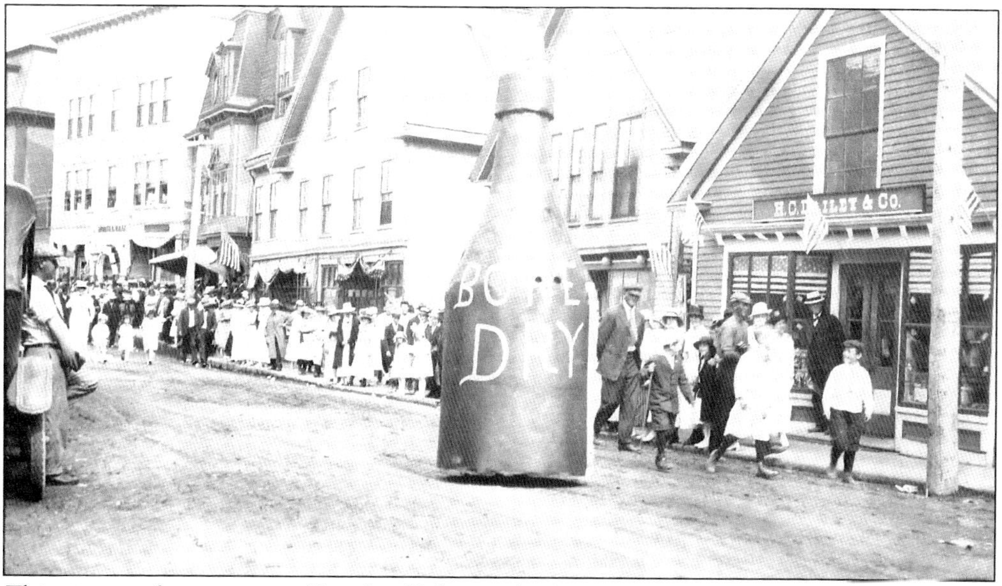

This picture of an entry in a Fourth of July parade, from about 1915, speaks for itself.

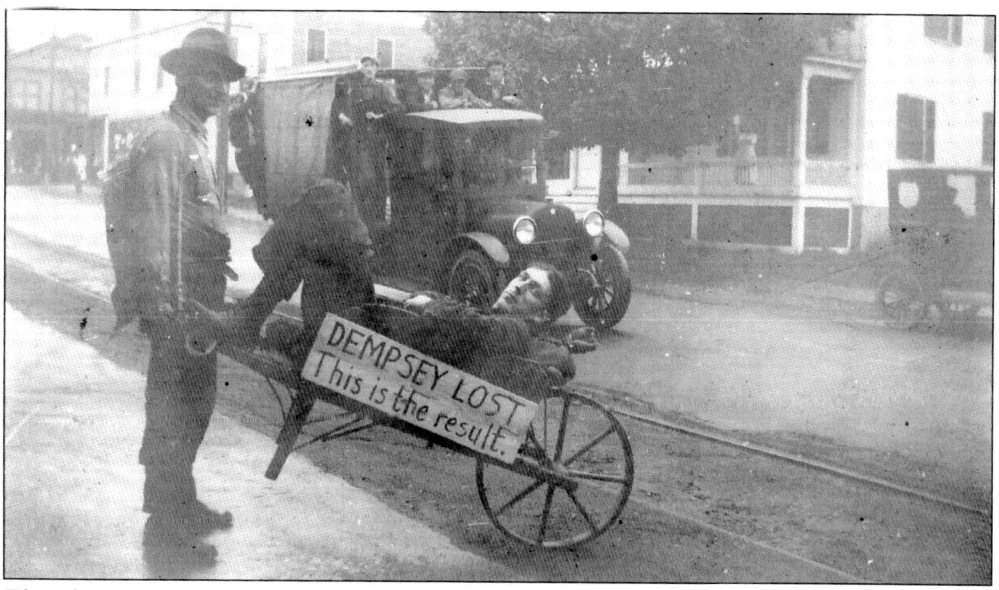

This photograph was taken the day after Jack Dempsy lost his heavyweight title to Luis Angel Firpo on September 14, 1923. These two unidentified men most likely gambled, and lost, on Mr. Dempsey's reputation in the ring.

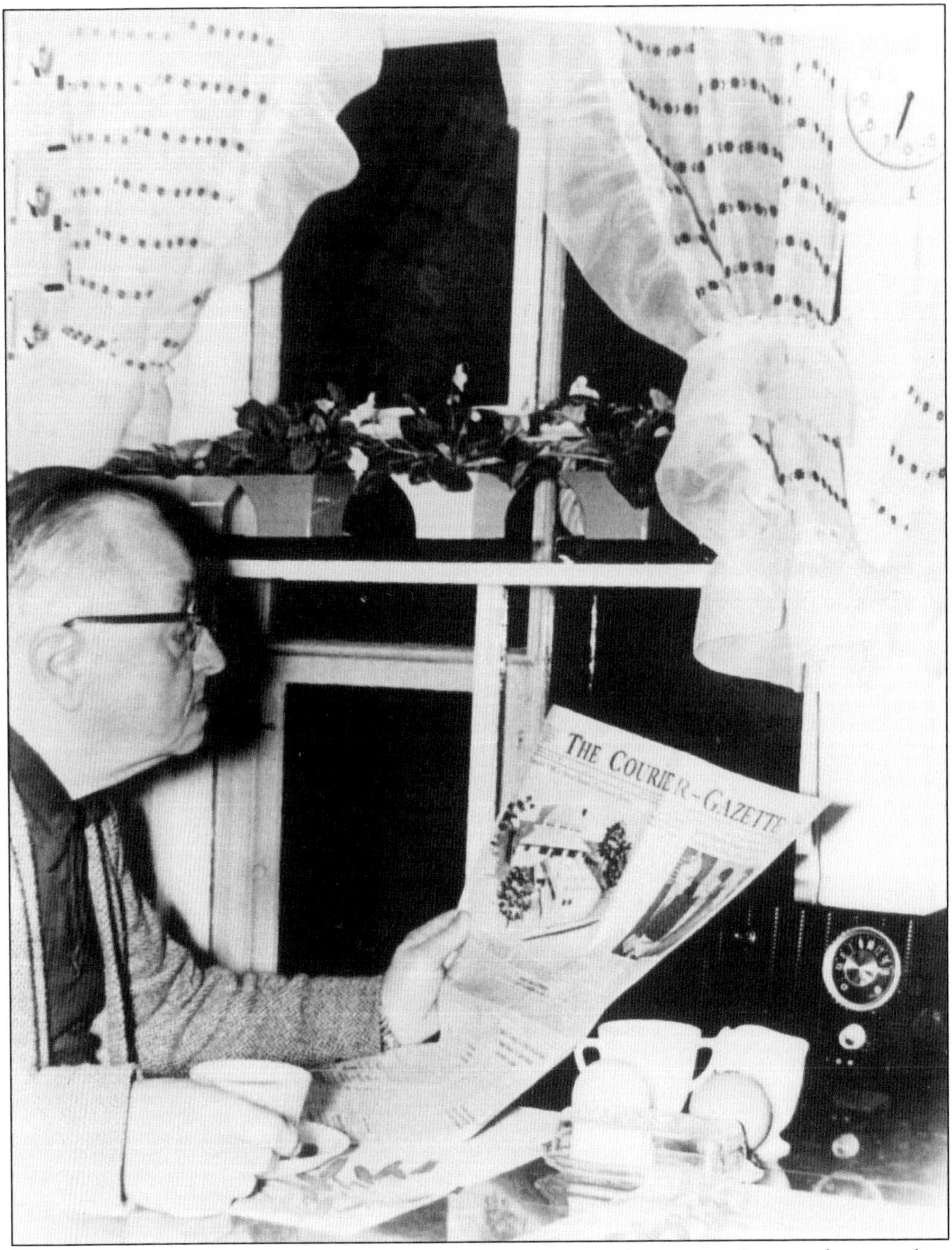

"Yesterday's news in tomorrow's paper tonight," a self-portrait by *Courier-Gazette* photographer Elmer Barde.

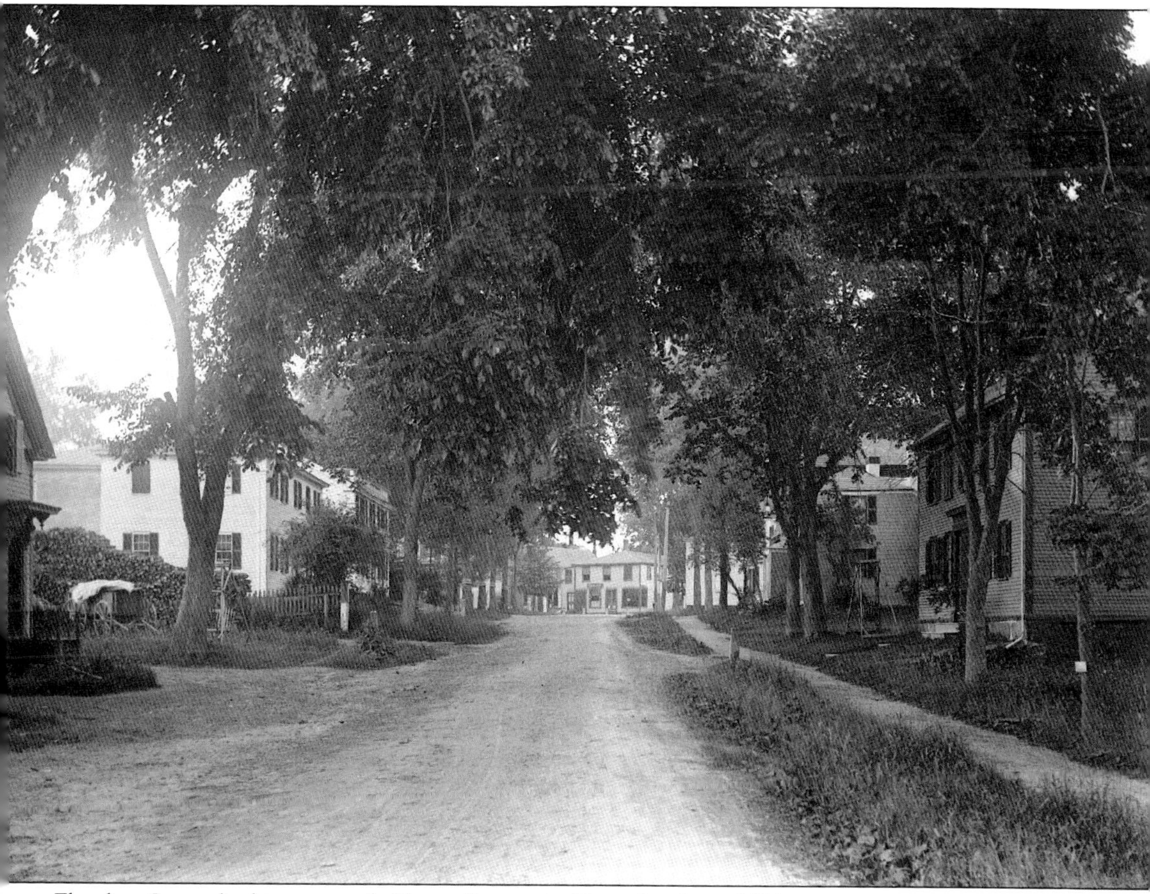

Fletcher Street looking towards Upper Square in Keenebunk, c. 1880.

HISTORICAL SOCIETIES

Arcadia would like to thank the following organizations for their contributions to this volume:

Acadia National Park
Aerial Survey & Photograph Inc.
Albert F. Totman Library
American Legion Post #57
Androscoggin County Historical Society
Atkinson Furniture
Auburn College
Auburn Library
Bethel Historical Society
Bethel Historical Society
Bloomfield Academy
Borestone Mountain Sanctuary
Bridgton Academy
Bridgton Historical Society
Bridgton News
Bridgton Public Library
Casco Public Library
Dennett, Craig & Pate
Dyer Library
Elm City Photograph
Family of Nettie Cummings Maxim
Franco-American Heritage Collection
Great Harbor Collection
Greenwood Historical Society
Harrison Historical Society
Hiram Historical Society
Historical Society of Wells & Ogunquit
Holden Cyclery
James Burns Collection
Kennebunk Free Library Association
Kittery Historical & Naval Museum
Knight Library
Lewiston Library
Lewiston Sun-Journal
Libby Memorial Library
Lincoln County Cultural & Historical Association
Maine Aviation Historical Society
Maine Historic Preservation Commission
Margaret Chase Smith Library
Maritime Research Center
McArthur Library
Mid-Maine Medical Center
Museum of Our National Heritage
Muskie Archives at Bates College
Naples Historical Society
New England Electric Railway
North Bridgton Historical Society
North Bridgton Library
Northeast Harbor Library
Ogunquit Playhouse
Ogunquit Public Library
Old Orchard Beach Historical Society
Otisfield Historical Society
Phippsburg Congregational Church
Phippsburg Historical Society
Portsmouth Athenaeum
Portsmouth Masonic Museum
Portsmouth Naval Shipyard
Raymond-Casco Historical Society
Redington Museum
Robert W. Traip Academy
Rockefeller Archives Center
Rockland Courier-Gazette
Saco Fire Department
Saco Police Department
Seal Harbor Library
Seashore Trolley Museum
Seavey Collection
Sebago Historical Society
Sebec Historical Society
Shawnee Peak at Pleasant Mountain
Shore Village Lighthouse Museum
Skowhegan Board of Selectman
Skowhegan Camera Club
Skowhegan History House
Skowhegan Savings Bank, Wyman Collection
Skowhegan State Fair Association
Square One
St. Aspinquid Masonic Lodge
Standish Historical Society
Star Island Corp.
Town of Skowhegan
U.S. Coast Guard Academy Museum
Wagner Collection
Waterford Historical Society
Waterville Historical Society
Windham Historical Society
Wiscasset Public Library
York Public Library